TURKEY AND THE ARMENIAN GHOST

Turkey and the Armenian Ghost

On the Trail of the Genocide

LAURE MARCHAND
AND
GUILLAUME PERRIER

Foreword by Taner Akçam

Translated by Debbie Blythe

McGill-Queen's University Press
Montreal & Kingston · London · Ithaca

This publication was made possible by a generous grant from the Dolores Zohrab Liebmann Fund.

English translation of *La Turquie et le fantôme arménien : sur les traces du génocide*
© McGill-Queen's University Press 2015

French edition © Actes Sud 2013

ISBN 978-0-7735-4549-6 (cloth)
ISBN 978-0-7735-9719-8 (ePDF)
ISBN 978-0-7735-9720-4 (ePUB)

Legal deposit first quarter 2015
Bibliothèque nationale du Québec

Printed in Canada on acid-free paper that is 100% ancient forest free (100% post-consumer recycled), processed chlorine free.

McGill-Queen's University Press acknowledges the support of the Canada Council for the Arts for our publishing program. We also acknowledge the financial support of the Government of Canada through the Canada Book Fund for our publishing activities.

Library and Archives Canada Cataloguing in Publication

Marchand, Laure
  [Turquie et le fantôme arménien. English]
    Turkey and the Armenian ghost : on the trail of the genocide / Laure Marchand and Guillaume Perrier ; foreword by Taner Akçam ; translated by Debbie Blythe.

Translation of: La Turquie et le fantôme arménien.
Includes bibliographical references and index.
Issued in print and electronic formats.
ISBN 978-0-7735-4549-6 (bound). – ISBN 978-0-7735-9719-8 (ePDF). –
ISBN 978-0-7735-9720-4 (ePUB)

    1. Armenian massacres, 1915–1923. 2. Armenian massacres, 1915–1923 – Historiography. 3. Armenians – Turkey – History. 4. Genocide – Turkey. 5. Collective memory. I. Perrier, Guillaume, author II. Akçam, Taner, 1953–, writer of supplementary textual content III. Blythe, Deborah Mae, 1955–, translator IV. Title. V. Title: Turquie et le fantôme arménien. English.

DS195.5.M36713 2015   956.6'20154   C2014-907712-2
                                                   C2014-907713-0

This book was typeset by True to Type in 11/14 Sabon

Contents

Translator's Preface

Translation is both an art and a science; there are no hard and fast rules. Depending on the type and purpose of the text and the target audience, translators must sometimes answer difficult questions about how faithful to be to the original, whether or not to correct errors, and how to adapt the text to a different language, time, and culture. The translation of a document of this complexity thus presented many challenges.

The subject of this book is emotionally charged – of deep significance to both its authors and its readers. Faithfulness to the tone and intent of the authors and awareness of the sensibilities of potential readers were thus vital. At the same time, adaptation was required to create a coherent and accurate whole in the target language. The book is based on a series of articles written over a period of several years by French journalists Laure Marchand and Guillaume Perrier, correspondents in Turkey for *Le Figaro* and *Le Monde*. It contains a wealth of background material, evocative vignettes, horrifying first-hand accounts, and intriguing anecdotes. The story it tells is both compelling and relevant.

To do justice to this maze of detail with all its historic, geographic, literary, and cultural references, I first had to understand it. Fortunately, this task was simplified by the abundance of online documentation, including the texts of many of the books quoted, historic documents, government websites, and articles that appeared in France, Turkey, and the United States reporting the events described. Based on this research, I was able to add relevant details and explanations as appropriate – always bearing in mind the needs and interests of the reader. In addition, I corrected minor inaccuracies in the original and added translator's notes to incorporate explanatory material and events that have occurred since the original articles appeared.

The Turkish names and titles presented their own set of challenges. For over a thousand years, Turkish was written using a form of Arabic script. This alphabet was well suited to Ottoman Turkish, which incorporated a lot of Arabic and Persian vocabulary, but it was poorly suited to Turkish vocabulary. In 1928, as part of the sweeping cultural reforms of Turkey's first president, Mustafa Kemal, the Law on the Adoption and Implementation of the Turkish Alphabet was passed, introducing a Latin-based Turkish alphabet consisting of twenty-nine letters, seven of them modified from their Latin originals for the phonetic requirements of the language. (An explanatory note on pronunciation is included after Taner Akçam's preface.) Following the example of the authors, I therefore retained the use of the Latin Turkish alphabet for proper nouns and also attempted to maintain consistency in geographic names, often supplying the Turkish or Armenian names for reference.

In 1934, Mustafa Kemal introduced the Surname Law, requiring everyone in Turkey to adopt a last name. He led the way by choosing for himself Atatürk, meaning "Father of the Turks." Prior to that reform, wives and children took the husband's first name as their last name, and this tradition is also reflected in the text. Finally, Turkish titles such as "Bey," "Pasha," and "Effendi" are placed after first names in the place of last names (for example, Talaat Pasha). The original version of the book is not entirely consistent with regard to the capitalization of such titles; for simplicity, they have all been capitalized.

In conclusion, it was my honour and privilege to translate this timely work. I have tried to do justice both to the original book and to the expectations of readers with the hope that this edition will play some small part in raising awareness of these tragic events and furthering the goal of genocide recognition.

Debbie Blythe

Foreword

TANER AKÇAM

Laure Marchand and Guillaume Perrier set themselves a daunting task: that of holding up a mirror to us Turks. But not just any mirror – a mirror that would allow us to see what we do not see and to know what we do not know. "Listen and look: this is your story," they say, while telling us the story of those who are not "us." Their goal? To enable us to see in our own reflection those whom, to be ourselves, we have condemned to disappearance and oblivion. So that, in the end, we will come to understand who we really are.

The first question raised by this book is: "Why do we Turks continue to deny the genocide?" I've been researching the question of the genocide since 1990, more than twenty years. Throughout all those years, this is the question that has arisen most consistently. It is a simple one, but as the years have passed, my answer has changed. At first, I tried to explain the denial through the concept of "continuity." The Turkish Republic was established by the Union and Progress Party (Ittihat ve Terakki), the primary architect of the 1915 genocide. The founding cadres of the young Turkish state were essentially members of that party.

A significant number of the founders of modern Turkey were thus either directly involved in the Armenian genocide or enriched themselves during that period by looting Armenian properties. But those individuals were our national heroes, the founding fathers of our nation. If we had recognized the genocide, we would have had to admit that many of our greatest national figures were thieves and murderers. Yet they created our state out of nothing. We see ourselves in them, and they define who we are.

This legacy holds true for the largest left-wing movement Turkey has ever seen, inspired by the 1968 student protests. The representatives of that wave and its political organizations strongly identified with the founding cadres of the republic. This strong identification was also seen in nationalist, Islamic, and other right-wing circles.

So recognizing the genocide would require us to disown our national identity as we currently define it. What nation could possibly do that? Instead of dealing with our identity crisis and the resulting fallout, isn't it much simpler just to deny the genocide?

Over time, my answer to the question "Why do Turks deny the genocide?" has evolved. Explanations based on moral values, self-identity, and other non-material considerations gave way to more materialistic motivations. I began to think in this way: If Turkey acknowledges that the genocide took place, it will have to make reparations. So there is more at stake than whether or not the events of 1915 were technically "genocide." Let's imagine that there was no genocide and that the Union and Progress Party simply deported the Armenians from a cold, mountainous region to a warm, hospitable one – to Florida, for example. Still, everything that these people owned was confiscated, and they received not a penny in compensation. Even if you refuse to view the events of 1915 as a genocide, you must still acknowledge that modern-day Turkey was founded on riches plundered from Armenians. So if Turkey acknowledges that something happened in 1915, it will be forced to pay compensation. To avoid doing that, it prefers to deny that the whole thing ever happened.

Now my thinking has again begun to change. I don't mean to suggest that my previous explanations were totally incorrect. Clearly the above factors play a major role in the denial of the Armenian genocide. However, I now think that the roots are deeper, more existential. The answer to the question seems to lie in a duality between existence and non-existence. Our existence – that of Turkey and many of its inhabitants – requires the absence of another entity: the Christians. To accept "1915" means accepting that Christians lived in this land, which amounts to proclaiming our own non-existence, because our existence is based on their absence, or disappearance.

To clarify what I am saying, I refer to the work of the great German philosopher Jürgen Habermas. According to Habermas, all levels of society and its institutions are imbued with what he calls hidden, or latent, violence. He suggests that this hidden violence creates a mode of communication that is adopted by the entire society. Through this "mode of collective communication," certain topics are excluded from public discourse, and certain invisible lines of demarcation are institutionalized.[1] What is significant here is that the warp and woof of society, its fabric, is not imposed from above by its leader but is on the contrary accepted and internalized by all, with no conscious awareness by either leaders or followers of what is happening. Over time, a kind of silent consensus forms around the society's dominant "mode of communication." Through this mode, what Habermas calls "hidden violence" – topics that society wishes to avoid by general consensus – can not only be relegated to the past but also forgotten.

To further clarify, I would like to borrow a term from author Elias Siberski. Siberski uses "communicative reality" to describe an important characteristic of underground organizations.[2] According to Siberski, underground organizations create a virtual reality, different from ordinary, shared reality, through a mode of communication that they use with their members and the outside world. The situation in Turkey today is much like that. As a society, we resemble an underground organization. Our institutions result from a "communicative reality" that we have created and that determines how we think and exist as a "state and a people." The belief systems that define our feelings shape our entire network of social relations or, in other words, our identity. What is important to grasp here is the gap between this "communicative reality" and what we call our actual, shared reality. A quick review of all the concepts and the value and thought systems that we use to define ourselves is enough to demonstrate just how far our "communicative reality" differs from what we call the "real world."

This "communicative reality" ultimately creates worlds that we can speak of and others that have been consigned to the depths of silence. It has created a collective secret that straitjackets our entire society and carves out a gigantic black hole in our reality. An extremely simple example of this phenomenon is found in the work of Idris Küçükömer (1925–1987), a scholar who has had a profound influence on Turkish intellectual life. His groundbreaking book *Alienation of the Order* is a cornerstone of our thinking. In that book, Küçükömer proposes a macroscopic model that is key to explaining the Turkey of today and tomorrow. The mainspring of his model is the dialectic between civil society and state. Küçükömer examines the reasons for the absence of a civil society in Turkey (or the fact that it has not developed successfully here); his analysis of the right- and left-wing forces at work, as well as of their political ideologies, adds new meaning to the concepts of "right" and "left." He argues that the major obstacle to democratization is in fact the bureaucratic-despotic state, that Turkish conservative currents assimilated by the right represent the opposition of civil society to the state, and that these conservative forces could therefore lead to greater democratization and the creation of a civil society.

Now here's my point: a closer look at Küçükömer's *Alienation of the Order*, which has profoundly influenced Turkish thought and stimulated endless heated debates between the right and the left, reveals that nowhere in its analysis of Ottoman society is there any mention of Christians, who nevertheless constituted 30 per cent of the population at that time. That's right: Küçükömer describes an Ottoman society from which Christians are totally absent. My purpose here is not to question the relevance of an economic, social, and political study that completely overlooks 30 per cent of the population but rather to point to the existence of a "coalition of silence" or a "collective secret" created by society as a whole. All of us, leftists and rightists alike, have contributed to the creation of a black hole. We discuss everything under the sun while "ignoring" this black hole – or, to be more precise, this hole, or absence, actually defines our existence.

I believe this is the mystery explaining the denial of the Armenian genocide and the silence that surrounds it. What happened in 1915 is the collective secret of Turkish society, and the genocide has been relegated to the black hole of our collective memory. Since the founding of the Republic of Turkey, all of us, rightists and leftists, Muslims, Alevis, Kurds, and Turks, have created a collective "coalition of silence," and we don't like being reminded of this secret, which wraps us in a warm blanket. Such reminders are distressing, forcing us to face a situation to which we don't know how to react.

Confronting our history means questioning everything – our social institutions, mindset, beliefs, culture, even the language we speak. Our society will have to closely re-examine its own self-image. That is why we don't appreciate "reminders." We experience them as external pressure and deeply distressing. Whether rightists or leftists, we find various pretexts, but our reaction is the same: "We were doing just fine by ourselves, minding our own business, so just go away and leave us alone!" As a nation, our response is this: "If you think we're going to suddenly destroy the socio-cultural reality we have carefully built for the past ninety-five years, you're very much mistaken!"

For all these reasons, I think it is time to address the question of the genocide from a broader perspective: that of the Christians who once lived here and were annihilated. This problem is directly linked to the history of the republic and to our very existence. The republic was founded on the disappearance of the Christian population living in Turkey – in other words, on the annihilation of an existing entity. Since our existence was founded on the disappearance of another entity, any mention of that entity provokes fear and anxiety. In our country, the difficulty we have in speaking about the Armenian question is entrenched in the duality of being and nothingness.

In the following pages, Laure Marchand and Guillaume Perrier lead us in search of an existence that has been reduced to non-existence. Holding up a mirror to our reality, they show us the traces of what no longer exists and remind us that, until we free ourselves from this communicative reality, this imaginary world where we are held hostage by our own illusions, we will never find peace.

Note on Turkish Pronunciation

Turkish proper nouns have been transcribed using the Latin Turkish alphabet now used in Turkey. The letters b, d, f, k, l, m, n, o, p, r, s, t, v, y, and z are pronounced as they are in English. The letters q, w, and x are not used.

a is pronounced as in "father"
c is pronounced "j" as in "joke"
ç is pronounced "ch" as in "chimpanzee"
e is pronounced "e" as in "red" or "a" as in "cat"
g is always pronounced "g" as in "game"
ğ has no English equivalent – almost silent, prolonging the previous
  vowel
ı is pronounced "e" as in "open"
i is pronounced as in "machine"
o is pronounced "o" is in "more"
ö is pronounced "u" as in "turn"
ş is pronounced "sh" as in "shine"
u is pronounced "u" as in "ultimate"
ü is pronounced "u" as in "cube"

Timeline

894–96	More than 200,000 Armenians are massacred in Anatolia and Constantinople during the reign of Sultan Abdülhamid II.
1909	Some 30,000 Armenians are slaughtered during pogroms in Adana Province in southern Anatolia.
1915–16	In the principal phase of the Armenian genocide, lasting until the end of World War I, 1–1.5 million people die.
15 March 1921	Talaat Pasha, chief architect of the genocide, is assassinated in Berlin by Soghomon Tehlirian, a survivor.
1923	The Treaty of Lausanne defines the boundaries of the modern state of Turkey and replaces the Treaty of Sèvres, which recognized an independent Armenian state.
1942	A wealth tax, *varlık vergisi*, deals a heavy blow to non-Muslim Turkish nationals and imposes forced labour on those who cannot pay it.
2001	The Armenian genocide is recognized by a French law.
19 January 2007	Journalist Hrant Dink is assassinated in Istanbul.

2009   Turkey and Armenia sign protocols to normalize
                diplomatic relations and open the border, but the
                protocols are not ratified.

2012   The French Constitutional Council rejects the law
                passed by parliament in January making it a crime
                to deny the Armenian genocide.

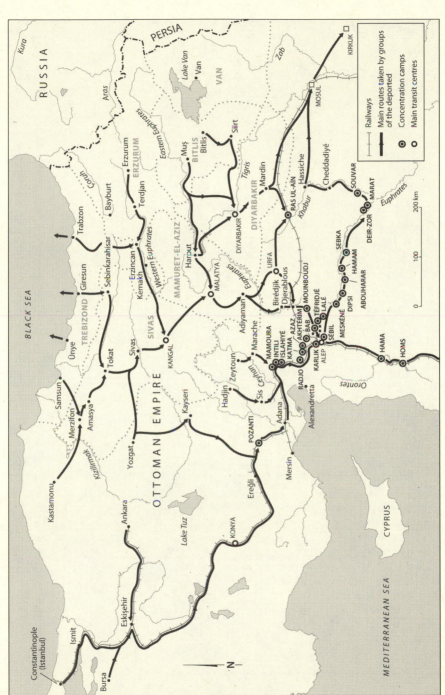

Centre of the Ottoman Empire in 1915, showing major routes of deportation and sites of genocide

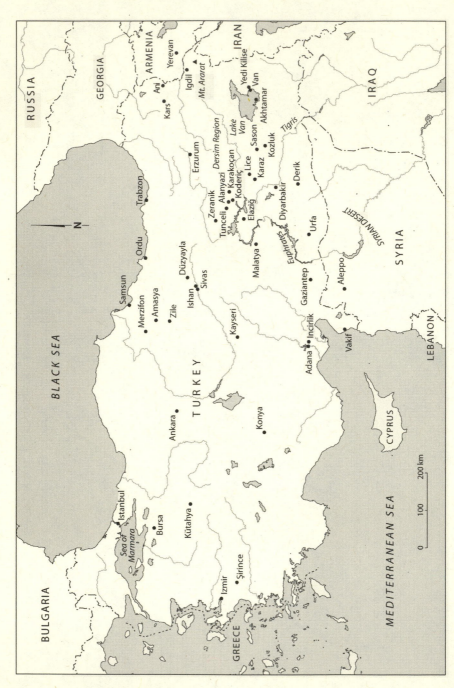

Present-day Turkey, showing the principal cities and places visited by the authors. (Maps by Bill Nelson)

Monument to Humanity, under construction. The Turkish artist Mehmet Aksoy created it in Kars, near the Armenian border, as a symbol of friendship and reconciliation. Turkey's prime minister called it a "monstrosity" and ordered its demolition in April 2011, five years after it was commissioned. (Photograph by Ggia–Own Work)

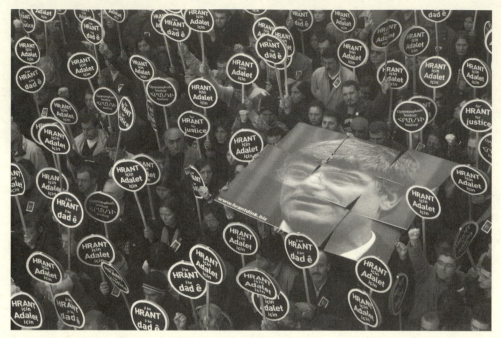

A crowd gathers outside the *Agos* newspaper offices in Istanbul on 19 January 2008, in memory of the Turkish-Armenian journalist Hrant Dink. He had been assassinated one year earlier. (Copyright Petitfrere/Dreamstime.com)

A ceremony in Istanbul's Taksim Square on 24 April 2012, commemorating not only the Armenian genocide but also the Turkish-Armenian soldier Sevag Şahin Balıkçı, killed one year earlier. (Copyright Sadikgulec/Dreamstime.com)

The remains of the Church of the Holy Redeemer (built about 1035) in Ani, a ruined Armenian city in the eastern Turkish province of Kars. (Copyright Witr/Dreamstime.com)

The small Chapel of the Virgins in Ani, perched high above the Akhurian River. (Copyright Asafta/Dreamstime.com)

Istanbul at dusk, looking up from boats on the Bosphorus towards the Süleymaniye Mosque. (Copyright Dreamstime.com)

TURKEY AND THE ARMENIAN GHOST

Introduction:
The Armenian Genocide and the Law

"Humanity can no longer live with the corpse of a murdered people in its cellar."

In 1897, the "Armenian question," as it was then called, was already creating a stir in the French National Assembly. With this ringing declaration, socialist deputy Jean Jaurès aimed to draw the attention of his colleagues to the massacres of Armenians in the Ottoman Empire by Abdülhamid II, known in the West as the Red (or Bloody) Sultan. These massacres were the forerunners of the 1915 genocide.

In 2011, the Armenian corpse emerged from the cellar in the form of a law that, one hundred years after the genocide, generated heated debate in France – and the latest in a long line of diplomatic crises with Turkey. In May 2011, with the support of French president Nicolas Sarkozy, Deputy Valérie Boyer tabled a bill to criminalize the "excessive" denial of "genocides recognized by the law." While general in scope, the legislation clearly targeted the denial of the Armenian genocide orchestrated by the Young Turks nationalist government. The bill was drafted by Philippe Krikorian, a Marseille-based lawyer of Armenian origin. Before its reworking by the legislative committee of the National Assembly, it was based on a European directive on racism, xenophobia, and historical revisionism and was intended to address a legislative gap. The French parliament had formally recognized two genocides: the Jewish Holocaust (Shoah) and the Armenian genocide of 1915. The first had been protected from the offence of historical revision (or negationism) by the Gayssot Act since 1990. The second had not.

The memory of the Armenian genocide has been a recurring subject of French parliamentary debate for half a century. In 1998, on behalf of the National Assembly's Socialist group, Didier Migaud sparked a legislative battle to have France recognize the 1915 events. After a stormy debate, this goal was achieved in 2001. Recognition of the genocide was fiercely defended by deputies and senators across the political spectrum in regions where the presence of descendants of Armenian survivors made it a shrewd political move: Marseille, the Rhodanian corridor, Lyon and its suburbs, and the southern inner suburbs of Paris. Votes for genocide recognition often appeared to be motivated more by short-term political gain than by a concern for historical accuracy – a sticking point that from the beginning placed France on shaky ground.

The 2001 law had no provision for prosecution. Its single article, "France publicly recognizes the Armenian genocide of 1915," identified no guilty parties, thereby making it unnecessary to put history on trial. For many French citizens of Armenian origin, the law was incomplete. France's recognition of the genocide did not prevent individuals or, worse yet, governments, from rewriting history for ideological purposes, thereby denying the suffering of the victims. French citizens who survived the Nazi concentration camps can prosecute anyone who denies the existence of the gas chambers, but those who survived the Armenian genocide have no recourse against denial of the 1915 deportations and massacres. This double standard was seen as an injustice.

In 2006, Christophe Masse, the socialist deputy from Marseille, sought to remedy the situation by introducing legislation to "penalize the negation of the Armenian genocide." Approved by the National Assembly, the bill met stiffer opposition in the Senate, which, without rejecting it outright, consigned it to oblivion to avoid offending Turkey. The law joined the Armenian corpse in the cellar – but it refused to stay buried. In 2007, Nicolas Sarkozy promised to unearth the bill and have it voted on by both chambers. As soon as he was elected to the French presidency, however, he sent Jean-David Lévitte, his diplomatic advisor, to Ankara to assure Turkey that he would do no such thing. Throughout Sarkozy's five-year term of office, nothing more was heard of the bill, until another presidential election loomed on the horizon. In the end, Valérie Boyer introduced a bill that was quickly passed by the National Assembly and the Senate but, after a fiery debate, was struck down by the Constitutional Council on 28 February 2012.

The council's decision did not end the debate – far from it. First, while justified by freedom of expression, the decision could be legally challenged. Second, politically, the issue was still on the table. During the election campaign, both major presidential candidates (François Hollande and Nicolas Sarkozy) announced their intention to introduce new legislation prohibiting historical revisionism. On 24 April 2012, the ninety-seventh anniversary of the 1915 arrest of hundreds of Armenian leaders and intellectuals in Istanbul, both men stood at the foot of the statue of composer and musicologist Komitas Vardapet, the Paris monument dedicated to the genocide. This gesture was a first. Upon his election, Hollande, who was close to the "Armenian lobby" and had been sensitive to the cause since the late 1990s, when he was first secretary of the Socialist Party, clearly reaffirmed his desire to legislate. For the third time, it appeared, deputies and senators would have to take a stand on this controversial issue. Yet despite this regular intrusion into public debate, the question of the memory of the Armenian genocide is still little known and poorly understood.

Is it best to legislate against historical revisionism or to fight it on the field of ideas, as suggested by the great historian Pierre Vidal-Naquet? The purpose of this book is not to answer this somewhat philosophical question: both options are valid. While clearly acknowledging the historic lie, Vidal-Naquet declared himself to be against the passing of memory laws. "In the case of the massacre of the Armenians, the Turkish state is clearly revisionist," he wrote.[3] That is the only intellectually valid argument in the face of opponents of legislative intervention.

By exploring the living reality of the genocide and its consequences for Turkish and Armenian societies sickened by a century of denial, and by following the twisted pathways of the memory of this "great crime" still denied by its perpetrators, this collection of our reports and inquiries gives the lie to all those who accept historical revisionism or take lightly this "ancient history."

It is not our purpose to write a history book. Historians have studied the events of 1915 in great detail; there is no need for any government to convene a commission, as Turkey and its lobbyists propose to do, to declare the truth about a subject that is no longer the subject of academic debate. The archives and documentary sources, whether those of the Ottoman Empire (now increasingly accessible) or of Germany, for example, provide sufficient evidence of the genocidal intent of the Committee of Union and Progress (CUP), the core of Turkish national power during World War I. In short, we have no interest in debating the reality of the genocide. It is a fact, amply supported by the countless interviews we conducted and testimonials we collected throughout Turkey over almost a decade. The disappearance of a million and a half Armenians from modern-day Turkey has left a corpse with gaping wounds that, like medical examiners, we examine in an attempt to give visibility to what has been erased.

Outside Istanbul, the Armenian presence has almost been erased. Yet in towns and villages throughout rural Anatolia, we collected stories and testimonials that are the best antidote to the poison of denial. We found survivors, forced converts, crypto-Armenians, so-called "righteous Turks," churches and cemeteries, tools, windmills, houses, songs, and traditions that have resisted assimilation and continue to tell the story of a century of existence, of fear, and of survival. We were there not as archeologists to dig up the past, but to learn more about the heirs to the legacy of the genocide and the contemporary manifestations of memory.

Our research often took the form of a criminal investigation, a jigsaw puzzle whose pieces gradually began to fit together. First-hand witnesses have almost all disappeared, but the story of the genocide has been passed down, through words and feelings, from father to son and, more often, from mother to daughter. Memories of the events still resonate in every home from Istanbul to Van, from Samsun to Adana. Armenian inscriptions are overgrown with moss and obscured by years of grime, but are revealed with a little scraping. Buried bodies appear around every corner of memory. The evidence is so overwhelming that its denial clearly stems from a collective neurosis. Together, all these testimonials and reports of the still-fresh traces of the 1915 genocide reveal the degree to which Turkey is haunted by the ghost of a murdered people.

"Humanity can no longer live with the corpse of a murdered people in its cellar." While Turkey was the major player in this drama, it is not necessarily alone in having to face it. By definition, a genocide – the murder of a people, the deliberate and systematic destruction of a community – is of universal concern, affecting humanity as a whole. The argument that the French parliament is interfering in matters that do not concern it is thus skewed. In fact, the origins of the Armenian genocide are closely linked to French history.

The Committee of Union and Progress was founded by a group of students at the imperial medical school in Constantinople (now Istanbul), on 14 July 1889[4] – the date clearly the affirmation of a French model. The first meeting of the Young Turks (calling themselves the "Jeunes Turcs") was held in Paris in 1902, with the young revolutionaries referring frequently to the Age of Enlightenment and the French Revolution. The movement was heavily influenced by the positivism of Auguste Comte in the first half of the nineteenth century and by the French school of sociology that developed just prior to World War I. The Young Turks favoured the Jacobin model of a centralized and unified nation-state. Even France's motto, "Liberty, Equality, Fraternity," was adopted after the 1908 revolution to overthrow the Turkish sultan. But, as Hamit Bozarslan explains,[5] this relationship is complex, intertwined with the nationalist ideas of that era and the German influence.

Some authorities believe that Turkey and Armenia should be left alone to sort out their history. But that is forgetting that modern-day Armenia is a recent political creation, having gained its independence in 1991 when the Soviet Union was dissolved, while the 1915 genocide involved the Armenians of the Ottoman Empire, citizens of a country now known as Turkey. The survivors of the Armenian genocide and their descendants are Turkey's children.

Another argument commonly used to oppose legislation is that the 1915 genocide is "ancient history," best left undisturbed. Jean Jaurès has already responded to that position. No statutory limitation applies to crimes of this kind. So the next question is: "In that case, why not pass a law about the extermination of Native Americans, or about the St Bartholomew's Day massacre?" The answer, quite simply, is that what sets the Armenian genocide apart from other such crimes is that it has been fiercely denied by Turkey, heir to the government of the Young Turks and the Ottoman Empire. Neither Germany, Rwanda, nor even Serbia has devoted so much energy to rewriting history. On behalf of Germany, Chancellors Konrad Adenauer and Willy Brandt both expressed contrition for Nazi crimes. France acknowledged its responsibility for the roundup of Jews at the Paris Vélodrome d'hiver. The Khmer Rouge, the Hutu militants, and Bosnian Serb General Ratko Mladić either have been or are currently being tried for their crimes. Each of these genocides has been recognized and commemorated by the countries involved.

None of that is true in Turkey, where genocide denial is alive and well in the form of a state ideology, or in the words of Turkish historian Taner Akçam, an "industry." As a result, a very real threat hovers over the few remaining survivors – "the leftovers of the sword," as they are commonly called today. In 2007, journalist Hrant Dink, founder of the *Agos* newspaper, was assassinated in Istanbul, and four years later, Sevag Balikçi, a Turkish soldier of Armenian descent, was also gunned down. Impunity is always an invitation to reoffend.

As long as it is denied by Ankara, the memory of the 1915 genocide cannot be laid to rest. Can you build peace over a gaping wound? Heal memories by trampling bodies? The answer is clearly no. As demonstrated by Vidal-Naquet, historical revisionism is the continuation of genocide – its final, most sophisticated phase. In *Assassins of Memory: Essays on the Denial of the Holocaust*,[6] he defined Holocaust denial as "an attempt to exterminate on paper that takes over from the physical extermination." The same mechanism is at work in the Armenian genocide: through denial, Turkey perpetuates the extermination process.

The Turkish state, the republic founded in 1923 by Kemal Atatürk, an extension of the government that orchestrated the 1915 genocide, remains committed to denial of the crime. In declaring itself to be neither responsible nor guilty, it prevents the wound from healing. The victims and their descendants still cry out for justice and reparation. A century after the events, the need for recognition, even vengeance, sometimes becomes an obsession. "They condemned the survivors to madness," said philosopher Marc Nichanian, speaking at the French Institute of Istanbul. At the other end of the sword, the descendants of the killers are equally unable to free themselves from this tragic heritage. In the words of Hrant Dink, the denial of 1915 fuels a double neurosis, poisoning the blood of both Turks and Armenians.

I

Marseille: Little Armenia

Rows of tiny houses are crammed together along the sunny slope of Verduron Hill in Marseille, offering a magnificent view of the sea below. Beneath them, beyond the high-rise towers of Cité de la Castellane, lie the quays of the self-sustaining port, where Panamanian cargo ships and ferries from Corsica and Algeria occasionally tie up. It was here, in Cap Janet, ninety years earlier, in 1922, that the *Hürriyet Pacha*, a Turkish ship from Constantinople, docked. On board were hundreds of Armenian refugees. "My grandparents and their little boy – my father – were on that steamer," says Patrick Chéguérian, contemplating the scene from his kitchen window. "In the beginning, they lived in a little hotel near the quays. But when they heard that small plots of virgin land were for sale up here, they came to build a new life. At the time, they had nothing. This area was called 'Strawberry Harvest.' My grandparents came up here on weekends to build their house."

The hilltop was soon covered with small houses built in the Anatolian style: low two- or three-room homes built in step formation with small vegetable gardens. Seen from below, Verduron resembles one of those little villages nestled in the mountains such as you see in the Turkish countryside. In Patrick's kitchen, the weathered floor tiles in geometric patterns are reminiscent of those found in the entrances to Istanbul buildings. "In the garden, there was a walnut tree, an apricot tree – the trees they had in the old country – and vines to make *dolma*, stuffed vine leaves," he recalls. "My grandparents disembarked in Marseille with the idea of continuing on to Argentina, but in the end they stayed. Grandpa Calouste was a cobbler – he had learned his trade in

Istanbul. My grandmother was a devout woman, totally devoted to the church. She embroidered the priest's robes with gold thread. No doubt it was her last refuge after the trauma of the genocide."

The entire hill became home to a small Armenian colony with a church, shops, and community life. Most of its residents were families from Sivas, a province in the centre of modern-day Turkey, where the raids left few survivors. Some 2,600 kilometres from their homes, the refugees came together. "They traded figs for hogweed. But those days are long gone," Patrick notes ruefully. One by one, the bakery, the cafés, Manouk the barber "who sold groceries" all closed their doors. In the 1960s, there were still twenty-five Armenian shops. But property values skyrocketed – the Armenian shacks are now worth €300,000 to €400,000, and with the mixing of the population, Marseille residents of all backgrounds have moved into the area. At the top of the hill, the St Garabed church, where no one comes to pray anymore, is all that remains of the community's Armenian roots – along with the house where Patrick lives, the last depository of the neighbourhood's memories.

The maritime transport line that had linked the ports of Istanbul and Marseille since 1830 became a route to exile. In just a few years, thousands of Armenians set sail for France. In November 1922, the first ship, the *Tourville*, unloaded four hundred refugees. One year later, Marseille had already accommodated eleven thousand newcomers. The first refugee camps were quickly opened. The Oddo military camp, originally built to receive White Russians, opened its doors to Armenians fleeing Kemalist Turkey on 27 November 1922, followed by Camp Victor near the Saint-Charles railroad station. The Armenians soon occupied the open areas on the city's outskirts. A steady influx of refugees continued until the late 1920s.

Hostility rapidly bubbled to the surface. In October 1923, *Le Petit Provençal* published a letter by Dr Siméon Flaissières, the socialist mayor of Marseille, clearly illustrating the city's feelings:

For some time now, there has been a seemingly endless stream of immigrants from the East – particularly Armenians. These poor wretches assure us they have good reason to fear the Turks. As a result, more than three thousand men, women, and children have already descended on the quays of our port. After the *Albano* and the *Caucase*, other ships will follow, and we hear that forty thousand more of these uninvited guests are on their way, meaning that smallpox, typhus, and the plague are also headed to our shores, if they have not already arrived in the form of germs carried by these immigrants: destitute, resistant to Western ways and basic hygiene, immobilized by their resigned, passive ancestral lethargy ... Exceptional measures are called for, and they are beyond the scope of the local authorities. The citizens of Marseille urge the government to vigorously deny these immigrants entry to French ports and immediately repatriate these pathetic hordes, who pose a huge public danger to the entire country.

It was a difficult adjustment for the new arrivals, most of whom had to rebuild their lives from scratch. The uprooted Armenians were discovering France and, with it, a racism for which they were unprepared. "We inherited the idea that we mustn't make waves, that we must play the part of the eternal victims – it's part of our genetic code," says Patrick. "Our parents were naïve and promoted the fantasy that the French had to be good people because they had taken us in. At school, they automatically separated the Armenian children from the 'good French boys and girls.' The local kids were told, 'Don't sit next to them. They're crawling with lice.' Cries of 'Dirty Armenians!' could be heard on the main street." The refugees' strange traditions were the object of ridicule. Patrick's cousin Françoise cites one example: "Our grandparents made *basturma*" – smoked dried beef covered with *tchemen*, a layer of paste prepared with cumin, garlic, and paprika. "My grandmother made the strong-smelling paste in a large bucket that she left out on the windowsill. And she told us that the French liked to say that the Armenians ate their own excrement."

Françoise's sister Nicole remembers their grandmother, just nine years old at the time of the genocide, who, seven years later, disembarked with her younger brother on the quay in Marseille. She ended up living in a shack next to the small Saint-Jacques church (Sourp Agop) on Arthur-Michaud Boulevard. The place was spartan, but she was happy in her two tiny rooms under the protection of a priest, and she lived there for many years. Nicole Matta recalls games of hide and seek in the church and hours spent playing in the small courtyard – where a monument to the victims of the genocide now stands. "When we were young, my sister and I would spend hours brushing our grandmother's long hair while she told us stories of her village, Khorkhon, near Sivas. The stories always ended in tears," Nicole recalls sadly.

"Before being deported, her mother had had no choice but to entrust her two children to the care of a Turkish farmer to save their lives. But her final words to her daughter were these: 'Remember who you are. Don't forget your language!' At night, in the barn where they slept, my grandmother would teach her little brother to speak Armenian and make him recite his multiplication tables. During the day, they worked like beasts of burden on the farm. The years passed until one day in 1918, Red Cross workers came to the village searching for Armenian orphans, and, ignoring the protests of the Turkish family, my grandmother went to speak to them in Armenian. 'My little brother also works in the fields,' she told them, and he too was freed." So many thousands of broken, violated, and traumatized lives; so many thousands who arrived in Marseille without a penny to their name.

In *Marseille, porte du Sud* (1927), Albert Londres describes the hordes of immigrants, or "human wrecks," "carried by the sea" to the quays of Marseille. Among this flotsam were the Armenians:

> The Armenians are inhabitants of Marseille, no more, no less. And Camp Oddo is their private corner of this shipwrecked kingdom. The camp represents the old corks, the discarded slices of lemon and orange, and the fistfuls of hair seen floating along the quays. It's the last place in the world you would want to end up. But I must take you there. Escapees from Smyrna, from Constantinople, from Batoum, from Adana, Armenians, always Armenians, still more Armenians disembarked and disembarked in Marseille. They first lined up in tight formation and set off to conquer the older neighbourhoods. Then they targeted the suburbs. But they had second thoughts. They returned to the city. Armenians are plants that thrive only between the cobblestones of city streets. Fresh air holds

no attraction for them. They just catch cold. So the Armenians took over the public gardens, the avenues, the public squares, and the staircases. When all that was occupied, another 2,700 Armenians arrived. They took over the city. Nothing was left unoccupied – not a single bench or curbside, not even a basin, which makes a fine home once you tip out the water. The 2,700 Armenians began to get angry. Fortunately, the municipality understood that it was time to begin negotiations.

"Greetings, foreigners!" it said. "Not too far from here, I have a large piece of land."

"Let's go see it!" cried the Armenians.

The troops set out. They arrived at Camp Oddo. A dozen old army barracks came into view.

"They'll do," said the sons of Asia. "Now leave us!"

That was three years ago. They were left well alone! There are two hundred of them in each of those barracks. Nothing but a rag separates one family's cubicle from the next. They sleep there – their heads with their neighbours on the right, and their feet with those to the left. They sleep with their neighbour's daughter thinking it's their wife.

Oh, my! Marseille, a word to the wise. You have forgotten them but, if you do nothing, their numbers will soon double – not counting twins! It's true that cholera may not be far away.[7]

Upon arrival, the Armenians were sorted on the Frioul Islands. Once on the mainland, they went directly to the Patriarchal church on Stanislas-Torrents Street, which served as the consulate. There they applied for a marriage or baptismal certificate – anything, as long as it bore the seal of the French Republic. They were considered to be "stateless": in Constantinople, next to "Purpose of travel," the words "Cannot return" or "No possible return" had been systematically stamped on their passports.

This is what had been written on one such document that came into our hands – that of Achod Malakian, alias Henri Verneuil, born in Rodosto, now Tekirdağ, Thrace, on 7 December 1920. He landed in Marseille in late 1924 and arrived at Camp Oddo in 1926. Thousands of other such identity papers preserved in the archives of ARAM (Association for Research and Archiving Armenian Memory) bear similar stamps. "The birth records were kept by the church," says Jacques Ouloussian, the association's president. "There was a strong desire to document, to record, an identity the authorities had tried to erase." The documentation centre, located in the Saint-Jérôme district of Marseille, not far from an Armenian church, is the only one of its kind in France. ARAM is a veritable Noah's Ark for French Armenians, both a library and an archive centre. It is a treasure trove of documents, registers, maps, newspapers, photos, and letters, all bearing witness to the exodus, reconstituting the memory of a people out of thousands of individual stories. In one corner, a box overflowing with old portraits of families in their Sunday best is labelled with a Post-it note: "To be sorted." Every week, new boxes arrive – gifts, bequests, slices of life in black and white.

Founded in 1997, the association "embodies our father's desire to preserve the memory of everything that had been passed down to us by word of mouth, to keep the Armenian memory alive," says Varou Christian Artin. Since his father's death in 2012, Varou has taken up the cause with his sister Astrid, a historian. From early childhood, their father, Garbis, had heard the story of his family's odyssey. His deported grandfather, Sahag, had learned Armenian in the deserts of Syria and Iraq by tracing letters in the sand. When he arrived in Marseille, Sahag began collecting "hundreds of photos and souvenirs. Anything written in Armenian could not be thrown away." His son Garbis by age twenty had opened a small carpentry shop that, many decades later, allowed him to retire in comfort. His workshop was then converted into a documentation centre.

Varou pulls out two large bound registers and opens them on the table, revealing the names of the five thousand Armenians who passed through Camp Oddo. In clear, round handwriting on fine paper, the camp secretary meticulously recorded the arrival of each person in surprising detail: age, place of birth, date of arrival, family ties, profession. Marseille natives with Armenian roots can now find here a condensed history of their ancestors and their arrival in this country. The first point of entry, Camp Oddo, was also a point of departure for the building of an Armenian community in France, rendered strong by the shared experiences of genocide and exile. The camp quickly took shape with a church, then a school and a scouting and fitness organization – the UGA Artziv. Its football team is still a cornerstone of the community.

In a period of labour shortages, factories around the camp were happy to hire Armenians: steel mills, soap works, cookie factories, the Saint-Louis sugar refinery, the Rivoire et Carré pasta plant. Women were employed at the Tapis France-Orient carpet weaving company, which did special orders for the ocean liner *Normandie* and Paris's luxury hotels. Some Armenians travelled up the Rhône to settle in the Lyon region, where they worked in the silk factories, as they had done in Turkey. Elsewhere, Armenian hairdressers, shoemakers, and grocers assumed their place in the city's mosaic. Near Camp Victor, a stone's throw from the Saint-Charles train station and the Porte d'Aix triumphal arch, was "the Terras," a five-storey building housing a multitude of small, windowless shops. It quickly acquired the ambiance of an Oriental bazaar, where Armenian craftsmen sold leather and leather products. "My father would come here to buy his shoes," Nicole Matta recalls. "As a little girl, I was amazed by all the noise, the smells, and the activity in this building."

When they left the refugee camps, the Armenians tried to acquire plots of land: as described by Albert Londres in 1927, the Verduron, Beaumont, Saint-Jérôme, and La Valbarelle districts were quickly sectioned off. "Schools and churches sprang up in each neighbourhood," says Varou. "Most of them were built in the early 1930s under the guidance of Bishop Grigoris Balakian." The bishop played a key role in structuring the nebulous Armenian community and consecrated seven Apostolic churches, all of them still active.

As soon as they set foot on French soil, the Armenians began organizing themselves by place of origin. More than simply being Armenian, what shaped the identity of these genocide survivors was their region, their town, their village: their stolen lands. Along with their memories of Turkey, they passed down their traditions, their language – Western Armenian – their recipes for *bureks* and lentil patties. The first community structures were naturally regional associations whose statutes were recorded with the diocese. "There were the Armenians from Adana, those from Angora [Ankara], and those from Césarée

[Kayseri]," says Varou. He pulls from a thick binder a few yellowed pages: the associations' founding documents. "The rural people from Sivas headed straight for the countryside and didn't mix with the city folk. The scholars came together and started recording the history of their region, throwing in a little hero worship of the resistance fighters along the way. Their identity was transmitted through those organizations. That was a consequence of the genocide."

Of course these weren't the first Armenians to arrive in this bustling cosmopolitan port so reminiscent of Constantinople. It was already home to a few merchants, publishers authorized to print since the issuing of Colbert's decree,[8] revolutionary activists. An identity centre had been established there since the mid-nineteenth century. The men responsible for the 1896 hostage-taking at the Ottoman Bank, the first action organized by the Armenian Revolutionary Federation, were expelled to Marseille. Following each series of massacres, a new wave of refugees would arrive. In 1909, a subscription was organized for the victims of the Adana massacre; the list of donors can be found on the shelves of the ARAM documentation centre. According to the register, even Ziyad Bey,[9] the Turkish consul general of Marseille, donated twenty francs for the Armenians of Cilicia.

So it was only natural that the refugees flocked to Marseille, and it was with the exodus following the 1915 genocide that "Little Armenia" was really founded, its memory composed of stories of decapitated men, disembowelled women, and babies drowned in the Euphrates, its identity forged of abandonment and uprootings. Two thousand kilometres from Constantinople, the survivors would found an obsessive, bruised, and battered community fiercely determined to protect what little had been spared them and to reconstitute an indelible memory of their existence.

One evening in September 2012, every dignitary and VIP in Little Armenia could be found in the courtyard of the Armenian Cathedral of Prado. Built in 1928 on the well-known Avenue du Prado, ironically just down the street from the Turkish Consulate General, this little cathedral is an exact replica of the Echmiadzine Cathedral, the mother church of the Armenian Apostolic Church. As always when the community comes together, the politicians jostled for position. A handful of elected representatives – both left- and right wing – were on hand, looking grave. Along with the religious leaders, representatives of the community's principal associations, chief among them the Coordination Council of Armenian Organizations of France (CCAF), gathered before the *khatchkar*, the stone monument dedicated to soldiers who died in the Nagorno-Karabakh War.[10] "We won't allow anyone to trample on our rights, our lands, or our dignity!" they cried. "We don't accept that the head of a criminal state be welcomed and honoured by France!" The next day, Ilham Aliev, president of Azerbaijan, was to be received at the Élysée Palace by French president François Hollande, and that visit was provoking the indignation of the Armenians. Aliev, the head of a country at war with Armenia, had just pardoned and granted a hero's welcome to Ramil Safarov, a soldier from Baku in the Azerbaijani army who, in 2004, had hacked to death an Armenian soldier in Budapest during a NATO-sponsored training seminar.

"Acts of barbarism are still being committed against Armenians," declared Éliane Kazandjian, chair of the CCAF. "We want the law criminalizing the denial of the Armenian genocide to be placed back on the agenda as quickly as possible." The deputies and city councillors agreed. In the front row of the crowd in the courtyard, wearing a red, white, and blue scarf, Valérie Boyer, UMP deputy representing the 8th Constituency, added, "The memory of the dead must be protected for the sake of the living."

Albert Londres was right: two or three generations after those thousands of "human wrecks" washed ashore in Marseille, the community of genocide survivors has swollen dramatically – doubled and tripled. Marseille is now home to some eighty thousand French citizens of Armenian origin – or about 10 per cent of the population of the second largest city in France, forming a not-inconsiderable voting bloc. The community has grown up far from its roots, and the yearning for its lost homeland and the thirst for justice have grown along with it. Armenian-sounding names have begun to emerge on the local political scene. These include Garo Hovsépian, mayor (Socialist Party) of the city's 13th and 14th boroughs and president of the Armenian cultural centre (Maison de la culture arménienne) and Pascal Chamassian, national secretary of the CCAF and city councillor (in alliance with the Socialist Party).

Not surprisingly, it was from this bubbling cauldron of identity that the first demands for recognition arose. "For cultural, historic, and political reasons, most campaigns on behalf of the Armenians have originated in Marseille," says Chamassian. "In 2006, a national appeal launched by left- and right-wing deputies led to an October vote in the National Assembly on a bill penalizing historical revisionism." Generations after the arrival of the refugees, the Armenian question has become a Marseille question.

In 2002, committed to ensuring that the memory of the victims was immortalized before it could be erased, the city erected a monument, a miniature replica of the Armenian Genocide Memorial in Yerevan. Every year, on the 24th of April, a ceremony at the base of this monument is attended by every elected official in Marseille. A walk along what is now known as the Avenue du 24-avril-1915, through the Beaumont district, the city's Armenian stronghold, takes you to the office of Valérie Boyer. This fifty-year-old deputy became a household name in France in 2011 when she tabled a bill in the National Assembly outlawing the denial of genocides. "It's a commitment of all Marseillais representatives, whatever their political stripe," she declared. A member of the popular right, the right wing of the UMP (Union for a Popular Movement), Boyer was elected in 2007 and re-elected in 2012 in this historically left-wing constituency. The outgoing deputy, socialist Christophe Masse, had also been involved in the Armenian cause and served as spokesperson for the first bill, which in 2006 proposed to criminalize denial of the Armenian genocide. Boyer took up that torch. "I'm not personally involved in the question, but my parents are Pieds-Noirs,"[11] she says. "When you've been on the losing side, you're more sensitive to such tragedies."

The "Boyer law" began to take shape in June 2011 in Marseille, Boyer recalls. "One night, the deputies were gathered at the Coordination Council of Armenian Organizations of France. We were just sitting around, shooting the breeze, talking about who had been to Armenia the most times – nothing specific. It was 11 p.m., and I was just thinking that my kids were going to complain that I was getting home late again." But before she could leave, attorney Philippe Krikorian pulled Boyer aside and told her his plan. Legally, they could penalize denial by transposing into French law a European directive condemning racism, anti-Semitism, and the denial of crimes against humanity and genocides. "In October 2011," continues Boyer, "I asked Nicolas Sarkozy if I could accompany him to Armenia to present this idea to him. Two days before he left, he agreed, and I flew to Yerevan." There, the French president denounced Turkey's revisionism and called upon it "to revisit its history and see it for what it really is, with all its highs and lows."

In Marseille, as elsewhere, elected representatives come and go. But the Armenian cause remains, and no one personifies this demand for justice better than the tenacious Philippe Krikorian. One bright fall day, he met us in his office near the Old Port, the cramped room piled high with papers. The flashy suits and cheerful Marseillais banter of his fellow bar members are not for him. Austere, precise, an expert on procedure, Krikorian is all law all the time. He keeps his distance from the city's Armenian organizations, which he views as "communitarian." The son of a history teacher and Grégoire Krikorian, police chief of Marseille, he fights injustice using Roman law. "The memory of victims of crimes against humanity must be protected by criminal law," he says. "This was confirmed by the European Union's November 2008 framework decision on racism, xenophobia, and historical revisionism. According to this legal decision, publicly condoning, denying, or grossly trivializing crimes of genocide, crimes against humanity, and war crimes is punishable as a legal offence. It follows that there is an obligation to transpose this principle into French legislation."

In June 2011, Krikorian filed an appeal before the Council of State and informed the CCAF's member associations of his action. He recalls that Valérie Boyer was there, and she said, "That interests me. I'm going to draft a bill." While Krikorian allowed her to give her name to the bill, which was eventually refused by the Constitutional Council, he was its original author. "I sent a bill to Valérie Boyer," he says, "but it was distorted by the National Assembly's Law Commission. This made it easier for the Constitutional Council to invalidate it. The council's decision on 28 February 2012 was clearly political." The big mistake, in his view, is to see the Boyer law as a "historical memory law." "Parliament is not rewriting history, as our adversaries claim. It is recognizing historical facts." Is that the case, we ask, even if the facts in question have not been confirmed by a decision of international justice? "Using the criterion of international justice to oppose the law is arbitrary and without foundation," he says. "The concept of genocide did not exist in 1915. But during World War I, the allies described the massacre of the Armenians as a 'crime against humanity.'" Furthermore, he notes, when coining the term "genocide" in 1944, Polish jurist Raphael Lemkin referred to the Christians of Rome, the Armenians of the Ottoman Empire, and the Jews of World War II. Krikorian hopes the Council of State will rule in his favour.

If a new bill is presented to parliament, it will have to pass through Marseille. "It's the cradle, the capital, of European Armenians, a vigilant guardian of memory," declares Pascal Chamassian. When Armenian president Serzh Sargsyan visits France, Marseille is as vital a stop on his itinerary as the Élysée Palace. Even Karekin II, patriarch of the Armenian Apostolic Church, has visited this Mediterranean city. But Little Armenia can sometimes be tough and unbending, as it was in 2006 when it jeered journalist Hrant Dink as he tried to explain why allowing Turkey to join the European Union was the best way to force Turks to confront their past. Paralyzed by its pain, it forgot that Dink was a brother and that part of his wife's family had emigrated to Marseille. (Just a year later, Dink was assassinated in Istanbul by a Turkish nationalist.) Today it is the Armenians of Armenia who come to these shores, fleeing poverty. These modern-day refugees are often met with indifference by those who came before them and who cling to the ideal of a fantasy Armenia, a substitute Promised Land. Politician Garo Hovsépian characterizes the Franco-Armenian identity this way: "The local community seeks its Armenian identity in its culture, its community organizations, and its associations. But with the passing of time, that identity is becoming less authentic. The glue that holds us together is 1915: that's what nourishes the spirit, the soul of Armenians."

Hovsépian continues: "The Armenian diaspora was triggered by the genocide, but they must not allow the cause to become a business. How can they avoid that? That's the whole problem of the Armenians and their schizophrenia. By returning to Turkey to reclaim their lost identity? The idea is tempting, but many are still paralyzed by the thought of taking that step." Henri Verneuil put it this way: "I'd be too afraid that when I walked across my land, I'd hear the cracking of bones."

"I can't set foot in a country that denies my existence," declares Chamassian, whose family roots are in Kharpert and Diyarbakir, between the Tigris and the Euphrates. "My grandparents came to Marseille but remained silent about their past. In our family, they didn't talk about it, to spare future generations the horrors of the genocide. Only fragments of the exodus were passed down. Every once in a while, after a Sunday dinner when he'd had a little too much wine, my grandfather would dig out the old 78s of Turkish and Armenian music he had brought with him. He'd play the records and start to cry."

In the family of Nicole and Françoise Matta, on the other hand, the story of the genocide was passed down in a less painful way. "Suddenly I needed to put images to all the stories my grandmother had told me while I was brushing her hair," says Nicole. "To make real all those places and details: the house in the village of Khorkhon, its wooden staircase, the apricot and walnut trees. I wanted to revive my memories so I could pass them down to my children, in a peaceful way. I feel it's my duty, out of respect for all those who were buried with no gravestone."

2

Armen Aroyan,
Archeologist of the Genocide

"When you look at this peaceful village, it's hard to imagine what happened here," exclaims Nicole Matta. The Marseille-born granddaughter of genocide survivors is visiting her ancestral homeland for the first time. A sleepy town of two hundred, Düzyayla, in the province of Sivas, lies on a hillside irrigated by a river where a few cows come to drink. At the top of the hill, the Turkish flag flutters in the wind. A few elderly men with white beards pass the time of day on a stone bench in the shade of an ancient oak.

Tourists are rarely seen in Düzyayla, so when a minibus full of foreigners, cameras slung over their shoulders, rolls into the square, the children come running. "Hello! Hello! Wotsyorname?" they cry. Uncertain of their welcome, the visitors introduce themselves. "Our families came from this village," they say hesitantly. "Children from this little hamlet, which used to be called Khorkhon."

"Are you looking for the Armenian houses? There were sixteen or seventeen in all," says a short, middle-aged man who has immediately guessed the reason for the visit of these *yabancı* (foreigners). "There was Vartouk's house – his grandson comes once in a while. He lives in Germany; his name is Mehmet Şeker. There's also a church over there, a little further down in the village. Come on, I'll show you!"

Nicole and her sister Françoise gaze around, wide-eyed, filling their lungs with the clean air of Khorkhon, the little village so dear to their hearts, thanks to the stories told by their grandmother in the small church courtyard in Marseille. This was where their grandmother, just nine years old in 1915, used to run and play. And it was in this village that her family was arrested, that she and her little brother were placed in the hands of a Turkish farmer. In one of these old barns, the two children slept at night and whispered in Armenian.

Nicole keeps her eyes out for a farm that might fit her grandmother's description. The villagers' welcome is almost courteous, curiosity winning out over suspicion. The group of tourists is disarmed: the village's Armenian past does not seem to be as taboo as they had expected. They follow their guide past dilapidated houses smelling like cowsheds to a pile of rocks covered with dirt and wild grasses. It takes the visitors a few moments to realize that they are looking at a church. Over time, the building has been almost completely buried. The front is the least obstructed, with inscriptions on a stone monument and the pediment confirming (if there was any doubt) that this was indeed an Armenian church. The main door is almost blocked by earth, leaving a gap of no more than fifty centimetres.

The visitors squeeze through and find themselves standing beneath a vault some fifteen metres high. From floor to ceiling, everything has been destroyed. A small hole in the roof opened by pillagers allows a ray of pale sunshine to enter. Only a few arches and the rounded shape of the chancel can be distinguished in the gloom. One member of the group stands quietly in a corner, stunned by the discovery. "It's very moving. Our grandfather was baptized and married in this church," whispers Rose-Anne, an American from New York. Her grandfather sailed to the United States in 1910, before the genocide, leaving his family behind and planning to reunite with them later on. But his wife and children were all killed in this village during the 1915 massacres. "He built a new life," Rose-Anne says.

Of her family history, Rose-Anne had heard only a few vague stories. She knew of the grandfather who had left for America and of a great-grandfather who had served as priest in the Armenian Apostolic Church in the Kayseri region. She wanted to understand, to see with her own eyes, to retrace the footsteps of those from whom she had inherited her Armenian identity. As with many members of the diaspora, born and raised far from their roots, her decision to return to Turkey was not an easy one. Right up to boarding time, she was filled with anxiety.

Turkey was the land of abundance, the land of creamy cheese made from buffalo milk, of walnut and cherry orchards, and of spinach treats baked by aunts and grandmothers. But it was also the land of ghosts and executioners: the scene of the crime. After years of hesitation, Rose-Anne finally took the big step. The desire to return to Khorkhon and to smell the earth of her ancestral homeland won out. She made the journey along with her cousins Nicole and Françoise from Marseille, with Claudine and Astrik, two sisters from Décines, in the Rhône-Alps region of France, born of second-generation survivors, and with Donnie, a photographer, who had flown in from New York with her son Chris. In the sweltering heat of August 2010, the little group met up in Istanbul, the departure point for their adventure, planned with Armen Aroyan, their Los Angeles–based "memory tour operator."

The group gathered at tea time in the Sultanahmet Hotel in Istanbul's tourist district. It was time to meet their guide. A white-haired sixty-something Armenian in a plaid shirt and suspendered khaki pants, Aroyan is a romantic character, a detective out of a crime novel. For the past twenty years, he has been organizing custom tours for the descendants of genocide survivors searching for souvenirs, details of their family's past, traces of their existence, and – above all – their identity. His tours are attracting more and more Armenians from the diaspora, visitors to a Turkey that is gradually opening up and becoming more accessible.

Aroyan began his travels for personal reasons. "I first came to Turkey in the 1980s," he says. "I had my own history to explore. When I returned to California, I shared my discoveries. My grandmother had often talked about life in Aintab,[12] about the beauty of the place. She always said it had the juiciest fruit, that life there was so sweet. I grew up hearing about those places, and I had always been curious to see them." Born in Cairo to a family that had fled Aintab, near Syria, during the genocide, Aroyan moved to California as a child. There the family found a sizable Armenian community, especially around Fresno. Aroyan studied engineering and began a successful career with McDonnell-Douglas, the aircraft manufacturer. But in 1990, just before his fiftieth birthday, he was laid off. "Perhaps it was a sign," he says with a smile. "By the following year, I had begun organizing trips for groups of Armenians."

Since then, Aroyan has travelled the length and breadth of Turkey, making four or five trips a year. He takes his groups from village to village, on the trail of Armenians who survived or disappeared. From the front of a minibus, seated next to his faithful driver, Cemal, a Turk from Antep, Aroyan criss-crosses the country from west to east. His business runs like clockwork now. In Los Angeles, he prepares a custom itinerary based on the wish-lists of his clients: a few days in Istanbul plus visits to some of the high points of Armenian heritage – Van, Kharpert, or Ani. But his clients are most interested in finding traces of their own history. "Everyone who has undertaken this journey has found something," he says: "a house, a school, a vineyard … Some have reconnected with a long-lost branch of their family."

His role is to organize these encounters with their ancestral homeland, to find a village such as Khorkhon, a farmyard, a bakery. Since 1991, he has led more than seventy-five groups and almost nine hundred people in search of the remaining traces of the Armenian genocide. Armed with a camera and a small camcorder, he records everything he finds: he has dozens of personal stories, more than four hundred hours of videotape. From Izmir to Kars, he unearths the remains and compiles the clues left by the perpetrators of the genocide. He has filled dozens of notebooks and inventoried more than six hundred Armenian villages in Turkey, including their original names. In some thirty cities, large and small, he has found small Armenian communities – hidden, forgotten, or assimilated – and recorded their stories. Through these repeated expeditions, he was one of the first to document the presence of descendants of genocide survivors who remained in Turkey – "the Armenians who had not lost their faith," the "leftovers of the sword."

Aroyan is not seeking fame. Possibly a little publicity among members of the diaspora – since he is also running a business. But, first and foremost, he is strengthening ties. In the *Armenian Reporter*, the community magazine in Los Angeles, Alexandra Bezkedjian writes that "Aroyan is one of the few historians who not only studies the issue but also shares his knowledge through tours of historic Armenia. He is a time traveler who unravels the threads of our scarred history to leave memories for the younger generation." He is "the one who unearths the dark fragments of our past, who leads those wishing to take a healing journey in search of the places we once all called 'home.'"

The group we join one Sunday morning in Istanbul is preparing to embark on a fifteen-day odyssey. Since 2005, retired sisters Claudine and Astrik have taken many such tours with Aroyan. "We visited the little village of Ishkhan, the hometown of our parents. We found the church and the home of our grandparents. All we knew was that the village of Ishkhan was near Sivas, that there was a large bridge crossing the river, and that there was a well and a small vegetable garden near the house," says Astrik, the elder sister. "The rest of the family is now discovering Turkey for the first time, and we offered to travel partway with them."

Our presence at first caused some concern. Why would journalists, who weren't even Armenian, be interested in these stories? Some fears, as well: "We don't want any problems, and we want to be able to return to Turkey after this trip," said one group member. Aroyan, who has spent almost twenty years exploring Turkey, was able to reassure them. In the early 2000s, it was still impossible to walk through a village investigating Armenian history without immediately being stopped by the police, but things have changed. The paranoia of the Turkish state has faded. Finally, the group agrees: we will join them in a few days in the city of Sivas (formerly Sebastia) in east-central Turkey, a key stop along their route.

Many genocide victims were originally from Sivas Province. "In 1914, the huge *vilayet* of Siva,[13] one of the most densely populated in Asia Minor, had about one million inhabitants, including 204,472 Armenians and 100,000 Greeks and Syrians."[14] The Armenian presence in 240 communities is confirmed by the Patriarchate, which inventoried 198 churches and 21 monasteries. According to the Turkish publisher Osman Köker, some 100,000 Armenians lived in Sivas before the genocide, and there were six churches in the downtown area: Sourp Asdvadzadzin, Sourp Sarkis, Sourp Pirgiç, Sourp Minas, Sourp Hagop, and Sourp Kevork. There were also Armenian schools for 25,000 children and an Armenian hospital.[15]

Today, Sivas is a city of about 300,000 in east-central Turkey. Freezing and snow-covered in winter, dusty and suffocating in summer, it is one of those charmless cities that one leaves without regret. In fact, *Sivasli* have moved en masse to Istanbul, France, and Germany. Modern-day Sivas is built around a wide main street lined with horrible square buildings of the kind that disfigure the entire country. Stores flash garish signs. At one end is an open space surrounded by historic buildings: the archeology museum; the newly restored mosque and its adjoining *madrasa*, both dating from the Seljuk period;[16] and, finally, the building where in September 1919 Mustafa Kemal laid the foundation for the Turkish Republic at the Sivas Convention.

More recently, Sivas made headlines for more shameful reasons that earned it a reputation as a conservative, nationalist stronghold. On 2 July 1993, thirty-six people died in a fire at the antiquated Madimak Hotel, just a few blocks from the historic square. Turkish intellectuals, mostly Alevis,[17] attending a conference in the hotel were attacked by a mob of Sunni fundamentalists. One of the speakers that day was Aziz Nesin, guilty in the eyes of extremists of having translated into Turkish excerpts from Salman Rushdie's book *The Satanic Verses*, then condemned by the Muslim world. An angry mob gathered in front of the Madimak, and the assailants, including deputies from the Islamic Refah (Welfare) party, set fire to the building. Neither the police nor the firefighters intervened. The image of Sivas is still linked with this tragedy, and the guilty parties have not been punished.

As Donnie, Rose-Anne, Françoise, and the others wander through Sivas, they have a hard time finding any traces of Armenians. The expedition resembles a treasure hunt. Aroyan leads them to the city exit, one of three stone bridges over the Kızılırmak River. He tells them that the bridge dates back to the twelfth century and was designed by an Armenian architect. Climbing down under the bridge in search of an inscription, he finds one on the south end written in old Ottoman. But on the north end, obscured by reeds on the river bank, the group finds another inscription in Armenian characters.

The exploration continues as the minibus heads back into town to Bezirci *mahallesi* (neighbourhood). This small working-class district, home to Sunni Turks, is made up of modern buildings, concrete cubes painted pink and green. Vendors hawking cheap clothing line the sidewalks. The neighbourhood is being redeveloped, as witnessed by the pounding of jackhammers and the dust and noise of construction work.

Bezirci was once a wealthy Armenian business district, and Aroyan is hunting for the last remaining houses dating from before 1915. There are about a dozen: dilapidated homes abandoned to cats, rats, and empty beer cans. But one impressive residence stands apart from the rest. One of the neighbourhood's best-preserved homes, it sits proudly in the middle of a vacant lot, its engraved pediment revealing the status of its owners. The name of the architect is written there in Armenian along with the date: 1890.

What happened to the owners? They were probably deported in 1915 along with most other Armenians in the city: "Between Monday, July 5, and Sunday July 18, 5,850 Armenian families were deported in 14 convoys, at the rate of one per day and an average of 400 households per convoy," reports French Armenian historian Raymond Kévorkian.[18] The surrounding houses were razed, and multi-storey buildings sprang up in their place. Only these few ruins have survived, as though the developers had qualms about destroying the last remaining evidence of the Armenian presence. Very little remains. "There are the houses in Bezirci and Tachan, the Sourp Nishan monastery church on the grounds of a military garrison, the Sourp Anabad monastery in another military zone, two houses and two millstones in the former village of Pirkinik," says publisher Osman Köker. "Aside from those, there's nothing left to see. It's all been reduced to 'once upon a time.'"[19]

The next morning, Aroyan and his memory tourists set out to explore the neighbouring villages. Twenty kilometres east, they drive through Koçhisar, once home to a prison with a sinister reputation, and on to Govun and Hafik, former Armenian towns. They then reach Düzyayla, the former Khorkhon, with its buried church. Before the genocide, half of its three hundred inhabitants were Armenian. A few survivors returned to the village and stayed until the 1960s. The Nishans left for Istanbul in October 1964, according to the village elders. "And now?" asks Aroyan. "There's no one left?"

It takes some time to get a clear answer, but after an hour of chatting, the old Turks suddenly recall that an Armenian by the name of Hovaghim still lives in those parts, and the visitors set off to find him. Half an hour later, an old hermit dressed in rags hobbles into view, bent almost double over his cane. The old man, who they learn is eighty-five, is surprised to be addressed in Armenian. "You mustn't speak Armenian here! It's too dangerous!" he cries. But he continues talking in Armenian as Aroyan questions him.

"My name is Hovaghim Karagozyan. But forget the 'yan.' They took it off. Now it's just 'Karagoz.' No, I'm not married. I live alone. I own nothing at all, not even a change of clothes. No, I have no family. I had a brother and a sister, but they left a long time ago." His eyes clouded by cataracts, he gazes fearfully around as if caught in the grip of unspeakable terror. "If I talk too much, they'll cut off my head. Take me with you, and I'll tell you everything." Then he asks fearfully, "But who are those people behind you? What are they thinking? What will they do to me?" The small group of members of the Armenian diaspora stands mute before the old man, the living incarnation of the pain that is their legacy. Their encounter with this Armenian descendant of genocide survivors, living alone in his village without being Islamized, is a shock. Tears running down her cheeks, Nicole slips a few bills into Hovaghim's hand and squeezes it. Then the minibus sets off again.

How many more are there like him, scattered throughout Anatolia, the last remaining survivors who have never left? It's impossible to say. "In Amasya, there are a few Armenians who have converted to Islam, married Turks, and been assimilated," Aroyan says. "I met one in the 1990s. During my travels throughout Anatolia, I've found about thirty places with Armenian communities." In the small town of Gümüşhacıköy in western Sivas, population 15,000, four households remain. "When I came here in 1995, there were still seventeen Armenian families," he adds. "Gradually, they are all leaving for Istanbul."

The group finds Kaspar Artin, one of the last remaining Armenians in Gümüşhacıköy, working behind the ovens in a bakery. "We've been working together for years," says Mustafa, pulling a tray of *pide* (Turkish flatbread) from the wood-fired oven. "He taught me my trade. The Armenians have always been the bakers here." Earlier, Robert Koptaş, editor-in-chief of the Istanbul-based newspaper *Agos*, had told us that his family came originally from the Sivas region before moving to Istanbul in the 1960s. "The Turkish soldiers needed bread, and my ancestor was a baker, so we were spared," Koptaş explained. Sivas was a large garrison town, so the entire bread production chain was preserved in 1915. The villagers of Tavra, millers who supplied the city and the army with flour, were also spared. But the farmers of Prkenik, Oulach, and Tetmadj, who supplied most of the wheat to the *vilayet* (province), were all killed once the grain was harvested.

Like other towns, Gümüşhacıköy was gutted of its merchant activity. "In the lower town, which used to be the Armenian quarter, they made wine, and there were butcher shops," recalls the baker. "And I remember the Hamparustan brothers, who were blacksmiths." Aroyan takes his group to visit the shop of Şhahan, an Armenian whose grandfather converted to Islam to save his life. Among the overflowing shelves of brightly coloured trimmings hangs a portrait of Atatürk. Şhahan is uneasy. The sudden arrival of this group of Armenians in his shop makes him nervous. "There are no problems here," he assures his visitors. "We live together peacefully, side by side. You see, my wife is Muslim, and I'm Armenian. There's no problem," he adds in his most persuasive manner. Şhahan acknowledges that "everyone was deported except us, because we converted." He's afraid to say more – a survival reflex in these Anatolian regions, where people don't shout their non-Turkish origins from the rooftops. Murat, an elderly Turk who happens to be in the shop, is more outspoken: "The Armenians hid in the mountains and the forests, and they were slaughtered. My own grandfather killed Armenians," he admits gravely. A heavy silence falls in the shop. "But things are better now," he says with a sigh. He seems relieved when the group turns to leave.

The tourists then meet an elderly man who timidly introduces himself in Armenian: "My name is Gabriel." Videocam at the ready, Aroyan doesn't miss a beat. This seventy-three-year-old former carpenter says that he still has a sister in Istanbul. He has remained here with no ties to Istanbul's Armenian community since the last visit of Patriarch Kalustyan in 1985. How did his family escape the genocide? "They came to arrest my grandfather, to deport the family to Arabia," he answers, his voice quavering. He starts to cry. "I don't want to talk about it." But then he takes up his story again, speaking rapidly in clipped sentences. "My grandfather hid in the fields. He never slept in a bed. We endured all kinds of suffering. The Turks got us all. They kidnapped the most beautiful women to marry them."

Gabriel's grandfather, Hagop Balian, a stonecutter, managed to slip through the net and return to his home in the town once the roundup was over. "He's the one who built the best *hammam* in the city. It's still in operation. Come on, I'll show you!" Gabriel leads us to the bath house, a beautiful building of grey stone. "I remember when I was a boy, the children carried the sacks of dirt and rubble." On the façade of this impressive building built by an Armenian, the municipality has installed a modern plaque, the words engraved on a blood-red background: "The nation's hammam." The nation it refers to, of course, is the Turkish nation.

In Zile, a few kilometres further on, the tall, upper-class homes in the old Armenian quarter are falling into ruin. The shutters are closed, the doors padlocked. The new owners don't live here. On the other hand, antique shops are flourishing, happy to sell the knickknacks, carpets, furnishings, and tools of the former inhabitants – as if they had only just departed. One of these secondhand dealers has collected dozens of Greek amphorae, a few religious objects, clocks, and a box carved with an Orthodox cross. On one wall of his shop hangs the mended cassock of an Armenian priest, who we can only imagine met with an untimely end.

The paternal grandparents of Nicole and Françoise both came from Zile. "Our grandfather was a boot-maker," says Nicole. "His workshop was probably around here." A few tiny wood-panelled shops have survived the urban renewal, but a merchant explains that the old shoe market was torn down a few years ago to make way for a parking lot. Zile is a pretty town at the foot of a hill crowned by a ruined fortress – a stop on the old Silk Road – and must once have been lively and prosperous. But today, the town seems to be in decline. The cheap Chinese goods displayed outside the shops attract no customers. The building that once housed the flourishing jewellery market has been converted into a mosque.

The next stop on the tour is Merzifon (Mersovan) to the north. "Before 1915, the city was home to more than five thousand Armenians," says Aroyan. "Today, not a single one. Many survivors moved to Fresno, California." At the time of the genocide, Merzifon was famous for its high school, Anatolia College (also known as the American College), run by American missionaries. "Its principal moved to Cairo, where he opened a school." The impressive building still stands and is even being renovated. Seized by the Turkish government in 1924, it served for many years as an army barracks. It was finally "returned" to the Ministry of National Education, which, since the beginning of the 2010 school year, has used it as a public school, complete with its regulation bust of Atatürk.

Across from the school, the dilapidated chapel and its wooden belfry sit abandoned. Down below was the Armenian quarter. The houses have the characteristic rounded silhouette with second-floor overhangs. On the right, Aroyan points out a house facing the street. In the centre of a small courtyard grows a strong fig tree whose branches have lifted one corner of the roof. A large room on the ground floor has been walled off. "That house was owned by the Dildilian brothers – they were photographers, and that room was their studio. I came here with their grandson in 2002," Aroyan says. The family of Tsolag and Aram Dildilian was originally from Sivas. The two brothers opened the studio and quickly became the official photographers not only of the American College but also of the province's governor. Some family members were able to emigrate to the United States. In 2002, with Aroyan's help, Tsolag's grandson, Dr Armen Marsoobian, chair of philosophy at Southern Connecticut State University, visited his ancestor's house. Since then, he has gathered as many photos from that period as he can, family pictures that depict the forgotten splendor of Merzifon and Anatolia College up until its tragic end. In the summer of 1915, Armenian students and teachers were rounded up and sent on death marches.

With its large Armenian population, the city had several churches, which have since vanished. Just before the deportation orders were issued in 1915, the Armenian community built a large Protestant church in the downtown core. There was no time to inaugurate it, however, and the Turks later converted it into a movie house. In the 1980s, patronage declined, and the movie house is now being converted into an auditorium. The street name – Cinema Street – recalls the movie house, but the pre-existing church has faded from public memory.

The minibus heads east, its passengers silent. The vehicle veers from side to side as the driver navigates the mountainous terrain of loose rocks and purple-hued cliffs, passing fewer cars than flocks of sheep with their shepherds and Kangal dogs. The sun sparkles on streams in the valley below. Next on the agenda is the village of Ishkhan, once home to the parents of Claudine and Astrik, the two sisters from the Rhône-Alps region. They recall the stories told by their parents, who were children in 1915.

"Our mother was born about 1910," says Claudine, the younger sister. "Her older brother, Stéphane, disappeared during the genocide. Together with a cousin of about the same age, she was taken in by a Turkish family, but she ran away. She often talked about the river, the colour of blood, where they could see hair floating. One day when she was very young, she was sitting on a donkey loaded with baskets. When she lifted a cloth covering one of them, she saw a human head." Another story the sisters heard was of a grandmother who, during the deportation, collapsed under a tree, too exhausted to continue.

On the paternal side, their grandfather was a priest. "Evidence of his fate was discovered in the Armenian archives in Jerusalem," continues Astrik. "He was arrested by the Turkish police, imprisoned, and tortured. He was forty-three. He was freed with the help of the archbishop of Istanbul, but they were relentless. He was finally executed on a hilltop. Our great-uncle, his brother, was an intellectual. They cut off his head in front of the entire family. Our grandmother dressed all her children as little girls." That's how their father, nine at the time, was able to escape.

The village of Ishkhan ("prince" in Armenian) was renamed Ishan in Turkish, meaning "workplace" or "office building," but all that can be seen there now are concrete houses, fields, and stables. Walking through the streets of this rural village, half Sunni and half Alevi, the group looks for the church where Claudine and Astrik's grandfather officiated. They identify it by its minaret; in 1984, the church was converted into a mosque, and the frescos were covered with a lime wash. In this village, their grandfather once held mass, taught school, and lived with his family in the adjoining house. "My father played in this yard; he ran in this dust," says Astrid, smiling sadly. Women living next to the mosque hand the visitors a plate of freshly picked tomatoes and peppers. Removing their shoes, the group enters the former church. To the bewilderment of the imam, they improvise a few Armenian devotional songs in what was once the chancel, now a broom closet.

Like most of the tourists Aroyan has brought here, this group of cousins is discovering Anatolia for the first time. After a return trip in

2000, Charles Hardy wrote of his experience: "Every place visited during our pilgrimage was a link uniting us through our shared heritage. Everywhere we went, we found evidence of the Armenian presence. We walked the same earth as our parents and grandparents, their words 'Mer Yerkir' [our country] ringing in our ears. We relived the memories they had shared with us and that we had shared with each other. Together, we set out in search of treasures from the glorious past bequeathed to us by our ancestors."

With each new encounter, the shock is great and the emotion intense. These cousins have also come to explore the traces of their past, their history. The creamy *ayran* (yoghurt drink) and savoury *bureks*, the aroma of Turkish coffee simmering over the fire all evoke a thousand memories. "We're seeing everything our grandmothers used to tell us about: the flocks of sheep, the fields of wheat," murmurs Donnie, the New Yorker. This country is also theirs, even though they can't yet put their feelings into words. A few handfuls of dirt, carefully packed away in small jars, will make the homeward journey with them. "It's really the trip of a lifetime."

3

Of Grandmothers and Grandchildren

A battered samovar steams on the stove in the living room. Frail as a hothouse flower, Emine spends her days bedridden, enjoying the gentle warmth of the room. We are in Sason, west of Lake Van. The old woman was born near the dawn of the last century and still belongs to it. Her grandson Nihat takes her hand and leads her back to her childhood in 1915. "Tell us, Grandmother. What happened?" [20]

Emine can't remember. The unexpected intrusion of a foreigner has upset her. Her tiny blue eyes gaze inward, to her forgotten past. "When it began, Granny was about seven," begins Nihat. "She has often repeated the same story. She was in the arms of a tall, blue-eyed man with a moustache, standing near a cemetery, when he was killed. She began to cry." All her life, Emine has asked the same question: "Was that my father?"

Her tragedy, says Nihat, a history professor, can be summed up in those few words. "Her life spared, she was adopted by a Kurdish family and Islamized. She was given a Muslim name, and her Armenian name was carried off by the genocide; she eventually forgot it: 'I don't know my name.'" Nihat feels a special tenderness for his Armenian grandmother. "I've always felt it was important for her to talk about her experiences." Emine rocks back on forth on the bed, squeezing the stranger's hand. "Do you have a mommy and a daddy?" she asks, before disappearing under the large flowered quilt. She is back in 1915.

Like Emine, thousands of Armenian children escaped the massacres by joining Muslim, Turkish, or Kurdish households. Whisked away from the death marches, they were pressed into service as housekeepers for families or as field workers for large landowners – or adopted by childless couples. Often they were young girls. The prettiest ones were forced to marry or shut up in harems. A few luckier children were hidden, taken in, and finally adopted by compassionate neighbours. In 2004, these invisible survivors emerged from the shadows with the publication of *My Grandmother: A Memoir*[21] by Fethiye Çetin, a lawyer, human rights activist, and attorney for the family of murdered journalist Hrant Dink. In writing her book, Çetin shattered a century of silence.

Every spring, her grandmother, Seher – a good Muslim woman who never left the house without her head scarf and said her prayers five times a day without fail – would make her little pastries. Fethiye would happily gobble them up, knowing nothing of this Easter tradition and never suspecting that they were in fact symbolic of her hidden origins. The little girl believed implicitly that she was a Turkish Muslim, but in fact she had Armenian blood in her veins. It was only later that she understood the words her exasperated grandmother would say when angry with her husband: "Oh, you Muslim!" And Fethiye finally understood her grandmother's reassuring words as they walked by a cemetery: "Don't be afraid of the dead, children. They can't hurt you. Evil comes from the living, not the dead."[22] Seher waited until she was past seventy to reveal her secret.

In 1915, this woman was nine years old, living with her family in Habab, and her name was Héranouch. All the men of the village "were tied together in pairs and led away by the police at gunpoint."[23] The old men, the women, and the children were deported on foot to the deserts of Syria and Mesopotamia. At the first stop, in Paulu, some of the men had their throats slit behind the high walls of the church, and their bodies were tossed into the river. Along the way, soldiers and bands of Kurdish brigands paid by the government harassed and murdered those who were not overcome by illness and exhaustion. Héranouch's younger brother, Herair, never returned from this death march; the body of her pregnant aunt, stabbed with a bayonet, was left to rot on the side of the road; her grandmother drowned two of her orphaned granddaughters before being swept away herself by the swirling waters. Héranouch herself was ripped from her mother's arms by an officer whose wife was unable to have children. The little Armenian girl – now Muslim – was raised by Constable Hüseyin as his own daughter.

"My parents knew the truth," says Fethiye, "but the facts were hidden from the younger generation, the grandchildren. For the adults, hiding this painful past was their way of protecting us." Knowing that she was near death, Seher (Héranouch) finally decided to reveal her secret to her favourite granddaughter because she had a mission to entrust to her: to find her mother, father, and older brother, Horen, who had fled to the United States. Fethiye successfully completed the mission, locating her long-lost American family. When she announced that her grandmother's brother Horen had named his daughter Héranouch, the old lady cried, "So they didn't forget me!" That day, Fethiye heard her grandmother sing for the first time. Héranouch died before meeting her American stepsister, Margaret, but Fethiye flew to New Jersey, where she placed flowers on the graves of her great-grandparents, reuniting the Turkish and American branches of the family, torn apart on that terrible day in 1915.

Lifting the veil on this hidden past forever changed the life of Fethiye Çetin and those of thousands of other Turks with their own family secrets. When her book came out, says the author, now sixty-three, "I received an amazing number of letters with the same message: 'My grandfather – or my grandmother – told us the same story!'" Her book has sold thirty thousand copies and has already been reprinted ten times. Turks aren't big readers, so that speaks volumes about the scope of the phenomenon.

Since then, hundreds of similar stories have emerged, shining light on hidden corners of the past. How many people have buried their Armenian roots, like a hidden treasure or a shameful secret? In some parts of Anatolia, it is whispered that every family has one Armenian ancestor, but the studies on the subject are inconclusive. "For 1915 alone, the number of children involved varies from 50,000 to 200,000," says Selim Deringil, history professor at Bosphorus University in Istanbul. One thing is certain: these children, these little girls, were the source of an invisible branch of genocide survivors. In Turkey, they have no official existence, but a popular Turkish expression indicates that everyone knows about their existence. They are called the "left-overs of the sword."

After telling the stories of the grandmothers, Fethiye Çetin part-nered with sociologist Ayşe Gül Altınay to tell those of their descendants, all those who, two generations later, are finally questioning the official version of history and the silence imposed on their own lives. In *The Grandchildren*,[24] the two women recount twenty-four personal stories, portraits of families that, in one way or another, have all been stamped with an Armenian seal. This thoughtful work has preserved from historical oblivion a collection of harrowing testimonials that might otherwise have been killed by secrecy, if not by the sword.

The stories reveal the suffering of women who endured the last century in silence – their "lips sealed" by pain. Mute witnesses to the horrors inflicted on their people, they spent a lifetime gazing out a window from dawn to dusk as if awaiting someone's return, or lying motionless on a bench, never uttering a word. These survivors, who carried within them "the reflection of pain," in the words of Ali, one of the grandsons, have bequeathed to us their tears, sliding down wrinkled cheeks, terrifying bedtime stories littered with bodies, gruesome fragments from 1915: a baby nursing at the breast of its dead mother, a woman poisoning her milk so that her two sons would die in her arms, not at the hands of an executioner, throats slit by swords, screaming children thrown into the Euphrates.

Çetin and Altınay collected dozens of testimonials from grandchildren throughout Turkey. The vast majority did not want their stories to appear in the book, even with their names changed and any reference to their location removed. "Fear is omnipresent in this book," says Altınay. "It's at the heart of all the stories. The grandchildren were afraid that revealing their secret identity would create havoc in their lives – some are still afraid. But by sharing it with us, they were able to face their fears, to go beyond them, and to say, 'Enough is enough!'"

For a long time after hearing her grandmother's story, Fethiye too felt uncomfortable about sharing it. An extreme-left militant, she had spent three years in prison following the 1980 military coup. "Resisting the soldiers, hunger strikes, torture – all that, I was able to talk about. But when it came to talking about my grandmother, I held back. How could that be?" Over time, she began to understand that, beyond the fear, there was shame. These grandchildren have mixed blood: sometimes that of the victim and her saviour, more often that of the victim and her oppressor. "It was this sense of shame that caused us to contribute to the culture of silence." And to their own disappearance – how many still choose to remain silent? "There are millions of grandchildren of the genocide, and we have inherited the suffering that has been passed down from generation to generation," Fethiye says.

"Where are they?" asks Altınay. "You might see them in schools, in the hallways of the National Assembly, in hospitals, in factories, in the fields, in the prefect's office, or in the mosques. They could be anyone: your bus driver, the nurse who drew blood from your arm, the journalist whose articles you like to read, the technician who upgraded your computer … your accountant, the official who issued your identity papers, the fruit seller in the market, your favourite actor, the janitor in your office building, the iman at your local mosque." In short, "they are everywhere."

And she is not exaggerating. Elif is one of those people. She cleans houses in Istanbul to pay the university tuition for her second-oldest son, who passed the difficult entrance exam. The small pension of her husband, a retired bank clerk, is not enough. Every Wednesday, she takes the bus to Kasımpacha, a racially diverse neighbourhood on the banks of the Golden Horn, on her way to the Bohemian neighbourhood of Cihangir. An extremely kind woman, Elif has two passions: smoking cigarettes on the balcony while watching the tankers sail down the Bosphorus – and talking about Armenians. She first became interested in the subject when dusting a sign carried at the funeral of Hrant Dink demanding "Justice for Hrant."

Elif was born in the Erzincan district, in the foothills of the Dersim Mountains in eastern Turkey, where "there were once many Armenians." There are still a few left, she says, but every time she mentions her village, she adds that "it's much less religious than others in that area." One year, on the eve of Bayram, marking the end of Ramadan, we wished her the traditional "Happy Bayram!" She thanked us, tied her scarf, and said with a wistful smile, "Our family doesn't really celebrate

Bayram." One day, when she was again talking about the Armenians in her village, we asked her if there were by any chance Armenians in her family. "Well, yes," she replied, "my father's mother was Armenian."

Denize, fifty-five, agreed to tell us her story over a cup of tea. A well-known figure, she wishes to keep her identity secret. She doesn't recall exactly when she realized that her paternal great-grandparents were Armenian. It has taken time to fit together the pieces of the puzzle, and there are still gaping holes. She has little to go on. She knows that her grandfather was born in Van, and her grandmother in Erzurum, and that they may have met on the road to deportation or in an orphanage in Urfa, near Syria. At least she finally understands the sense of unease that has disturbed her since she was a child. The daughter of a civil servant, Denize moved around often as her father was transferred from posting to posting and always lived in staff housing. Unlike the other children, she didn't "come from" anywhere. This lack of a sense of belonging made life difficult in a country where the first question you are asked is "Where is your *memleket* (country)?" "I always asked my parents, 'Why don't we have a village?'" she recalls. Her friends were lucky enough to have homes of their own. Even if they were just wooden houses with gardens or vines, they were "magical places" to the little girl.

Another question that tormented her was "Why don't we have any cousins?" In Turkey, family is sacred. Weddings, births, and deaths are all occasions for countless relatives to descend on a household. Denize has seven brothers and sisters but just one uncle. "I finally understood that it just made my parents sad when I asked such questions, so I stopped," she says. In time, she also understood the unspoken worry behind her parents' warnings to "never bring a police officer to the house." She never did, but she did become an activist and faced police violence in the 1990s during the "dirty war" waged by the Turkish army in the country's Kurdish southeast. Taken into custody, she was bombarded by the insult "Filthy Armenian!" At the time she never suspected how it specifically targeted her, but the Turkish civil status records keep tabs on this "fifth column."

The discovery of her family history triggered "enormous rage and pain": the foundations of her identity were shattered. Who was she? Today, she seems to have made peace with her identity, reclaiming every part of it – "a little Kurdish, a little Armenian, a little Alevi, a little Zaza"[25] – and she harbours a fierce hatred of nationalism of any kind, since it implies the denial of the other parts of her. Yet she can't help blaming her parents for choosing the path of silence. She feels that she never knew who they were, so has always lived a lie. "My mother and father are both dead. There's nobody left to answer my questions."

Berke Baş determined to avoid that situation by asking questions of those who knew the answers before they could take them with them to their grave. Nahide Kaptan, the second wife of Berke's great-grandfather, was an Armenian. Berke always knew this, but never understood what that meant. "I only knew that one of my great-grandmothers was of Georgian origin, and that we were all descended from her, and that the other was Armenian. That's all." For Berke, Nahide was the great-grandmother who knitted dresses for her dolls and was a hypochondriac who never went anywhere without a little bag of medicine. The opening of the debate on the genocide in 2005, meeting Hrant Dink, reading *My Grandmother* – it all piqued her interest in the life of her own great-grandmother, who had died in 1993 at the age of eighty-nine. A documentary filmmaker, Berke began asking questions of her family, knocking on neighbours' doors, and exploring the back lanes of the town of Ordu on Turkey's Black Sea coast, seeking the hidden face of the Armenian woman who had lived there. From this inquiry emerged *La Chanson de Nahide* (Nahide's song), a documentary paying gentle posthumous tribute to her Armenian great-grandmother.

To her great surprise, some Ordu residents still remembered Nahide's story and were willing to tell it. In 1915, the little girl known as Keganoush Bulbuldjian had found herself alone. Her uncle Dikran, who had connections, had entrusted her to the protection of the Turkish official who was drawing up lists of deportees. Nahide was taken in by a Turkish family. After the war, her uncle returned to Ordu to reclaim her, but she refused to leave her new home. In the course of her inquiry, Berke learned that Nahide's little brother, Kégham, had been thrown into the river next to the family home. All her life, that's what Nahide would say every time she crossed the bridge.

In telling the story of her great-grandmother, Berke shed light on the Armenian past of the entire town. "The official discourse is silent on

the question," she says, "but as soon as I began asking questions, people could not stop talking." She discovered that the quarter known as
"the National Victory" (Zafer-i-Milli) had once been home to Armenians. They had been the owners of those beautiful half-timbered Ottoman houses. Her father showed her a sepia-toned photo of the town
at the turn of the century. The picture, on which was written "Souvenirs d'Ordou," shows a large church. Today the building is still standing, but it has been converted into a mosque.

Her father told her that he had had many Armenian friends as a
child and that his father's accountant was Armenian. Maryam, a neighbour and one of Ordu's four "official" Armenians, said that the survivors and their descendants, who were numerous until the 1960s, had
ended up moving to Istanbul or Argentina. And Berke herself became
aware of buried memories emerging from the past. One summer day,
she and her family, including her great-grandmother, had taken a pic-
nic into the countryside outside Ordu to a place known as "the cliff of
the Armenians." The adults knew the grim story behind the name: that
was where Armenians had been thrown to their deaths.

The quantity of information conveyed by word of mouth began to
weigh on Berke. "We had never talked about it before. I had never
asked questions. How could that be? But we didn't even know there
had been Armenians in Turkey. They were never mentioned in books.
We only heard about them through ASALA [the Armenian Secret Army
for the Liberation of Armenia]."[26] Berke concluded that the explanation for this collective amnesia was the conditioning imposed by the
system: "We have been programmed not to ask questions. In this
country, the past is meant to be forgotten – except for the military
victories."

Berke had attended Bosphorus University in Istanbul, cradle of the
Turkish elite, but her awareness only began to grow when she left to
pursue her studies in the United States. By the time she returned to
Turkey, the nationalist stranglehold on the Armenian taboo had begun
to weaken, and she felt an urgent need to preserve the memory of her
great-grandmother's tragedy. Berke's generation is the last to have direct access to those who have known the survivors. "Our right to remember these men, women, and children has been denied. That's the
worst part. Today, it would be an exaggeration to say that we are able

to look the past in the eye. Let's just say that we have begun to catch a glimpse of it."

Turkish ideology is not solely responsible for obliterating the memory of these genocide survivors. They have also been erased from the stories of the Armenian diaspora. Scattered throughout the world, the members of the diaspora have left for dead those who remained behind. Having converted to Islam, those women and children are souls that have been lost to the community. "The silence has also been incorporated in Armenian historiography, which considers that their conversion destroyed their identity," says Altınay.

The disappearance of these survivors was all the easier to accomplish because they were mainly female. "Their existence raises questions," says Altınay: "Who is a genocide survivor? If you survive with a different identity, are you still a survivor? Since their children are Muslim, they are considered to be dead." It's no coincidence that it was two women, Fethiye Çetin and Ayşe Gül Altınay, who became interested in their fate. "For the first time," Altınay says, "these women are the subjects of the story, not the objects of a narrative composed by men and produced by a patriarchal system. They are the ones who whispered their stories to us." *My Grandmother* and *The Grandchildren* shook up the diaspora, which is starting to reintegrate these forgotten daughters and sons into the community.

Altınay, a Turkish expert on questions of nationalism and gender, dismisses both the Turkish and the Armenian histories. "The nationalist vision of some of our Turkish and Armenian historians, which is based on race or ethnicity, refuses to take into account the Armenians who have been converted, since their experience shatters the illusion of 'purity' on which nations are built."

The grandchildren of the survivors, in the book written about them, reveal that their sense of belonging varies greatly. They may self-identify as Armenians, Turks, or Kurds, as Muslims, Christians, a mix of both, or atheists, or recognize one identity as dominant without denying another. But most often they claim multiple identities, an infuriating state of affairs for promoters of the "Turkish race."

Yıldız Önen, a forty-two-year-old human rights activist, was one of the few women who agreed to speak to Berke and Altınay under her own name. Now living in Istanbul, she grew up near Syria in the city of Derik – "little church" in Kurdish. Before the genocide, it was home to four thousand Armenians. Afterward, fewer than forty remained, including her grandmother, Tano. Born into a wealthy family, Tano had a 100 per cent Armenian son from her first marriage, but her Armenian husband disappeared in 1915. Perhaps he died in the "Armenian oven" – "That's a cave outside Derik," explains Yıldız. "The Armenians were shut up inside and burned alive. For a long time, it was walled up. It was full of skeletons. My mother saw them." A vulnerable widow in the postwar years, Tano was forced to marry a Kurd who wanted her land. Her second son, Yıldız's father, was born of this union, marked by violence. "My grandmother raised two sons, one in the Armenian tradition, the other as a Kurd. My father, who was Muslim, had an Armenian brother."

Yıldız's history and her origins have never been taboo. As a child, she was warmly welcomed by her Armenian cousins in Istanbul. She loved the curious chocolate liqueurs that were never seen anywhere else. Her family is a microcosm of the various attitudes to the genocide. For Christian celebrations, her mother, who was 100 per cent Kurd, prepared special dishes for her Armenian cousins. And when Yıldız visited them, the Armenians always placed a prayer mat at her disposal. On the other hand, the hostility of some of her Kurdish uncles was almost palpable. "They refuse to accept us as Kurds because of my grandmother's religion. Everything that happened in the past is cloaked in silence."

It was the murder of Hrant Dink that caused Yıldız, like many others, to question her identity. "When that happened, I began to think that I too should feel Armenian," she says. But she has embraced only part of her paternal Armenianism. "Intellectually, I know that I am Armenian. Emotionally, it's harder, because I was raised as a Kurd." But she believes that her grandmother Tano, who died long before she was born, is to thank for the liberal education she received. Yıldız was the first girl from Derik ever to attend university. Her two younger sisters will follow in her footsteps. This was her parents' choice: in this region, heavily influenced by the Shafi'i school of thought,[27] girls are supposed to marry as soon as possible and start having sons. But Tano's determination was passed down to her children. On her deathbed, this strong-willed woman made a last request of her Kurdish daughter-in-law: "Above all, don't let them recite the *chahada* [profession of Muslim faith] over my body." Until the very end, she refused to convert to Islam and remained faithful to her Christian roots.

For Yıldız, demanding that the genocide be recognized is a matter of both intellectual honesty and solidarity with her grandmother. Like thousands of others, her grandmother may have survived, but at what cost? What suffering, what physical and psychological violence, did she endure? "Of course the genocide resulted from a policy of the Ottoman Empire. But it's not enough for the Kurds to recognize its existence; they must assume their share of responsibility. Yes, they abducted many girls, saving their lives. But they converted them to Islam."

All these remarkable stories, dredged up from the silent past, defy the anti-Armenian ideology. "They raise many questions," says Çetin. "And if you start asking questions about yourself and your family, 'the other' can no longer be 'the other.' The person you were told was your 'enemy' can no longer be your 'enemy' – because that person might be your grandmother!" The previous night, Çetin had been invited to talk about her first book, *My Grandmother*, at a local high school. "The discussion lasted three hours. The students' nationalistic education was evident, and there were lots of 'buts,' but at the end of the evening, we sold seventy books," she says proudly.

Historical revisionism is difficult to fight, but grandmothers are sacred. The strength of these stories is that they use inoffensive grandmothers to break taboos, becoming part of a historic reconciliation process. By studying the micro-history of families and communities, civil society and Turkish intellectuals may have found an effective answer to the official revisionism that surrounds the Armenian question.

Bekir Coşkun, a prominent journalist, summed it up well in an editorial titled "My Armenian Question," published in the daily newspaper *Hürriyet*. "I have no personal information about what happened to one million Armenians," he wrote. "I know just one Armenian. My father was a civil servant. When our mother died, he took my sister and me to live with our grandmother. We lived there with her in a big house in Tülmen, near Urfa. I don't remember much about my childhood, but I know that she loved us and took good care of us. My grandmother wasn't like our aunts and the other women in the household. She was tall and thin, with blond hair and grey-blue eyes. Her name was Ummuhan. The whole family loved her and treated her with respect. I was particularly struck by how much my father, a strict, authoritative, learned man, trusted and cared for her. Time passed, and we grew older. And we learned that she wasn't our real grandmother, that she had entered our home after our real grandmother had died. She was an Armenian.

"When my real grandmother died, my grandfather picked her up on the Euphrates plain, in Syria, where entire convoys of Armenians had been deported, and he married her. When we grew up and learned the truth, we understood the sadness in her eyes. And that is my personal Armenian question. What was done to the Armenians, why people don't want to talk about it, what really happened – I don't know. But what I want to know is who took my grandmother away from her home, from her safe place, when she was just a young girl. I want to know who is responsible for the pain she tried to keep from us, for the homesickness she tried to hide, for the tears she must have shed on her pillow every night, behind closed doors. I don't know anything about one million Armenians. Just this one woman. This terribly sad woman I loved so much. My Armenian."

4

Converts: The Hidden Armenians

"In Anatolia, any remaining Armenians are at best in cemeteries, at worst in mass graves." While the description seemed harsh, it reflected the views of the elderly journalist. He was categorical: the genocide left nothing in its wake but a gaping wound. According to a slightly exaggerated but commonly accepted figure, only seventy thousand Armenians are still living in Turkey. A handful remain in Izmir (formerly Smyrna), but the vast majority – the remnants of an exterminated people – fled to Istanbul.

It was 2006, and we were visiting the dusty offices of *Marmara*, an Armenian-language newspaper that stubbornly continues to publish an eight-page daily. Five years later, a service would be held at the newly restored Sourp Giragos Orthodox church in Diyarbakir. Officially, the town is now home to just two Armenians. Yet, during the service, the priest baptized some twenty adult Muslims. In recent years, men and women have been emerging from their self-imposed silence, revealing a hidden reality in Turkey – that of Islamized survivors.

After our meeting with the journalist from *Marmara*, we put our search for forgotten survivors on hold – until one early evening in January 2009, when we met up in Istanbul with an Armenian, Sadık Bakırcıoğlu, as he left work. A violent rainstorm hammered the sides of the bus as it inched its way through rush-hour traffic. The steam-room atmosphere of the crowded vehicle reinforced our feeling that we were about to enter a secret world – a long-awaited encounter with history on the outskirts of the metropolis.

At the end of the line, in Sultançiftliği, we left the bus with the few remaining passengers, who disappeared into the shadows of the ill-defined concrete neighbourhood. Dinner awaited us on the third floor of a small building, painted blue. "Thank you, Lord, for giving us this food. Please bless this meal we are about to eat," Murat,[28] the head of the family, intoned in Armenian. "In the name of the Father, the Son, and the Holy Ghost. Amen." Their heads covered with the white veil of Kurdish peasants, Murat's children, wife, and grandmother made the sign of the cross and dipped their spoons into the yoghurt chickpea soup. The heavy iron front door hid the conversation from the ears of curious neighbours. If overheard, it would have provided an inexhaustible source of *dedikodu*, gossip. In the corner of the living room, tinsel glittered on a plastic Christmas tree.

During the day, Murat runs a business selling plexiglass windows. "At the shop, I observe Ramadan," he says. "Here, everyone is a conservative Muslim. Being Christian would be bad for business. No one would want to buy from *gavur* [infidels]; that would be sinful." So is he Christian? Muslim? Both? He shows us the Bible in his shirt pocket and says that, under his roof, alcohol is forbidden. "My identity is in my heart. Only God knows what it is," he says, smiling ruefully. "Christ is in my heart." Above all, there is the Armenian genocide and the family tragedy, whispered from generation to generation: as a teenager, his grandfather had been forced by Ottoman soldiers to drown his four-year-old brother in the Euphrates. His six-year-old sister was already dead. He himself escaped the sword by becoming a shepherd working for "Turkish masters" and later adopting Islam.

Murat's grandfather was not alone. Tens of thousands of Armenians converted to Islam to escape the massacres ordered in the late nineteenth century by Sultan Abdülhamid II, dubbed the "Red Sultan," and those planned by the Young Turks government. "People were prepared to give up a lot to save their lives," says one of their descendants. They are known as the *dönme*, the "converts." Submitting to pressure that continued after 1915, some changed religions later on. For decades, they remained underground, threatened by the government's determination to eradicate all trace of their existence in Anatolia. These hidden Armenians found it all the easier to remain so since neither Ankara nor the diaspora had any interest in seeing them emerge from the shadows.

For the Turks, they are living proof of the darkest period in the country's history. For the diaspora, they raise two issues: first, Armenians who publicly renounced their Christian faith were lost to the community; second, recognizing their existence could raise doubts about the official genocide figures. But after a century of silence, these "hidden" Armenians are cautiously starting to lift the veil of secrecy.

In 2009, searching for *dönme* was still akin to hunting for ghosts. But on a rainy Christmas Eve, after some tough questioning in Istanbul's Kara Kedi (Black Cat) bar, a favourite haunt of the extreme left, Ari, one of the city's "official" Armenians, agreed to help us. Had we gained his trust with our skilful arguments, or was it perhaps the Efes beers? Whatever the case, Ari finally promised to ask Damla, one of his acquaintances, to meet with us – on condition of anonymity, of course. Ari was careful not to mention that she was also his cousin, a member of the "converted" branch of his family.

One Saturday afternoon, we met Damla, a management student, in a trendy pastry shop on Istiklal Avenue, Istanbul's main pedestrian mall. Like people in all such families, she uses a Turkish name to avoid attracting attention. "I've always known that I was Armenian," she says, "but when I was little, my parents made sure I understood that I mustn't talk about it." As a child, she was careful to obey this rule, and in college she learned from her history books that it was "the Armenians who had massacred the Turks." The great-granddaughter of a bishop, Damla self-identifies as "an Armenian Muslim," while continuing to practise a number of Christian traditions. "At Christmas, we bake a special raisin bread; at Easter, we soak coloured strings in holy water to make *basimbar*, good luck bracelets. And when someone is sick, I light a candle at the church." Damla is describing a hodgepodge of faith and superstition. Like other crypto-Armenians, she lives with a unique combination of religions and cultures.

The pastry shop is crowded and, despite the noise, Damla is careful not to speak too loudly, interrupting her story whenever the waitress brings more tea. "My father would kill me if he knew what I've told you, even though I didn't give you my name," she says. Over time, the converts have become masters in the art of concealment. Nothing looks more like a Turk than a crypto-Armenian. Wherever we went in Anatolia, we would amuse ourselves by trying to flush them out. Of course it didn't always work, but tongues are finally starting to loosen, especially with foreigners, and some regions are more prone to this than others. Eastern Turkey, home to the six *vilayet* (provinces) that had large Armenian populations before 1914, is the best place to play this game. Here, pulled from our notebooks, are a few stories illustrating the persistence of the Armenian presence.

According to his certificate of civil status, duly stamped at the town hall of his birthplace, Abdurrahim, fifty-one, is a Muslim – as are his brothers and sisters. This is what has been written on all family documents since his father, Abdullah, was forced to convert to Islam in 1927, when he was sixteen. His grandfather, Usip, son of Dono and Meryem, both Christian Armenians, as stated on the certificate, was killed in 1915 along with other family members. His grandfather's date of death is also recorded.

The discovery of his family tree and of the stark reality of the genocide in the official records devastated Abdurrahim. A nervous man, the youngest of five children, he has since devoted much of his life to unravelling the past, which he has made his own, despite the panic that engulfs him whenever he discovers a disturbing fact. For twenty years, he has collected files and documents, spending his evenings piecing together the stories of Armenians in the region of Diyarbakir and searching for family members who have disappeared to the United States or France. For many years, Abdurrahim hid his family secret, sharing only parts of it with a few trusted confidants. In 2010, he finally decided to leave his job as a municipal employee to devote all his time to exploring his identity.

Abdurrahim is fascinated by everything Armenian. First, he became a Christian. Then he began signing his text messages with the Armenian name he chose for himself: Armen. In 2011 he was one of the first to register for a course in the Armenian language offered by Sur Municipality, the old city of Diyarbakir. "There were about forty of us last year. I know them all. Some will tell you they are Kurds or refuse to talk about it. But they're all *dönme*," he says haltingly. More than fifty students are already registered for the 2012 course. In his spare time, Abdurrahim also delivers the Turkish-Armenian weekly *Agos* to its twenty-five subscribers in Diyarbakir.

From this large Kurdish city in southeastern Turkey, we catch a taxi to the neighbouring town of Batman. "Who are you? Where are you from? Where are you going?" The friendly thirty-something driver reels off the traditional litany of questions asked of any foreigner. In return, we ask whether he might by any chance be Armenian, there are so many in this region… "Oh, no, I'm a 'good Muslim,'" he replies quickly. Indeed, the visible evidence is all there: a closely cropped beard, a miniature Quran suspended from the rear-view mirror that jerks up and down at every pothole and, on the back window of his yellow Renault, a wide "May Allah Protect us" sticker. For a few kilometres, he concentrates on the road. Then, "I'm a good Muslim, but it's true that on our mother's side we're Armenian." Really? After a few more kilometres staring at an imaginary white line: "In fact, on my father's side, we're also Armenian."

"So everyone is Armenian, then?"

He switches lanes, passes a tractor, then: "Well, yes, actually."

Sunday, 19 September 2010, near the eastern border of Turkey, not far from Iran. Hundreds of joyful Armenians, mostly from Istanbul, pile into boats headed for the Holy Cross (Akhtamar) Church, a small architectural gem built in the tenth century on an island in Lake Van. For the first time since 1915, the Turkish government has authorized the holding of a religious service there. The service will be led by Arem Ateşyan, the deputy patriarch, who has come from Istanbul – and whose family also includes converts to Islam.

The building is not large enough to hold all the faithful, and plastic chairs have been set up outside. Some neighbouring farmers have also arrived, picnicking off to one side. Officially they are Kurds, but their presence alone is enough to raise doubts about that. Sitting under a tree is an old man wearing the embroidered cap of a *hadji*, the distinctive mark of a Muslim who has made a pilgrimage to Mecca, and wearing a pair of *şalvar*, the traditional baggy pants worn by Anatolian peasants. Suspended in the tree above him is a loudspeaker from which a crackling hymn is blasting at full volume. Is he Armenian? "Oh no, I'm a Kurd," he says. Next to him, a younger man, his nephew, bursts into laughter. "No, he's a *dönme*. Why else would we have travelled three hours to attend a service?"

Inevitably, some converts have tried so hard to hide their Armenian roots, to relieve the social pressure or simply to save their lives, that they have been completely assimilated. Becoming more Turkish than a Turk was the best way to survive. Implacable and insidious, time has been denial's best ally. Ari tells us about one of his uncles: "He's very pious. As soon as he hears the call to prayers, he hurries to the mosque. During the Festival of Sacrifice, he slaughters a sheep. Who would ever guess that he and his wife speak to each other in Armenian or that they visit us on Christian religious holidays? No one." The rural exodus to Istanbul has helped the Armenians to cover their tracks and lose themselves in the anonymity of a city of fourteen million inhabitants. Neighbours know nothing about one's family tree. Externally, Ari's uncle has retained a single clue to his hidden identity: he's a jeweller. But his daughter has buried hers beneath her chador and does not want to hear about her impious origins. "When you do everything in your power to bury the past, your children become nationalist and religious," Ari says.

One drizzly evening, Sadık Bakırcıoğlu takes us to the Sultançiftliği quarter, explaining that one of his distant relatives is an imam, but that another member of his family has an even more interesting story. Today, Sadık is a peaceful family man, but like tens of thousands of Turks of his generation, his youthful commitment to leftist causes led to his incarceration after the 1980 military coup. He spent eight years in Adıyaman prison in the east. In the 1980s, that prison was populated by novice Trotskyists, Maoist revolutionaries, Kurdish separatists – in short, a cross section of Turkish communist movements. But that wasn't all. "My family would visit me in prison," recalls Sadık. "And I realized that some of them were also visiting another prisoner: a cousin who belonged to IBDA-C [Great Eastern Islamic Raiders' Front – an Islamic militant organization]. In 1988, that cousin participated in an attack on Urfa."

To preserve the secret of their Armenian identity, people resorted to a number of stratagems. To stay under the radar, husband and wife – both from *dönme* families – would be married in a mosque, passing their secret down from generation to generation. But when and how could that secret be revealed? Hatice remembers her "initiation." She was twelve years old and believed she was Muslim, like her classmates.

When she began to pray at home, her father told her that Islam was not her true religion, but that she had to keep that secret to herself. "He told me, 'You're Christian.' It was strange, because I didn't know what that meant." Even when their parents don't tell them, children generally learn the truth from someone else. This is particularly true in rural areas and small Anatolian towns, where everyone knows everyone else. The taunt of *gavur* (infidel) never goes out of style in the playgrounds of the republic's schools, all proudly displaying a Turkish flag and a bust of Atatürk.

The government keeps a close eye on these "leftovers of the sword," viewing them as a fifth column. Occasionally, these "hidden" Armenians discover that, during their military service, they have been classified as such in the official records. "I went to the military barracks where my father had done his service to pick up his certificate, which he needed for his pension," recalls Damla. "The paper they gave me had the word 'foreigner' written on it. When I asked what that meant, the word was scratched out. We've been living here for two thousand years, and we're still foreigners!" This was particularly distressing to Damla since, when she was a little girl, she had wanted to be an airline pilot. "My father told me that wouldn't be possible." It seems that senior positions in the Turkish army and civil service are off limits to converts, as they are to non-Muslim minorities.

Ahmet, twenty-eight, is a telecommunications engineer, originally from Adana, in the south. In April 1909, thirty thousand Armenians were exterminated in that province in a prelude to the 1915 massacres. Having recently moved to Istanbul, Ahmet relishes "the freedom" of the big city, where he does not have to hide his Armenian identity. The seven hundred kilometres that now separate him from his hometown allow him to distance himself from the pain he felt when he discovered his origins at thirteen.

His family's nickname for his sister Asli was "Julia" (obviously not a Muslim name), but he was never aware of their "otherness." His middle-class Turkish family was totally committed to nationalist values – in fact his older brother was named Ata, after Atatürk, meaning "Father of the Turks." Raised to revere the founder of modern Turkey, Ata had one burning ambition: to serve his country by becoming an army pilot. At fifteen he met the tough entrance requirements for the military academy – but that's where his patriotic dream ended. "The examiners told him they couldn't accept him because of a large birthmark on his chest. They said it was a distinctive mark that would allow the enemy to identify him." Two years later, after having a bit too much to drink, an uncle blurted out the truth: "They didn't want you because you're Armenian. We chose to become Turks during the First World War, but we're Armenian." But Turkish propaganda had done its work on the teenager's mind: Ata refused to accept that he was one of the "traitors" who had stabbed the Ottoman Empire in the back by colluding with Western powers. "My brother first started to believe that he had been chosen by Mohammed and that his family had mistaken him for an Armenian. Then, that our family was descended from the prophet and that others wanted to turn us into Armenians." Ata began to suffer from schizophrenia, and his identity delusions led to regular admissions to a psychiatric hospital.

The state is not alone in harbouring animosity toward Armenians. In some parts of Anatolia, that same hostility is ingrained in the population, like a veiled threat. In the small town of Sason in eastern Turkey, Giyasettin Gelir has collected testimonials from the last genocide survivors. "Everyone told me that at the time they thought their conversion was temporary, just until things blew over." But things never really did blow over. In the late nineteenth century, the Armenians here participated in rebellions that erupted in the Ottoman provinces against an oppressive tax targeting their community. In 1894 and 1895, those protests were quashed in bloody confrontations ordered by Sultan Abdülhamid II. In 1915, tens of thousands of Armenians hid in the mountainous region of Sason. Besieged and starving, the majority were slaughtered where they stood. About five thousand escaped to the Russian lines.

The war between the PKK (Kurdish acronym for the Kurdistan Workers' Party)[29] and the Turkish state has led to further casualties. Isolated, off the beaten path, the little town of Sason has turned in on itself and its past. But as the long winter draws to an end, the flowering fruit trees seem to hold out a promise of better things to come. Metin Özmen, a young journalist who single-handedly produces the local paper, *Yeni bahar* (New spring), waits for us at his office next to the gas station. In addition to his reporting activities, Metin circumcises little Muslim boys in a room next to the mosque on the other side of the road.

Today Metin has offered to be our guide, delighted to be of assistance. His benevolent attitude toward the converts is apparent. Despite the reigning hostility, he is quick to jump to their defence. "I tell them they shouldn't be ashamed to say they are Armenians, to reveal their true identity." He also recognizes the genocidal nature of the events of 1915. But as a devout Muslim, he has trouble understanding that the conversions were not motivated by the love of Islam, and he misses "the sense of brotherhood between peoples that existed in the days of the Ottoman Empire." This is not the time to disillusion him, because he knows a *dönme* who has agreed to speak to us.

Halil has assembled all of the adult family members in his living room. The room is austere, like all those where we have been invited to take tea during our travels throughout the region. A naked light bulb hangs from the ceiling. A television set sits in one corner. Rugs cover the concrete floor, and colourful floor cushions line the walls. But this household differs in one important way from those of conservative Sunnis, where wives rarely appear before strangers, male or female: here the men and women sit side by side. They can tell us little about why their grandparents converted to Islam; all they know is that their grandfather, the only one of six siblings to survive, converted soon after the end of the First World War. That didn't protect him completely, however: "He left to do his military service, which lasted four years at the time. When he returned, the villagers had taken his land." The knowledge of the seizure of this valuable property has been passed down from generation to generation like a festering sore. "My grandfather always told me, 'You won't see it in your lifetime, but perhaps the dream will come true for your children. Maybe one day their rights to that land will be recognized.'"

Halil is determined to show us the extent of his family's former grazing lands. At the foot of a valley at the end of a long, muddy road outside the village, the lands are irrigated by a mountain stream swollen with melted snow. "You see that lush grass? We owned the best land. It went all the way down to the plateau, over there. We've got just two plots left," he sighs. Halil barely manages to feed his family with what he earns as a minibus driver. The loss of social standing is hard to take. A man riding a tractor waves as he goes by, and Halil returns the greeting. "It was his clan that took our land," he says, his troubled blue eyes fixed on the horizon. The descendants of the *aghas*, the village heads who helped themselves to the fertile land, are still in charge in Sason. "The truth is that, even though we're Muslim, we're still Armenian," says Halil's wife, whose flowered scarf tied behind her head reveals a bare neck. "We have problems because we're Armenian. This summer, I wanted to draw water from our old well for the tobacco plants, and they called me a 'filthy infidel.'"

The fifty families still living in Sason were terrified by an incident in 2004 when an Armenian man fell to his death from the top of a cliff. No one believed it was an accident: it was whispered that "the police investigation showed he was pushed by friends who wanted his property." But nobody dared file a complaint. The man's wife and children fled to Istanbul, and Halil is also thinking of leaving. "The worst is that I couldn't even sell what little land I have left. They've already got their eye on it, just waiting for me to leave."

How many converts are there? Counter to the official ideology, Turkish researchers are trying to rescue these crypto-Armenians from oblivion. Dr Selim Deringil is studying consular and missionary archives for clues. Conversions to Islam were massive during the Hamidian massacres in the last decade of the nineteenth century.[30] "The estimates vary greatly," he says, "from 20,000 to 150,000." The figures for 1915 are unclear – they vary from province to province and from village to village. "In the beginning, the authorities accepted the conversions, making deportation unnecessary. But when there began to be too many, they stopped accepting them, claiming they were not genuine. So converts were also deported." After the war, some reconverted to Christianity and opted for exile. Many Armenians who were able to save their lives and their religion during the genocide had to embrace Islam later on. Between those who were totally assimilated and those who retained their identity, it's impossible to know how many of their descendants now live in Turkey.

On Sunday morning, the small church in the town of Boyacıköy on the banks of the Bosphorus is packed. Seated on benches, the members of Istanbul's Armenian community are instantly recognizable. The women's blow-drys are impeccable, their husbands' suits freshly pressed. Here and there, believers dressed in their Sunday best fervently cross themselves. But when the notes of the hymns rise to the brick roof, they hesitate, stumbling over the words. Some twenty new-comers, still Muslim or newly baptized, are rediscovering the faith of their grandparents. They're not familiar with the rituals, can't speak Armenian, and are struggling to renew ties with the community of their ancestors.

To be understood by his flock, the bishop preaches in Turkish. These "new" faithful embarrass the Armenian Patriarchate. The prelate acknowledges the phenomenon of reconversion but remains discreet about it. "It's a new phenomenon," he says after the service. "More and more people are breaking their silence and knocking on our doors. The atmosphere of democratization is favourable here, but the fear is still present: the subject is still politically sensitive. We're not quite sure how to handle it." The bishop stresses that his church does no evangelizing in Anatolia for fear of being confused with the highly active Evangelical missionaries who are targeted by radical Turkish nationalists.

"As it was under the Ottoman Empire, religion is still the backbone of our identity. In a society structured around Muslim and Turkish propaganda, setting yourself apart from the majority is akin to treason." A more democratic Turkey could possibly open doors to missions in Anatolia. In the meantime, the bishop explains his caution by citing a well-known Turkish proverb: "If you chase after bulghur at the bazaar, you risk losing the rice you have at home." The Armenian community has lost a lot of rice since 1915.

The youngest generation of *dönme* feels less need for caution. Having been suppressed for so long, their "Armenianism" is demanding its due. Damla has made her choice: she will marry an Armenian – a real one. This is a disappointment to her parents, who would have "preferred a convert to protect her." Her children will be given Christian names. Hatice, twenty-seven, a fine-art restorer, has just been baptized and is known as Karine to those she has entrusted with her secret. "Our identity is bizarre. Our grandparents were Armenian, our parents are Muslim, and now we're returning to our roots." She still doesn't dare wear her cross around her neck when shopping in her neighbourhood, she says. "But at work, I've told all my colleagues that I'm Armenian; they've been very understanding and ask me for pastries at Easter. Now I want everyone to know that I'm Armenian!"

"No good will come of this," her veiled grandmother predicts. "Of course, I worry," she murmurs, her eyes on the pink slippers she is knitting.

Deeply disturbed by his brother's tragedy, Ahmet is also determined to learn more about his past and has decided to question his uncle, the last guardian of the family's history. "I don't even know our name." He's not sure how to define himself, although he knows that his "blood and genes are Armenian." On the other hand, he "never" calls himself Turkish. Each in their own way, these young people are inventing new ways to be Armenian, with or without religion, whether Christianity or Islam. They are expanding the limits of the Armenian identity, however the adherents of Orthodoxy might feel about it. They are also shaking up the Turks.

While following the route of the Baku-Tbilisi-Ceyhan pipeline as part of a film project, young documentary filmmaker Mehmet Binay came across Geben, a small town in the Taurus mountains of southern Turkey. There he discovered a liberal and culturally open community that stands apart from the more conservative settlements in the region. At a wedding, girls and boys held hands while dancing and spent time together without hiding from their parents: an Armenian legacy. Binay interviewed a young woman who spoke freely about her roots and allowed him a glimpse of a reality that was foreign to him. "In Geben, Turks and descendants of Armenians coexist peacefully, no doubt because the town's isolation has sheltered them from propaganda," he says. "This social mix gives me hope for Turkey. It shows that if we leave people alone, they learn to accept their differences."

One October day, members of Istanbul's Armenian community watched the forty-two minute documentary, *Whispering Memories*, that was born of this chance encounter. Moved that a young Turk sympathized with the plight of their people, the audience gave Binay a standing ovation. Dedicated "to those who stayed behind," his film shows Turks the pathway to accepting responsibility for the genocide.

5

Dersim: Land of Rebels

"From this promontory, men and women were thrown into the river.
Some jumped to escape the Turkish soldiers," says Enver, a sixty-year-
old man with a greying moustache. He kneels on the canyon's edge;
below, the raging waters of the Munzur River send mists of spray high
into the air. "In 1915, the inhabitants of the Armenian village of Vank
were massacred here. The water ran red with their blood." A river of
legendary strength, the Munzur runs through the region of Dersim
and holds the bones of thousands of Armenians from the Ottoman
Empire. Almost a century later, it still carries the memories of that tragic history of crackdowns and massacres. Yet, at the source of the Munzur, the icy torrent that spews from the rock is as pure and white as
milk. For centuries, Kurds, Armenians, and Alevis in the Dersim region
have celebrated the powers of this nourishing waterway.

From the hills above it, the town slumbers peacefully on the valley
floor. Dersim is a small, isolated settlement, the capital of the country's
least inhabited province, known since 1935 by its Turkish name of
Tunceli or "bronze hand." On the mountain slope lies what was once
an Armenian quarter, renamed Kalan – leftover – after the genocide.
Enver shows us a number of gravestones scattered among the wild
grasses in a tiny cemetery. Some of his family members are buried here.
"That's Boghos, my grandfather's brother," he says. Enver was originally Armenian, but he explains that after the 1915 massacres most of the
survivors were Islamized: Uncle Apraham became Ibrahim, Sarkis took
the Turkish name Şakir.

"Here, everyone knows about it," he says. But the burial place itself gives no sign – except perhaps for the wire fence erected by an Alevi family to separate their own dead from these *gavur* (infidels). Enver would like to believe that times have changed: "Today, it's finally possible to take an Armenian name."

On the civil status certificate he removes from its plastic sleeve, his first name, Enver, is followed by the Turkish last name Devletli, "statist." This surname was given to his family in the 1950s. In the box indicating religion – long compulsory on all Turkish IDs – it says "Islam." But in the past few months, Enver has begun calling himself "Assadour," an Armenian name. He has also begun studying the language spoken by his forebears and reading *Agos*, the weekly newspaper founded by Hrant Dink. Sometimes he attends church in Istanbul. "I want to officially change my name, and I'll be able to do that in a year or two. I've discussed it with my children, who are finishing their studies, and they've asked me to wait a bit longer." He sighs. "It's hard to find work with an Armenian name." Reclaiming his identity has become an obsession with Enver. Some of his ten brothers and sisters have taken similar steps. Mehmet now goes by the name Kevork, and their sister Nurcan, who moved to France, has been calling herself Jeannette for the past decade. Others are more hesitant. Despite what Enver wants to believe, in Turkey the process is not without risk. "Some people filed a complaint against me because I was claiming to be Armenian," he says.

He's not alone, however. Some hidden Armenians in Dersim, officially Alevi Muslims, have begun to demand their right to an identity that has long been denied to them and considered shameful. Mirhan Pırgiç Gültekin, a former political activist, was one of the first to take this step. He converted to Christianity, legally changed his identity and, in 2010, founded the Dersim Armenian Association, headquartered in the heart of the Beyoğlu district of Istanbul. "We must protect our identity and our culture, assert our origins," he declares. His efforts are supported by more than six hundred people, a few dozen of whom have reclaimed their Armenian identity. But how many others still hide their ancestry for fear of reprisals? Mirhan boldly claims that "75 per cent of the Dersim population is of Armenian descent." While exact figures are hard to come by, that number is clearly exaggerated.

For centuries, this mountainous region has also been home to Kurds, Alevi *zazas*, and *kizilbaş*, whose unique religion is a blend of Islam, Zoroastrianism, and Christianity.

The road to Hozat, running alongside the Munzur River, winds around the mountainside before dropping back down into a swampy valley. It's a blistering hot day in May, almost 30°C, and the road is surrounded by snow-capped mountains. On either side of the car, flocks of goats and sheep graze on lush grass. Enver whistles as he confidently manoeuvres the vehicle across the rugged terrain. We are accompanied by the Kurdish mayor of Hozat, who wants us to meet a family of Armenians still living in his village at the foot of Mount Zeranik.

In 1915, there were massive deportations from this valley. After that, the old watermill in Zeranik stopped turning. In fact, very little turns now in this poor village. A few cattle provide a subsistence living. Half of the village is in ruins; the other half lies ankle-deep in mud when the river floods, as it does every spring. Even the army barracks built in the centre of town have been deserted since a deadly attack by the PKK. The retreating soldiers left nothing behind but camouflage-painted walls, barbed-wire fences, and punctured sandbags. At the crossroads of the rutted dirt roads – the "downtown" area – a few wooden tables with tiny stools stand outside the only café. The old men don't look up from their cards as we approach. They have nothing to say.

A few cups of tea later, a farmer admits that, until the 1950s, the dilapidated house at the end of the road was inhabited by Natalia and Manik, an Armenian couple, and their children. The conversation is interrupted by Taylan, a serious young man of twenty-five. He speaks fluent Armenian, the language of his ancestors. "I've been studying it since I was sixteen," he says. He converted to Christianity in a church in Istanbul attended by crypto-Armenians from Dersim. For him, identity is a matter of conviction. "It's become fashionable in Turkey these days to say you have Armenian roots. But you've got to walk the talk," he says firmly. "To be Armenian, you must be Christian and speak the language." He takes us to his home for yet another cup of tea and introduces us to his girlfriend, whose family, like his, was forced to convert to Islam after the genocide. "The neighbouring villagers never let us forget we're Armenian," jokes Uncle Celal. "For them, we're *gavur*."

"I can't talk about it," says his father. "We were left with nothing – not a tradition, not a folk song."

When Taylan learned he was Armenian, he rebuilt an identity for himself from whatever he could find. In his small, bare bedroom, an Armenian flag hangs above the desk. He hopes to go to Armenia some day, without knowing exactly why. For him, Dersim is home, part of a former Ottoman *vilayet* where the Armenian minority was once firmly established. From an envelope he pulls out a 1912 map of Armenian villages in the region. "I bought it online from a specialized bookstore in Paris," he says. He unfolds the map, revealing dozens of villages with Armenian names, evidence of the Armenian presence in Dersim before 1915.

According to historian Raymond Kévorkian, there were 157 Armenian churches in the area before the genocide.[31] In Halvori, what remains of a church is still attended by Armenians and Alevi. The Mazgirt basilica, one of the few to be spared, was converted to a mosque in 1980 with the addition of a minaret; the frescos and inscriptions were obliterated. In Ergen, surviving fragments of engraved walls from a magnificent tenth-century basilica can be seen at the edge of a field. "It was a major place of worship dating from the Byzantine period," explains a farmhand with a bushy beard, his tools slung over one shoulder.

"No, it's Armenian!" insists another. "When we were kids, they used to take sick children there to wash them in that church. It relieved their suffering and cured illnesses. Widows would go there to pray." But the church began to attract interest of a more practical nature after it was visited by a group of Armenian tourists in 2010. To promote local tourism, the village applied to the Ministry of Culture in Ankara to have the church restored. Are there any Armenians left in Ergen? The response is a chorus of "no"s. An elderly man of about ninety recalls that there used to be about a dozen families in Ergen. "Some died, and the rest left for Istanbul; the last ones left in the 1960s."

The ruins of a more modest church can be found in the village of Koderiç a few kilometres away – no more than a pile of stones buried under trash and overgrown vegetation. Not all stones from dismantled Armenian churches have disappeared, however. Hard wearing, well cut, and carefully polished, they were often used as cornerstones in houses built after 1915. Here and there, in the wall of a farmhouse or a sheep pen, it's not unusual to find fragments of pillars, or stones engraved with Armenian characters. At the entrance to the former Armenian village of Alanyazı, a ninety-one-year-old woman proudly shows us a beautiful cross on the wall next to her front door – before describing in detail the atrocities committed by Turkish soldiers in 1915, the looting and the killing. The block of stone carved with an Armenian cross came from the church across the street.

In Koderiç, the house nearest to the former church is occupied by Muslims. On the doorstep stands a heavy-set woman in peasant dress, hands on her hips. She assures us that the pile of stones next to her house "was a mosque, not a church." There's some truth to what she says. Damaged after 1915, the Armenian church was torn down in 1920 by Sunni Turks who had been relocated there to occupy the village and prevent the return of any Armenians who might have survived the roundups and deportations. The goal of the genocide was to radically alter the ethnic balance in central and eastern Anatolia and ensure a Turkish majority. The new residents of Koderiç used some of the old stones from the church to build a mosque on the site. But the Turks left town in 1927 and were replaced by Dersim Alevi, including some Armenian converts, and the mosque was in turn demolished. The woman says that her family arrived much later, and she can't tell us any more than that, so we take our leave. As we round the corner of the house, our attention is caught by the metallic blue door of the shed. On each side of the door are stones from the church, carved with a cross and a rosette.

Along the road, we pass the village of Kilise (the church), now known as Yenidoğdu, "newborn" in Turkish. The town of Der Hovannessian, named after an Armenian saint, is now Dereova (the valley of the river). But in Dersim, more than elsewhere, the former village names persist; while you won't find them on any signs, they are still used by locals. Many people, for example, still refer to the village of Nazmiye by its former name: Kızıl Kilise (the red church). According to Mirhan Gültekin, the origin of the name Dersim was actually Armenian: Der Simon (Saint Simon).

In 1915, the Young Turk government issued deportation orders throughout Anatolia. But in Dersim, the prefects met with opposition from the Kurdish tribal leaders, who often refused to deliver the Armenians. Many sought refuge in the mountains, especially those of Kharpert, "the slaughterhouse province," as it was dubbed by American consul Leslie A. Davis, who spent several weeks exploring the area on horseback at the time of the massacres.[32] In the rebellious region of Dersim, where Ottoman sultans had been unable to collect taxes for centuries, at least fifteen thousand Armenians found shelter.[33]

Entire villages converted or continue to hide their identity to this day. Always reluctant to obey the central authority, the region has continued to resist the assimilation policies of the Turkish Republic, which has made it pay dearly for its obstinacy.

In 1926, the Honourable Hamdi Bey, a Turkish deputy, called Dersim "an abscess requiring urgent medical attention from a surgeon of the Republic." This operation was carried out in 1935, when a law was passed declaring a state of emergency in the province, renamed Tunceli (the bronze hand) and placed under martial law. Dozens of military barracks were built during that time, along with a rail line and a road to open up the valley. In 1937, Mustafa Kemal Atatürk launched a brutal military crackdown, officially to crush a tribal insurrection. But was the Turkish government punishing Dersim for protecting the Armenians? Was it aiming to "finish the job" begun twenty-five years earlier?

The Dersim massacres of 1915 and of 1937–38 bear many troubling resemblances. The locations and methods were often the same. The same hiding places used in 1915 saved entire families twenty-three years later. In 1938, Turkish soldiers searched some villages for uncircumcised children. The stories told by the elders around the fireside at night sometimes confuse the two periods. The "second wave" left 15,000–20,000 dead (sources vary considerably) out of a population of 100,000, mainly Alevi, including thousands of crypto-Armenians. For Hasan, eighty-seven, from a small village in the Dersim region, there can be no doubt: "There were two genocides," he declares firmly, stooped over his cane. "The soldiers came in 1915, and since Armenians found refuge here, they returned in 1938 to kill everyone."

Ismail Beşikçi, a Turkish sociologist, was one of the first to study the records of the Dersim military campaign. In a book published in Turkish in 1990, *Tunceli kanunu (1935) ve Dersim jenosidi* (The Tunceli Act [1935] and the Dersim genocide), he qualifies the events as "genocide." Dutch anthropologist Martin Van Bruinessen, an expert on Alevi issues, prefers to speak about an "ethnocide" against the inhabitants of Dersim.[34] Hasan Saltık, an ethnomusicologist who has spent ten years researching this bloody episode, believes the taboo is being lifted. The silence around what is discreetly referred to as "the Dersim events" has been partially broken. "Thousands of people were massacred," says historian Cemal Taş. "In the Pulümür River, you can still see the skeletons of bodies thrown into the water. As the grandchildren of those who were massacred in 1938, we want to see those events commemorated each year. The state must apologize to the people of Dersim, who were victims of genocide." Commemorations and torchlight parades have already been organized to mark the arrest and hanging of Seyid Riza, a powerful Kurdish Alevi chief and member of the Abbas clan. The eighty-one-year-old leader of the local uprising was executed in November 1938. Today, his grandson, who also believes that the origins of the second massacre date back to 1915, is demanding truth and justice. Riza himself is said to have hidden Armenians and protected sacred books. Long seen as a uniquely Kurdish uprising, the Dersim rebellion is now being looked at more closely and acknowledged to be more complex than once believed.

It was primarily through the efforts of Hrant Dink and Sarkis Seropyan, editors at the weekly newspaper *Agos*, that stories and testimonials about this period were brought to public attention. Academics, publishers, and documentary-makers all rushed to examine the archives. The Islamic-conservative government of Recep Tayyip Erdoğan was not sorry to see the opening of a debate on this episode, one of the darkest in the history of the Turkish Republic and in line with the nationalist objective of ethnic purification in the early days of the republic. The military operations were planned and voted upon from the beginning, then officially endorsed in 1927 by the regime of Mustafa Kemal (later Atatürk). They were finally launched just prior to the death of the Turkish leader and directed by Ismet Inönü, his right-hand man. By revealing the historic truth of this "civilizing mission," Erdoğan and his Justice and Development Party (JDP, or AKP in Turkish) are further weakening the army and upsetting the model of the Turkish nation-state in favour of the ideal of Ottoman coexistence.

Dersim also served as a proving ground for military experiments. Chemical gas was probably used in caves that harboured fugitives, and planes were used for the first time to bomb the mountain hideouts of rebel groups. In fact the tons of bombs dropped from planes partly explains the huge toll on human life. One of the pilots was Sabiha Gökçen, the world's first woman fighter pilot, after whom Istanbul's second international airport is named. A national hero, Sabiha was also the adopted daughter of Kemal Atatürk. Born in 1913, she was adopted at age twelve from an orphanage in Bursa. At twenty, she earned her pilot's licence, and then continued to train as a pilot, first in Russia and then at the Eskişehir air base in Turkey. Her first mission was to rain fire on Dersim at the controls of her French-made Breguet 19. But, in 2004, in a series of articles published in *Agos*, Hrant Dink reported that, before being adopted by Atatürk, Gökçen was an Armenian orphan whose parents died in the 1915 genocide. Celebrated as a pioneer in the world of aviation, she gave her name to a medal "for women who have accomplished remarkable feats in aerial sports." Adopted by the "Father of the Turks," this orphaned girl became more Turkish than the Turks. She became the scourge of Dersim – and thus of thousands of Armenians who had survived the 1915 massacres.

In the villages of Dersim, the memory of the last century's massacres is still very much alive. In Alanyazı, former fief of the Mirakian tribe, one of Dersim's two large Armenian clans, "everyone is Armenian," affirms Hıdır Boztaş, a peasant born the same year as the republic, in 1923. But few admit it openly, for fear of repercussions. "My grandfather and his brother were killed here," he says. "My father was just a child, and he was hidden by Alevi Kurds in Cafer Agha's clan. When the soldiers returned in 1938, we were terrified. For us, it was the return of the genocide, but they just passed through. Since 1915, they've been killing us because we're Armenians! But I don't care! I've always been proud to say I'm Armenian. Nothing's finished. The genocide is not over. The state continues to persecute Armenians. And Armenians continue to curse the Turkish government."

Boztaş's nephew, Mustafa, fifty-seven, belongs to a generation that avoids talking about things that upset the authorities, a generation for whom Armenian roots are a weakness to be hidden. In his living room is a portrait of Caliph Ali, venerated by the Alevi. "My father didn't teach us Armenian, and I don't know how to do the prayers," he says with regret. "He told us it was dangerous." But Mustafa nevertheless inherited the rebellious spirit of the people of Dersim and has decided to fight to regain ownership of the three fields stolen from his grandfather, Bedros. Since 1915, the former apple orchards at the edge of the village have lain fallow. "But everyone knows they belong to Bedros!" Mustafa declares.

In Hirnek, "they grew wheat and the Armenians weren't killed," says Hussein, eighty-seven, grandson of Hampartsoum Boyadjian, a tailor. Hussein's mother, Shogat, miraculously escaped the massacres in another village and sought help from the Protestant mission in Kharpert. He speaks calmly, sitting on the terrace of his home. "They lined up the women and children to execute them, then finished them off with knives. She played dead, but she never lost the knife scars on her arms and shoulders." Hussein remained Armenian, but he gave his children Muslim names. The eldest was named after the prophet of Islam, Mehmet in Turkish.

The atmosphere is more relaxed today, and "grandchildren can be more open about their Armenianism," says Mehmet, a small-business owner. "In Dersim, there is less social pressure than you find elsewhere in the country. From my parents, I'm half Alevi and half Armenian. The two cultures are very close, but I feel more Armenian, if only because my father told me the story of the genocide." His sister says she feels Alevi – "But also Armenian … In fact, my daughter goes to pray at the church in Istanbul." In this region, explains Mehmet, "it was often the women who were Armenian and the men who were Alevi, so Alevism tends to predominate." A friendly, heavyset man, his features are marked by the twelve years he spent in prison for collusion with the PKK's Kurdish rebellion. He pulls from his wallet a yellowed photograph of his grandmother. This brave woman is his hero, and her symbolic presence is a comfort to him. Recently Mehmet discovered that a branch of his Armenian family settled in Marseille. "One day an Armenian woman in France sent a letter to my grandmother. She said that she knew about her past and that, if she wished, she could contact her."

Very few families in Dersim do not have an Armenian great-grandmother or great-aunt. Here, more than elsewhere, the people are of mixed ancestry, and hybrid identities are common. Some self-identify as Kurds, some as Alevi, while still claiming to be Armenian. Folk dances and songs, the Feast of Saint Sarkis are all shared. "We always thought the Kochari was a Kurdish dance, but now I know it's Armenian," says Mirhan Gültekin, founder of the Dersim Armenian Association. "And when I first heard the Armenian choir of Istanbul, I realized I had always heard those songs in Kurdish."

6

Genocide of the Stone

Never had there been so many comings and goings between the shore of Lake Van and Akhtamar Island. Filled to overflowing, small boats chugged their way across the four kilometres of water separating the Church of the Holy Cross from the shore. Happy crowds disembarked and began climbing the hill toward the conical roof looming above the almond trees. On Sunday, 19 September 2010, the honey-coloured island in a sea of turquoise was a hive of activity. Rows of candles glowed before the biblical scenes depicted by low-relief carvings on the church's outer walls. People everywhere made signs of the cross, and when the first notes of a liturgical hymn sounded in the nave, the mantilla-covered heads were lowered. For the faithful, it was an emotional experience. Shrouded in obscurity since 1915, the church had been restored to life. For the first time in almost a century, Ankara had authorized the holding of a service there. Torn between unwillingness to support the Turkish state and a strong desire to worship in the land of their ancestors, Armenians from Istanbul, Lebanon, Europe, and Armenia had come to attend this historic mass.

The Church of the Holy Cross was one of the lost jewels in the Armenian crown, and the Turkish government has wisely made it a showcase of its Armenian policy. The incidents marking its renovation and reopening were symptomatic of the advances, ambiguities, and reversals of Turkish policy in recent years. After the massacre of the monks and the destruction of the monastery in 1915, after being abandoned to looters, after being saved at the last minute from a prefecture-ordered demolition in 1951 through the intervention of Kurdish

writer Yaşar Kemal, and after being closed to foreigners for half a century, the building was renovated and reopened on 29 March 2007 with
great pomp and ceremony. Turkey's Islamic-conservative government
wanted to demonstrate good faith in its rapprochement efforts with
Armenia. Putting its money where its mouth was, it had spent two million Turkish lira (almost US$3 million) to restore the ancient cathe-
dral. Repairing the bullet-pitted façade was the most difficult part of
the work.

On the day of the dedication ceremony, a huge Turkish flag was un-
furled in front of the church. From a distance, it resembled a red carpet and seemed a strange way for the government to show its desire for
reconciliation. Next to the entrance hung a portrait of Atatürk with
the words "Respect for history; respect for culture." But there were no
signs indicating that the church occupied a place of great importance
in Armenian history.

A vestige of the Armenian kingdom of Vaspourakan, the church was
the last remnant of the royal complex built on the island by King
Gagik I in the tenth century. In his interminable speech, Culture Minister Atilla Koç, the master of ceremonies, declared that the "government wished to protect this cultural heritage." The audience remained
sceptical: in his speech, Koç achieved the astounding feat of never once
pronouncing the words "Armenian" or "church." His skittishness mir-
rored Ankara's unwillingness to fully admit the significance of the
restoration. Indeed, several sour notes limited the impact of the event.
First, the building was classed as a secular museum, not a place of worship. Second, the name "Akhtamar" was Turkified as "Akdamar," meaning "white vein." In fact, the name Akhtamar was inspired by an
Armenian legend: every night, a young man would swim out to the island, guided by a torch held by his beloved, Princess Tamar. When the
young girl's father discovered this secret love affair, he blew out the
flame, and the boy drowned. When his body was found on the
lakeshore, his dead lips seemed to be calling, "Ah! Tamar!"

Third, the building had neither bell nor cross – major omissions for
a church of the Holy Cross. In the land of the star and crescent, these
Christian symbols were threatening.

All of these failures inspired a biting editorial by well-known journalist Cengiz Çandar, who accused the Turks of committing "cultural

genocide." For their part, the Armenians in Armenia and the diaspora had denounced the event as a media stunt. To show its disapproval, Armenia had sent only a token delegation. Although Armenia is just 250 kilometres from Van, the delegation, led by the country's deputy minister of culture, had been forced to make an 830-kilometre detour through Georgia. Wishing to send a strong signal of reconciliation, Turkey's president Abdullah Gül had requested permission for the delegation to cross the border, closed since 1993, but the army had vetoed his request.

Finally, three years later, permission was granted for a service to be held in the church. At the airport, young people passed out tourism brochures about Akhtamar. Less reticent now, Turkey was starting to promote the church-museum as the centrepiece of the region's cultural heritage. With the holding of a single mass, an entire century of eradicating the Armenian presence in Anatolia would be made history. Only a week earlier, a group of pilgrims praying before the altar had been reprimanded by the guard: "You can't pray here! This is not a church!" But the conflict over the cross had not yet been resolved. The Turks had not kept their promise: the church's dome was still bare. Learning of this, hundreds of Armenians cancelled their travel plans at the last minute. Horrified at the prospect of the entire ceremony's being ruined, the authorities brought out the cross and placed it on a temporary pedestal at the entrance to the church.

Two weeks later, the cross would be moved to the dome without fanfare. Since then, an annual mass has been celebrated in Akhtamar without creating the slightest stir. The church has reclaimed its place in the landscape. But on 19 September, 2010, the day of the mass, emotions were running so high that the delay in installing the cross was enough to revive the feelings of mistrust. "I understand the emotional reaction of the Armenians but, above all, this renovation is important to Turkish society," says Ara Sarafian, director of the Gomidas Institute in London, who attended the event. "Yes, in a way, you could see it as a manipulation, since it's an exception to the rule. But it raises the question 'Who built Akhtamar?' It highlights the fact that people other than Turks once occupied this land." The church is opening a door to the past by "defying the Kemalist historiography," adds Sarafian, a British historian of Armenian origin involved in the Turkish-Armenian dialogue.

Focused on this long-term objective, Sarafian looks beyond these details to the glowing words of the Turkish prime minister. For Recep Tayyip Erdoğan, the mass was nothing less than a "demonstration of Turkish tolerance": "We want to show the whole world that we respect their [the Armenians'] places of worship and look after them." These words made an impression. Less than two weeks after the mass, hundreds of nationalists received permission to pray at the site of Ani, the former capital of the medieval Armenian kingdom, now situated in Turkey. Cries of "Allah Akbar!" (God is great!) rang out. Devlet Bahçeli, leader of the Nationalist Movement Party (MHP), flanked by a troop of Grey Wolves, the ultranationalist militants of the party's youth organization,[35] knelt before an imam amidst the cathedral ruins. These far-right militants were responding to the religious ceremony held in Akhtamar. Their message was clear: Anatolia is a Muslim, Turkish land with no Christians or churches. Even the stones must be assimilated.

The liquidation of the Armenian population, begun in 1915, was not limited to its physical elimination. It also consisted in erasing all traces of a people, of ensuring the disappearance of all evidence of a civilization that had thrived in Anatolia since ancient times, of denying the history of this land so as to reinvent it as the cradle of a modern nation-state. First the Young Turks, then the Republic of Turkey carried out a cultural genocide with an efficiency that would have been admired by Tamerlane, the vicious conqueror who razed ancient cities to the ground, and of whom the Turks claim to be proud descendants.

Since the Armenians' religious heritage was the strongest expression of their ancestral roots, it became a prime target for their oppressors. Since 1915, in the Lake Van region alone, hundreds of churches have been destroyed, burned to the ground, or simply abandoned to the ravages of time. Eighteen kilometres from Akhtamar, the residents of the tiny hamlet of Inköy recently used the stones of a church to build new houses. Twenty kilometres away, villagers dismantled the Sourp Tateos monastery. Thirty kilometres further on, the stones of the Sourp Partoghimeos church were also recycled in the walls of local homes. A newspaper photo published in September 2012 shows the church in Anaköy providing shelter for two cows. And these are just a few examples. Many churches throughout Turkey have suffered similar fates. Those that have not been torn down have been converted to mosques, prisons, barns, or stables. In the province of Kars, in the middle of a muddy farmyard inhabited by turkeys, straw bales are stacked in the remnants of a nave. "Tourists and journalists would come to visit the church, so soldiers destroyed it," says the farmer. "The villagers weren't happy about that – not because of its historic value, to be honest, but because they used it to store their crops. That was about thirty-five years ago."

In the last century, the Turkish army had a heyday with these churches: they served for target practice, were blown to bits, or were incorporated in military zones. Abandoned and left to disintegrate, they disappeared stone by stone from the landscape. Here again, time served the political agenda. On the eve of the First World War, the archives of the Armenian Patriarchate of Constantinople inventoried 2,538 active churches and 451 monasteries in the Ottoman Empire. This enumeration did not include the hundreds of deconsecrated churches and some three hundred places of worship belonging to Protestant and Catholic congregations. Today, the Armenians own just six churches in Anatolia. Muslim Turks own dozens.

East of Van, we drive up Mount Varag past fragrant fields of mown hay announcing the arrival of fall. Youthful shepherds chase after frisky goats. At a crossroads, we turn onto a potholed road that takes us to Yukarı Bakraçlı. The main street of the village, better known as Yedi Kilise (Seven Churches), is not even tarred. Children in plastic sandals stretch out their hands to visitors, hoping for a coin or two. The elderly Kurdish women hulling berries in the shade ignore the arrival of the strangers. It's a familiar sight to them. People come from neighbouring Iran and Armenia, from all over Europe and the United States, to visit the Varagavank monastery – or its ruins, to be exact. In the village square, a church with an entrance topped with three crumbling arches is all that remains of this important centre of Armenian spirituality.

Founded in the eleventh century, the complex was an important religious and intellectual hub – the largest in the region – until it was destroyed in 1915. It could house a hundred pilgrims, its seminary was full of vocations, its library contained valuable manuscripts, and it was home to a fragment of the True Cross. The monks were also pioneers in the field of printing. In this remote province of the empire, they were the first to own a printing press. They printed *Arciv Vaspurakani* (The Eagle of Vaspurakan), an Armenian newspaper. Uncomfortable with this clearly suspect behaviour, the governor confiscated the press around 1885, transported the subversive object to Van, and authorized the publication of a newspaper in Ottoman Turkish so that he could understand and thus control the content. The monastery's days were numbered. In 1915, 250 Armenians took up positions on its walls and faced the armed forces of the Ottoman Empire. In May, a fire ended their resistance. But the memory of their courage is alive and well in the national narrative. The monastery became a legend, along with the Van rebellion, because in this city the Armenians took up arms before the deportation orders arrived. Thanks to the Russian army, they held their ground until August, when they were massacred.

In front of the church is a small plot, its few rows of tomatoes resembling a priest's bedraggled garden. We're almost expecting a man of the cloth to appear. But it is Ahmet, eyes shining, who meets us in the shadowy nave. A ray of sunshine illuminates a pale fresco of Bishop Kirakos, who led the community in the seventeenth century. The dirt floor has been carefully swept, a rough wooden roof serves as a barrier against heavy winter snowfalls, and the walls have been propped up with metal bars. "I did all that," says Ahmet, proudly. "I've been looking after the church since 1975."

As it was then used as a stable, Ahmet convinced the peasants to move their cattle elsewhere. He's the one who keeps the church key, shows visitors the barely visible crosses engraved on the walls, and has them sign a gold book that he guards as if it were a Bible written in Aramaic. To tourists puzzled by his presence, he explains that he made a pledge to his father: "On his deathbed, he made my brothers and me promise we would take care of the church." What could inspire such devotion? We wait to hear the admission that, logically, should follow, but it is slow in coming. We prompt Ahmet gently, knowing he would like nothing better than to reveal the truth. Finally, he whispers, "I'm not really Muslim, if you know what I mean." We assure him that we completely understand. Here, life for those who are "not really Muslim" is less difficult than it was thirty years ago: "It was really hard then," he says. "But I still hung the Turkish flag in front of the church to avoid problems." He and the church are survivors. They have remained here, alone. The man protects the stones, faithful to the memory of his people, guided by his silent mission, ignored by all.

Ahmet was worried by the additional damage caused by a deadly earthquake in October 2011. Walls had collapsed, and restoration work was desperately needed. The province's Department of Culture and Tourism swore up and down that it would take care of the necessary repairs, but word eventually came that work could not be started without the authorization of the owner, a certain Hüsamettin Altaylı. Sadly, Altaylı had been dead for many years and, as luck would have it, his heirs could not be located.

Historian Osman Köker was disgusted. "In Van, everyone knows that Hüsamettin Altaylı owned not just the church but the entire village, and that he was the grandfather of Fatih Altaylı – one of the most high-profile people in Van. So I spread the word."

In September 2012, the situation was made public by the *Taraf* newspaper. It caused shock waves. Fatih Altaylı is the editor-in-chief of the Turkish daily *Habertürk*, a key player in Turkish media. His talk show *Teke Tek* (Face to face), the promoter of cheap nationalism, has been a permanent fixture for almost twenty years. The Armenian cause is not welcome there, either on the air or in the pages of *Habertürk*. In 2011, when French deputies adopted the law penalizing the negation of the genocide, Altaylı lashed out on live TV: "We killed Armenians; Armenians killed us … but let no one, anywhere in the world, accuse the Turks of committing genocide! I spit on anyone who says that. And if our parliament said that, and apologized for it, I would spit on the doors of parliament!"

Altaylı may not have regretted his explicit language, but the Yedi Kilise affair was embarrassing. The *Taraf* article openly addressed a subject that was totally off limits: the despoilment of Armenian heritage. Everyone knew about it, of course, but as long as no one spoke about it, there was no loss of face. Interviewed by a *Taraf* reporter, Altaylı responded, "Yes, the church is mine. I have the deed of ownership for the church. My father inherited it from my grandfather, and when he died, he passed it down to me." His announcement was met with a storm of controversy. Left-wing militants demonstrated in front of *Habertürk*'s Istanbul headquarters, carrying placards: "Give back the church!" "Who was the first owner?" "Heritage genocide." Altaylı was bombarded with indignant emails: "You have placed yourself in a shameful position. There's just one thing for an honest, intelligent, civilized person to do: take the deed of ownership to the Patriarchate and give back the church." "Do you realize you're a Muslim and a Turk and you own an Armenian church?"

So how did a Muslim Turkish family come to own a church? "The state gave vast expanses of land to the family in what is now downtown Van," explains Köker. "In the 1920s, when the authorities built the new town, they erected public buildings on the family's property and gave them the land on which the monastery stands in exchange." The Altaylıs were not spared in the First World War. "Hüsamettin's father and uncle were killed by Armenians. And they may also have killed Armenians. In Van, things happened differently than in other towns. Before the deportation orders were issued, the Armenians had already begun to rebel against Ottoman repression."

Fatih Altaylı was born in Van long after the final convulsions of the dying empire. He attended the Galatasaray French-language high school in Istanbul and rarely returned to his hometown. When he swears that he has never set foot in the village of Yedi Kilise, built over the monastery ruins in the 1950s, and that his family has never earned a cent from that property, he is no doubt telling the truth. He is probably also sincere when he says that the government made no attempt to contact him about restoring the church. "I have no plans to pray there, or to turn it into a discotheque, or to tear it down," he says. "If the Patriarchate asks me for it, I'll give it to them without hesitation. If the Ministry of Culture wants it, I'll give it to them."

After being totally indifferent to the crumbling church he had inherited, Altaylı would have been quite happy for anyone to take it off his hands. The Patriarchate appreciated the offer but said that the law would not permit such a transfer, even if Altaylı was the original owner. In one month, the media mogul was able to quash the debate. Through his secretary, he announced that he had nothing more to do with the church, that he had transferred its ownership to the Ministry of Culture, and that any further inquiries should be addressed to it. The media uproar had at least one positive result: the bureaucratic hypocrisy was ended, and the Van prefecture announced that restoration work would begin.

In recent years, attitudes have been gradually changing, and municipalities are starting to protect the Armenian religious heritage. In Kayseri, the Sourp Astvadzadzin church had been converted into a gymnasium, but athletic activities have now been moved to another location, and the building will be repaired. The same has happened in Antep, where the Fevkani church, once used as a garbage dump by the local residents, its roof overgrown with wild grasses, has been restored to its former splendor. But these churches are still owned by the state. According to Köker, "Provincial bureaucrats tend to restore remarkable churches and monasteries to demonstrate the government's tolerance and generate tourism revenues. But they're not very enthusiastic about it." The destruction continues: vandals know they can count on the justice system to be lax in this area. Last July, for example, a few days after a group of Armenians made their annual pilgrimage to the Chapel of the Holy Virgin on Mount Marouta, in Sason (Batman Province), the church was vandalized.

Akhtamar may be somewhat protected now by the tourism spinoffs it generates for the region, but the extraordinary medieval city site of Ani is less secure. Since 1996, the World Monuments Fund has included it on its list of the world's one hundred most endangered sites. After years of neglect, Turkish authorities have begun showing a mild interest in protecting what can still be saved, and financial assistance has been requested from UNESCO. The St Gregory of Tigran Honenc Church and the Manuhcer Mosque (previously a church) have been restored, but the other buildings continue to deteriorate.

The vast majority of churches have not been classified as historic monuments and so are not protected. Thus churches still standing in Turkey have been systematically stripped of their treasures. Cultural objects, Bibles, candelabra, paintings, and statues disappeared long ago, of course, but looting is still a national sport. When nothing remained but walls, the Turks and the Kurds began to dig. "They've been digging since 1915," reads the headline of the 12 November 2010 issue of *Agos*. A photo taken by hikers shows tents set up near a monastery in the Lake Van region: the pillagers had arrived. Dirt was being thrown through a hole in a wall made to remove debris that had piled up inside the building. When they were deported, the Armenians did not realize they were never coming back, so many hid money and other valuables inside the walls of homes and churches or buried them in fields, in earthenware jars, or down wells. Ever since then, Turks and Kurds have been obsessed with finding this "Armenian gold."

It was in Yüksekova, a small Kurdish village near the Iranian border, that we first heard of this obsession. In a grocery store, the clerk suddenly asked us if we had "maps." In Turkey, a foreigner in an out-of-the-way town obviously had maps. For the clerk, his meaning was so clear that he didn't bother to specify what kind of maps he was talking about. We innocently asked if he meant road maps. This only confirmed his suspicions: the foreigner doesn't want to admit it, but he obviously has "maps"– treasure maps to find Armenian gold, of course.

In the taxi between Aleppo and Antioch, the driver asked us knowingly where our "maps" were and then proceeded to tell us about a European who had arrived in his aunt's village with a plan to find money hidden in the crevice of a rock. In the minds of Turks and Kurds, under every rock, every gravestone, every apricot tree that has ever been owned by an Armenian lies a treasure chest full of coins and jewels. In Şirince, near Izmir, Sevan Nişanyan, a Turkish citizen of Armenian descent, was searching for buildings to convert into guest houses. The day after he visited one of them, you would have thought a giant mole had spent the night there. Every one of the heavy paving stones had been systematically overturned. It is well known that if an Armenian is interested in a property, it is because treasure is hidden there.

This vast treasure hunt stretching over 780,000 square kilometres may seem like a game – in fact, it's the favourite pastime of children in rural areas – but it's also a continuation of the pillaging.

The eradication of Armenian heritage has also been carried out quite literally through the Turkification of place names. Changing the names of villages, rivers, and mountains has been a priority for the republic, since the physical space occupied by the new nation-state obviously must be Turkish. Scientific commissions have hunted down Armenian, Greek, Arab, Kurdish, and Laz names and eliminated them. By the late 1970s, more than one-third of all villages had been given Turkish names. Names with meanings such as "pretty village," "stone village," "new village," "green village," "pretty source," and "new bridge" abound. In the process, people and places have been separated from their roots. The names may be unrelated to the past, but they are Turkish. Ani, for example, lost the dot over the "i" and became Anı, Turkish for "memory."

Turkification became an obsession. Any reference to historic Armenia was removed from maps, and it was made illegal to import maps that contained such references. In 1934, the Surname Law required all residents of the country to have a purely Turkish last name. Armenians were not allowed to add the suffix "yan" (son of) to their last name. In 2005, language purification extremists turned their attention to the Latin names of animals in Anatolia. The sheep *Ovis armeniana* became *Ovis orientalis anatolicus*. The deer formerly known as *Capreolus capreolus armenicus* became *Capreolus capreolus capreolus*. And the red fox, *Vulpes vulpes kurdistanica*, lost its reference to Kurdistan. The minister of the environment justified this purge in all seriousness by invoking the foreign threat: "Unfortunately, many other species in Turkey were maliciously misnamed in this way. This spiteful intent is clearly evident in the fact that names undermining Turkish unity were given to species found only in our country."[36]

Along the same lines, few Turks realize that many of the Ottoman buildings they are so proud of were designed by Armenians. Nineteenth-century Istanbul was shaped by Armenians, including the famous Balian brothers, architects of the Sublime Porte (site of the government of the Ottoman Empire), who followed in the footsteps of the great Mimar Sinan (Sinan the architect).[37] Their works include the Dolmabahçe imperial palace, the tomb of Mahmoud II, the military academy, the Beylerbeyi and Çirağan palaces, the Ihlamur pavilion, many mosques, and the rector's office of the University of Istanbul.

Fortunately, there are dedicated people working to make visible what the authorities have tried to erase. The Houshamadyan project, for example, aims to "reconstruct and preserve the memory of Armenian life in the Ottoman Empire … to reconstruct a rich but ignored and forgotten heritage." A website is used to collect documents of all kinds bearing testimony to daily life before the genocide in the towns of Palu, Maraş, Yozgat, Zeytun, Harput, and Van. Historian Osman Köker, founder of Birzamanlar (Once upon a time) Publications, is a pioneer in this field. His 2005 book *Armenians in Turkey 100 Years Ago* is a collection of hundreds of postcards from the early twentieth century. These yellowed images, mostly two-tone sepia and tan, show women in ceremonial dress, cotton factories, schools, village squares, cafés, shops, theatres, looms, cemeteries, and church towers. In post-card after postcard, Armenian social, economic, and cultural contributions to the Ottoman Empire are on display.

"In Turkey, encyclopedias and school books create the illusion that only Turks have ever lived here," says Köker. "The younger generation doesn't know there were other people here, or anything about the multiculturalism of the past. For them, anyone who is not Turkish is an enemy. That mentality does not lead to peaceful coexistence; it hurts society. With that view of history, non-Muslims are either invisible or enemies who suddenly appeared during the First World War. So I decided to write a book to shatter that illusion." Köker's book inspired the creation of an exhibition that can be adapted to each venue. First mounted in Istanbul, it attracted ten thousand visitors in eleven days – a record turnout for Turkey. In Diyarbakir, a town that has made great progress in its "duty to remember," the postcards highlighted the multi-ethnic nature of daily life. For Izmir, exhibition curators chose postcards revealing the multicultural life of the former city of Smyrna. Slowly but surely, the postcards are beginning their journey. While the exhibition still avoids the most conservative regions, it is bringing Armenians back to Anatolia.

The national symbol that continues to be more Turkish than a Turk is the signature of Mustafa Kemal: "K. Atatürk." These sacred letters, written with a firm hand on an upward slant, are everywhere: stickers decorate gas tanks of scooters, rear windows of cars, and cell phones. On national holidays, they are inserted in newspapers. The signature is worn on pendants and engraved on signet rings and watch faces. The latest trend is to have it tattooed on one's neck or forearm, as did a Turkish Airlines flight attendant we met. The famous graphic even has its own Facebook page. But where did it come from? Its creation coincided with the passing of the Surname Law in 1934, when the founder of the republic chose the surname "Atatürk" – "Father of the Turks." There was no signature to go with it, however.

Journalist Vercihan Ziflioğlu tracked down Dikran Çerçiyan, the son of the symbol's designer, Hagop Vahram Çerçiyan, for many years a professor of mathematics, geography, and calligraphy at the prestigious Robert College in Istanbul. His son Dikran, now ninety, recalls: "Early one morning, there was a knock at the door. Worried, my mother came to tell my father he was wanted by the police." It was the police commissioner of Istanbul's Bebek neighbourhood, with the official order. Some former students, now deputies, had thought of asking Çerçiyan – a man of Armenian descent – to carry out this heavy responsibility. He immediately set about the task. "I was tired from watching him work, and I fell asleep," continues his son. "When I woke up the next morning, I saw five models lying on the table, which the police soon arrived to collect." The identity of the designer of the well-known signature has long been forgotten, but when Turks have "K. Atatürk" tattooed on their bodies, they are recording in indelible ink a piece of Armenian history.

7

The Armenian Don Quixote

The stone tower he commissioned is one of his latest whims. Like a watch tower, it offers a splendid view of the domes of the old Greek churches in the hill town of Şirince and the only paved road leading up to it from the plain. It's an ideal observation point from which to observe an enemy's approach, and we are not disappointed. Sevan Nişanyan reminds us of Obelix observing the arrival of the Romans. Gleefully rubbing his hands together, he says, "Cool! The cops!"

Two soldiers amble toward us, flanking three officials in purple ties. The three representatives of the Şirince subprefecture have arrived for the umpteenth time to inspect ten guest houses that Nişanyan had built without permits. "How many are there? How many rooms?" The answers are meticulously recorded by their superior while the rest stifle yawns. "This has been happening three times a week for the past twelve years," sighs Nişanyan. "The bureaucrats would get bored without you," jokes a soldier. But their ongoing entertainment is assured. This Armenian intellectual will continue to cross swords with the Turkish administration with the conviction of a knight errant, because the battle is part of a much larger war he is waging against the Turkish state – "the last fascist regime," in his words, built on the genocide of his people in 1915.

It was in Şirince, near Turkey's Aegean coast and the Ephesus archeological site, that Sevan Nişanyan chose to organize his resistance. He discovered that the history of the village was reminiscent of that of the Armenians deported from Anatolia: a Greek colony was founded here in the eighteenth century by Ottoman authorities wishing to populate the brigand-infested area, and to collect taxes while they were at it. The architecture is typical of Albania, so the town's first inhabitants were likely brought here from northwest Greece and the Balkans – before being returned there two centuries later. In 1923–24, those who had survived or resisted the policy of terror to sweep Greeks from the region, implemented in 1913 by the Committee of Union and Progress, were sent back to their homeland. At that time, the governments of Greece and Turkey had agreed to exchange their minorities, each wishing to carry out a wide-scale ethnic cleansing to create racially and religiously "pure" nation-states. The great-grandparents of the current residents of Şirince were therefore expelled from Crete and Macedonia because they were Muslim. But according to Nişanyan, "These new inhabitants have never really felt comfortable here. The third generation still calls it the village of *gavurs* [infidels]. The spirit of the Greeks still walks among us."

Feeling solidarity with these persecuted minorities, Nişanyan immediately made himself at home here. In just a few years, he had turned it into a popular tourist destination. The "who's who" of Istanbul flocked to the guest houses that he designed from scratch, from their pantries to their chimneys. He quickly earned a reputation for serving the best breakfasts in Turkey, complete with views of the valley and classical music playing in the background. Success was not long in coming and, along with it, problems with the law for "illegal construction." "But everything in Turkey is illegal and would have to be torn down," Nişanyan argues. Indeed, construction without a permit has become a national sport. In Istanbul, 70 per cent of buildings have been erected outside the law. After a legal truce, the notices of demolition began to reappear three years ago. Nişanyan's criminal record now includes seven trials, sentences totalling eighteen years' imprisonment for illegal construction and resisting authority, the loss of his civil rights and the right to found a political party, plus a mysterious €70 fine (about $US100) for "good conduct."

"Armenians are only tolerated in this country if they grovel and hang pictures of Atatürk," he had declared a few months earlier. "By challenging the status quo, I broke the social contract." Nişanyan is as rebellious as his compatriots are discreet. A 2004 photo hanging above the hotel's front desk says it all: like a king with a mocking smile seated on his throne, he and his considerable bulk are ensconced in an armchair carried with great difficulty by police officers. It was the only way they could execute an eviction order. But this time he had to compromise, at least to some extent. To prevent his cottages from being bulldozed, he donated them to the Nesin Foundation, run by his friend Ali Nesin, a prominent mathematician and fellow disturber of the peace at the forefront of battles for democratic freedom in Turkey. The two men built a "mathematics village" in Şirince to serve scholars from Turkey and around the world whose passion is solving equations, and also to inspire a taste for math in Turkish youth. In the summer months, classes are held in an open-air amphitheatre in the shade of an olive tree. The goal is to share knowledge as it was done in classical antiquity. A theatre school followed last year – another slightly crazy project. But nothing pleases Nişanyan more than being called crazy.

Indeed, you have to be a bit crazy to contradict historian Yusuf Halaçoğlu on live TV. Elected to parliament on the ticket of the far-right, ultranationalist MHP, Halaçoğlu is the poster child for state-sponsored revisionism. For many years he served as president of the Turkish Historical Society, a public organization that denies the genocide. You also have to be a bit of a kamikaze to publish in the daily newspaper *Taraf*, another thorn in the side of Kemalist ideology, an editorial adapting Atatürk's "Address to Youth." Displayed on the walls of every classroom in the Republic, Atatürk's words have been recited by rote by generations of Turkish youth. But under the pen of this born provocateur, the rousing command "Your first duty is to preserve and defend Turkish independence" became "Your first duty is to be a human being." In France, Nişanyan's revision would have been seen as a harmless parody. In Turkey, where worship of the nation has replaced that of God, it was the ultimate insult. The declarations of the founder of the Turkish republic are as sacred as the chapters of the Koran. Outraged zealots responded with death threats: "We'll make you write the correct version of the 'Address to Youth' with your own blood. We'll kill you like that dog Hrant Dink." Nişanyan has no doubt that, in sentencing him to jail for his guest houses, the judges are really making him pay for his words.

At the guest house where he has welcomed us with a generosity befitting his own larger-than-life persona, we are enjoying an afternoon snack. Popping a last bite of fresh-baked cake into his mouth, he interrupts his story to excuse himself until supper time. He must finish a series of articles on the reform of Turkey's education system. Outside, the warm winter sun caresses the landscape, a dog slumbers in the middle of the road, a goat bleats in its pen, and smoke wafts gently over the rooftops. Far from the prevailing schools of thought, Şirince offers the ideal vantage point from which to observe the ills of society.

The next day, Nişanyan insists on showing us the replica of a Lycian cave tomb he has had carved into the rock in the hills above the village. In the pediment above the portal are chiselled, in Ancient Greek and Old Armenian, the words "Built by Sevan Nişanyan in 2012 AD." This project – which will no doubt lead to another conflict with bureaucracy (making us wonder if that is not the whole point of the operation) – is consistent with the man: over the top, astonishing, self-indulgent. But this attempt to provoke the authorities is also designed to challenge the country's official history, which has erased signs of all who lived here before the Turks.

Nişanyan's aversion to nationalism shaped his education. At seventeen, he left Turkey to study philosophy at Yale, then political science at Columbia. Hungry for knowledge, he soaked up languages like a sponge: in addition to Armenian and Turkish, he speaks English, Arabic, and modern Greek, gets by in classical Latin, Greek, and Armenian, and boasts a smattering of French, Hebrew, Ethiopian, and Syriac. As a child, he amused himself by memorizing the *Petit Larousse* encyclopedic dictionary and, early on, he developed a keen political sense. "By the time I reached college, I already detested everything related to nationalism, Kemalism, and militarism; in short, I had developed a deep disdain for our political system, which claims the superiority of the Turkish race." In this young rebel, the ideological propaganda hammered home by the education system had the reverse effect: instead of accomplishing the desired brainwashing, it taught him to use the extraordinary brain with which nature had endowed him "for political purposes."

Living in Istanbul's well-to-do neighbourhood of Şişli, his family had escaped the genocide. Neither his architect father nor his homemaker mother speaks of the atrocities of the First World War. Only his grandmother refers to them occasionally with flashes of bitter wit. But Nişanyan's childhood memories are full of daily acts of discrimination. The implicit message transmitted by newspapers and the radio was that "minorities are the enemies of the republic." When, as a student in the United States, he learned about the genocide, his "obsession with destroying the Turkish state" was fuelled. He became a Marxist. Now fifty-four, he has long since given up his Marxist beliefs, but his youthful rebellion has remained his intellectual compass. "All my books have the same objective: to deconstruct the racist Turkish ideology that overshadows the rich history of this country." This is true even of those books that appear at first glance to be inoffensive, since in Turkey everything is ideological.

In 2006, for example, Nişanyan published a tourist guide to the Black Sea region.[38] This Turkish Switzerland along the country's northern border is worth exploring for its magnificent mountains and multi-ethnic history. But the region is less famous for its alternative tourism than for being a stronghold of the Grey Wolves, the Turkish ultranationalist youth organization. In the section devoted to the town of Giresun, on the shores of the Black Sea, Nişanyan mocks a statue honouring Topal Osman, or Osman the Lame, a hero of nationalist literature. In 1915, Osman commanded a squadron of gangs in the pay of the Committee of Union and Progress that exterminated the local Armenian population. In 1919, history repeated itself, this time against the Greeks.

It was retired General Veli Küçük, suspected of being one of the instigators of the murder of Hrant Dink and now behind bars for his association with the so-called "Ergenekon" plot to overthrow the government,[39] who argued for the erection of the statue. In 2006, Küçük was still a free man, and the memory of Osman the Lame was not to be trifled with. Emotions in the country were running high, with the genocide taboo beginning to crumble. Atom Egoyan's film *Ararat* had been seen on television for the first time, and, confronted with its historic responsibility, the country was hit by a wave of paranoia. Nişanyan's tourist guide to the Black Sea was seen as a dangerous, subversive opus, and the province's governor called for its banning. Nişanyan was accused on television of doing evangelical missionary work and received thousands of death threats. "They stopped overnight," he says, "proving they were the result of an organized campaign." A few months later, on 19 January 2007, his friend Hrant Dink was gunned down.

For Nişanyan, Dink's funeral sounded the death knell for the racist ideology that had nourished the Turkish republic since 1923. On 23 January, more than 100,000 Turkish citizens marched in Dink's funeral procession carrying signs reading "We are all Armenians." Said Nişanyan, "Seeing that this spontaneous demonstration was not repressed, I understood that the regime had fallen with the death of an Armenian." He decided to deliver the final blow by publishing a manuscript that had lain waiting patiently in his desk drawer since 1994: *Yanlış Cumhuriyet* (The wrong republic),[40] an all-out attack on the foundations of the republic. Once again, the premise was sacrilegious: Atatürk had never intended to found a democracy and had created a dictatorship.

Nişanyan continues to deconstruct history with the same determination that he devoted to constructing houses. "An Armenian identity is a plus for criticizing the Turkish state," he says: "it helps to complicate the situation." Even his passion for etymology has been placed at the service of his political objective. His encyclopedic knowledge of linguistics led to the writing of *The Country That Has Forgotten Its Name*, a comprehensive survey of the Turkification of Anatolia designed to highlight Turkey's multicultural identity. The task is endless and, from his home in Şirince, he uses the Internet to pursue it. He has created the *Index Anatolicus*, an interactive tool for compiling a list of all the former Armenian, Syriac, Ottoman, Kurdish, Arabic, and Greek names of places and villages that have been renamed. By fall 2012, a total of 31,511 had been inventoried. An Armenian is thus "helping Turks to discover their country and their history."

In October 2012, during a prime time program on CNN-Türk, the Turkish version of the cable news channel, Nişanyan declared, "No one knows Turks or Turkey better than I do." With his characteristic blend of smugness and anxious awkwardness, he had come to defend his position on *Innocence of Muslims*, the US-made anti-Islamic video that had triggered violent protests in the Muslim world. As always, this Armenian intellectual challenged conventional thinking and political correctness. On his blog, he had said this about Mohammed: "It is not a hate crime to poke fun at some Arab leader who, many hundred years ago, claimed to have established contact with God and made political, economic, and sexual profit as a result. It is almost a kindergarten-level case of what we call freedom of expression."

In effect, this was a little online test of the new taboos of Turkey, a country increasingly ruled by bigotry. His Twitter account was flooded with insults: "Armenian dog!" Bekir Bozdağ, the country's deputy prime minister, called for the criminal prosecution of his "crime." A Turkish lawyer, politician, and theologian, Bozdağ declared that "only a sick mind could produce such madness." On CNN-Türk, Nişanyan fired back that "people with healthy minds are necessarily atheists," before launching into a brilliant but outrageous analysis of Turkish ills. "In Turkey, two monsters have been confronting each other for the past century. One is Kemalism, and the other is Islamism." Abandoned by some of the Turkish intelligentsia, who had tired of his boundless ego, and criticized by the Armenian community, who feared they would bear the brunt of the backlash, he was like a condemned man who has willingly entered the lion's den.[41] A free-thinking extremist, he confronts dogmas of all kinds. Sevan Nişanyan: intolerable, but oh so indispensable.

8

Vakıf: The Last Village

The engine protests loudly as the road winds up the side of Mount Moses (Musa Dagh). The minibus has been climbing for a good half hour on the way to Vakıf, our destination. To the left, orange orchards slope gently down to the sea. As the town comes into view, an official from the tourism office grabs the microphone and begins her spiel: "Vakıf was the first village in Turkey to benefit from an organic farming assistance program. All those oranges you see are organic."

"But what's the history of this village? What sets it apart?" someone asks innocently.

"Nothing special. It's just a village like any other in this region," she answers, chewing her lip. The explanation and the bus come to a stop, and the doors swing open. As the vistors climb down from the bus, they are greeted by about a dozen community leaders lined up in front of the church. Soldiers with automatic rifles strapped across their chest are posted every hundred metres along the main street. Vakıf is far from being a village like any other. In Turkey, it is known officially as "the last Armenian village" – for good reason, since all the others have been wiped off the map.

It's January 2011, and the delegation has arrived with great pomp and ceremony in this peaceful village, population 135. Earlier in the day, three Turkish ministers took their places at the front of the minibus: Egemen Bağış, minister for European affairs, who appears to be in charge; Sadullah Ergin, justice minister, the local hero, who loosens his tie and adjusts his Ray-Bans; and Cevdet Yılmaz, minister of planning, who discreetly folds his long legs behind the driver's seat.

Behind them are twelve rows of advisors and technocrats, a busload of Turkish and European deputies, and a few journalists.

The semi-annual meeting of the Turkey-EU Joint Parliamentary Committee (JPC)[42] has just wound up in Antakya (formerly Antioch on the Orontes). Two days of rarely constructive debate on Turkey's application to join the European club have just been held in the basement of a hotel. As generally happens at these meetings, the members of the European Parliament (MEPs) for Cyprus and far-right Dutch MEPs made clear their opposition to any negotiation, acting as obstructive and confrontational as possible. It was time for some fresh air. To relieve the tension, the organizers planned this afternoon excursion to visit the Hatay mosaics.

The Hatay region, at the southern end of Turkey very near the Syrian border, is a tangled web of origins and beliefs. Largely Arabic-speaking, although Turkish is gradually emerging as the dominant language, Hatay Province is home to many Alawites, members of a heterodox branch of Islam said to be an offshoot of Shi'ism. Historically, Hatay was also the seat of the first Christian community founded by St Peter, first bishop of the city of Antioch, and it is still home to hundreds of Syriac and Armenian Christians. Indeed, the former French consulate in Antakya is now a Protestant church. Its congregation is headed by a dynamic Korean evangelical minister, who has quickly become a leading figure in Antakya. The old city is also home to a tiny Jewish community of about thirty-five people and a few synagogues.

That morning the delegation visited the oldest synagogue in Antakya, where the deputies were shown a set of priceless leather Torah scrolls dating from the thirteenth century. Only two sets of these scrolls are now in existence: the other is in Jerusalem. During the visit, Minister Bağiş launched into a long-winded speech praising the religious tolerance of his country. "In Hatay, mosques, churches, and synagogues coexist peacefully – proof of the respect and harmony between beliefs and communities that exist in Turkey today," he declared with a straight face. Part cynic, part spinmeister, Bağiş often dilutes the facts, presenting a picture-perfect image of Turkey to the outside world, and that is clearly the objective of this little excursion.

Of course all these fine folk have not been brought to Vakıf to admire its organic orange and lemon trees. With its Armenian mayor and one of the few churches in Turkey that have not been converted to a mosque or a barn, Vakıf is a curiosity: living proof, according to Bağiş, of the leniency of the Turkish Republic toward its non-Muslim minorities. This is the traditional broken record played by the Turkish state for decades. Bağiş talks about the openness of his government to the Armenians: the renovation of the church on Akhtamar Island in Lake Van and the rapprochement efforts with Armenia launched in 2009 through "football diplomacy."[43] He leads the group into the tiny Holy Mother of God Church, where the women's cooperative, which sells handicrafts and local produce, is permitted to give a brief tour. In twenty minutes, it's over.

The Greek and Cypriot Euro MPs lag behind, bombarding the town's mayor, Berdj Kartun, with questions that appear to make him uncomfortable. "We know the true situation. Freedom of religion exists only on paper," declares a Greek MP. "Vakıf has been without a priest for ten years now because the government is standing in its way." In fact, Turkey does not allow foreign clergy to perform religious services in the country. Only home-grown Christians can officiate, but their numbers have fallen drastically over the years. Since the death of the last priest in Vakıf in 2000, no replacement has been found. Despite its orange trees, the survival of the village is in question. But it's already time for the visitors to leave. Bağiş takes his place at the front of the bus, the soldiers climb back on board, and the town is left to itself again.

After seeing the village through the eyes of the Turkish officials, we had to return to Vakıf to take a closer look, to learn more about its inhabitants, their daily life, and their tragic yet romantic past. Today Vakıf is indeed "Turkey's last Armenian village," but in 1915, before the genocide, it was one of seven Armenian villages on Mount Moses (Musa Dagh) along with Kebusia, Idir Beg, Bitias, Yoğunoluk, Hablak, and Yezur. In 1914, there were 8,500 Armenians living here. The 150 current residents of Vakıf are the last remaining descendants of that community, whose fate has been described in great detail by historians. In 1915, refusing to submit to deportation orders, some 4,000 to 5,000 villagers fled to the top of the mountain overlooking the bay. From there, they defended themselves from the Turkish army for more than a month before being rescued by French and British ships.

These events were made famous by the 1933 novel *The Forty Days of Musa Dagh* by Austrian author Franz Werfel.[44] Written during the rise of Adolf Hitler and Nazi Germany, the novel achieved great international success and has been credited with awakening Europe to the scope of the century's first genocide.

On 30 July 1915, when the Ottoman governor issued orders to deport villagers from the region, the inhabitants were unsure how to react. According to historian Raymond Kévorkian,[45] many chose to obey: 332 families, including almost all those from Kerbusia, were escorted to Antioch and from there deported along the Euphrates route to Deir ez-Zor[46] in the Syrian Desert. Haroutioun Nokhoudian, the pastor in Bitias, thought the idea of resistance was "folly." But in Yoğunoluk, the villagers were already on the defensive. Five days earlier, on 25 July, the Reverend Dikran Andreassian, who officiated in Zeytoun, returned to his native village with the assistance of American Protestant missionaries. He brought with him alarming news: what he had seen in Zeytoun and now reported to families in Yoğunoluk played a decisive role in the Musa Dagh rebellion.

Here, we digress briefly. Before the First World War, Zeytoun, another emblematic location for Armenians in the region, had been a bustling Armenian city of more than ten thousand people. An eagle's nest on the side of the mountain near Maraş, it was a rebellious fief that made life difficult for the empire's soldiers throughout the nineteenth century. During the Hamidian massacres in 1895, Zeytoun's inhabitants put up a brave resistance. But this time, the Turkish authorities took steps to quash any possible uprising. On 8 March 1915, a group of twenty-five military deserters had ambushed a battalion of soldiers to obtain arms and then sought refuge in a monastery in the hills above the village. This was the incentive needed to launch an attack: five thousand men were sent to crush Zeytoun.

The plan had been in the works for some time, according to Arnold Toynbee, a British diplomat hostile to the Turks, who notes that many backup troops – *muhacir* (refugees), Muslims who had fled the Balkans and been resettled in the place of Christians by the Turkish authorities – had previously been sent to the region. In three months, long convoys of deportees emptied Zeytoun of its population. The city was then renamed Süleymanlı, after one of the officers killed in the attack on the monastery. According to Kévorkian, Zeytoun's fate "no doubt marked the symbolic beginning of the program to Turkify Anatolia, from the annihilation of the Armenian people to the renaming of its towns."

The pastor's report of these events was enough to convince the Armenians of Musa Dagh to resist the deportation orders. On 31 July, hundreds of Armenian families from the mountains above Antioch abandoned their homes. On 12 and 13 September, 4,092 people, including eight wounded, running short of food and ammunition, were rescued by the third squadron of the French combat fleet in the Mediterranean under the command of Admiral Gabriel Darrieus. The *Dessaix*, the *Amiral Charner*, the *Foudre*, the *Guichen*, and the *D'Estrée* each picked up hundreds of refugees. The *Guichen* was the first to spot smoke signals and, as it approached shore, saw groups of men gathered on the beach. The desperate Armenians on Musa Dagh had lit fires and written the words "Christians in distress" on a sheet. To be seen by the ships, they had painted a huge cross on a piece of white fabric – a "relic" that can still be seen in Jerusalem.

During the brief tour of Vakıf led by the Turkish ministers, we had had no time to visit Avedis, an elderly man who is the guardian of the village memory, for the officials had not deemed it useful to include him in their program. Avedis was likely born in 1914, although he likes to tack on another year: "I was born in 1913, but it says 1914 on my ID card," he told us. He is the last survivor of the epic Musa Dagh standoff, the last direct witness of that famous episode in Armenian history and of almost a century of life in Turkey: an invaluable repository of memory.

On our return to Vakıf six months later, we went directly to see Avedis, anxious to hear his story. We had been assured that he was still lucid. The old man was lying on a straw mattress on the veranda of his house on the main street, surrounded by a loving group of children and grandchildren. Physically, he seemed frail, pale and thin with a gaunt face. He fanned himself with an old issue of *Agos*, the Istanbul-based Armenian newspaper to which he has subscribed for many years and that he has someone read to him. We introduced ourselves. After sizing us up carefully, Avedis motioned us to take a seat near his bed. His thin voice emerged as a whisper, and we strained to hear his words.

Avedis was just a toddler in July 1915. At the time, his family name was Demirdjian but, under the republic, Turkey forced all its Armenian citizens to Turkefy their surnames. "Later, they stole the 'ian': now all we have left is the 'Demirci,'"[47] he joked. ("He has a great sense of humour," said his family.) Avedis was barely walking when the Turkish soldiers approached Musa Dagh. "We gathered a few belongings and headed up the mountain," he explained. To make fires and be seen from the sea, the Armenians cut down trees. Then they were rescued by ships. "The inhabitants of Vakıf were loaded onto those ships, and our family left for Port Said, in Egypt. I spent a few years in the refugee camp, until I was five." The exile was temporary; Britain, which ruled Egypt at the time, was reluctant to take in Armenians.

"In 1918, after the war ended, we returned," he recalled. "Everyone was hungry." Most of the inhabitants of the seven Armenian villages conquered their fears and returned to Musa Dagh, then under French protection. The region, the Sanjak of Alexandretta, was attached to the state of Syria. After the First World War and the establishment of the French mandate of Syria, it passed under French control. "I remember a French captain who came to the village," said Avedis. Life returned to normal, as it was before the war and the genocide. "We began farming. My father began to plant orange groves, down there, behind the house." He gestured vaguely. "But nobody looks after them now."

The orange crops didn't support Avedis who, in the 1930s, was a shepherd by day and a journalist by night. Artin Demerci, one of his three children, explained: "He wrote for one of the Armenian newspapers that were printed in Bulgaria in those days. They published his stories about peasant life between the wars."

"I was their Vakıf correspondent," said Avedis. He had filled pages of notebooks with details about rural life at the time.

"It's wonderful to have a father like him," declared his son proudly. "He passed down all that information to me, all that rich history that makes up the Vakıf adventure. In his notebooks, he even wrote down the surnames they gave all the inhabitants, neighbourhood by neighbourhood." The old man is the living memory of the village, which is slowly dying. "In 1938, there were seventy-three Armenian homes and families in the village. Now there are barely twenty," Avedis said sadly.

In 1938, Turkey was on the verge of being plunged into another world war. Kemal Atatürk, who had guided the country, had just died in Istanbul. More than fifteen hundred kilometres away, in the Sanjak of Alexandretta, Ankara's nationalist demands were becoming increasingly strident. Kemalist Turkey had encouraged Turks to settle there to shift its demographics. In 1918, one-third of the population was Turkish-speaking, and one-third (mostly Alawite, but also Sunni and Christian) spoke Arabic. The prospect of an independent Syria worried Turkey, which supported the separatist demands of the Turkish minority in the Sanjak. An ephemeral Republic of Hatay was founded with its own flag and parliament. In May 1937, a survey indicated that 47 per cent of voters in the Sanjak were Turkish. This number grew to 55 per cent, and in November of that year, Paris finally decided to separate Alexandretta from the rest of Syria. In September 1938, the region was given the Turkish name Hatay and became a Turkish province. On the eve of a global conflict, France and its ally, Great Britain, wished to appease Turkey, and Hatay was used as a bargaining chip. The Armenians saw this agreement as a betrayal. The genocide was still fresh in the minds of its victims – and in those of their executioners, who remained unpunished. No one doubted that the past could easily be repeated.

Mount Moses witnessed a second exodus, with many families moving to Syria and Lebanon. "Our culture was largely Arabic – it was easier," said Avedis. A new community was built in the village of Anjar, on the Bekaa plain at the foot of Mount Lebanon. That town is still inhabited almost exclusively by Armenians from Musa Dagh, and the Armenian dialect from this region is still spoken there. Those few Armenians who could not afford to leave the now-Turkish mountain came together in a single village: Vakıf.

In the other villages, Turks and Turkmens[48] resettled there by the government took possession of the empty houses and the deserted streets. Today, it's as though the Armenians just left. In Yoğunoluk, the beautiful stone houses and the public fountain used to wash clothes are almost intact. Two or three Armenian families may have blended into the background, converting to Islam to escape detection, but little can be known about that: the distrust runs too deep.

The most astonishing site in Yoğunoluk is the mosque, built by the newcomers on the roof of the church in the village square. Stacked one on top of the other, the two places of worship fit together like a jigsaw puzzle, united by history. The little mosque with its pale green concrete walls, its tin roof, and its white minaret sits on one section of the church, like the top tier of a wedding cake. A stone staircase once used to reach the church tower serves as the mosque's entrance. Amazingly, on the pediment of the church, built in 1896, a beautiful inscription in Armenian letters has been preserved, as if to leave some small trace, some evidence, of the building's tumultuous past. Inside the church are only the stone arches, the bare floor and walls, and, here and there, a few engraved crosses left by pilgrims who came here to pray. Small groups of Armenians, descendants of the former residents, regularly visit the church, and the Turkish villagers do not object.

The Turkmens who were moved to the village of Yoğunoluk in 1940 following the departure of the Armenians between 1915 and 1920 first used the church as a mosque, according to Hatay's local newspaper. After a while, disturbed by the dampness, they built the structure of reinforced concrete right on top of it. But in recent years, there has been talk of restoring the historic church, which would mean destroying the mosque. The eight hundred villagers find themselves between a rock and a hard place. "The village is small, and there are very few places to build a mosque," says Osman Gücük, the *muhtar*.[49] "That's why we originally built it above the church. Moreover, we're poor. Our livestock are our only source of income, and we can't afford to build a new mosque. The villagers can't agree to let this mosque be destroyed without a guarantee that another will be built. What's a Muslim village without a mosque?" Mustafa Arik, one of the villagers, insists, "The state must build a new mosque before authorizing the destruction of this one."

According to Ali Kaya, an administrator in Hatay, the restoration of the church in Yoğunoluk could boost tourism and yield positive economic spinoffs for the village. In Turkey, that's often the primary reason for restoring Armenian heritage. In Vakıf, it was a different story. The church building there is modern and well maintained but, without a settled priest, it was being used more as a living space than a place of worship. The last priest died in 2000, and, for eleven years, an Ar-

menian priest had been sent from Istanbul by the Patriarchate to celebrate mass almost every Sunday. For those eleven years, from 2000 to
2011, Turkish bureaucracy opposed the appointment of a new priest
for the the parish.

But that all changed in 2011. On that beautiful Easter Sunday, the
trees were in flower and Vakıf was in a festive mood. Students had
come home for the weekend, and families gathered in the small courtyard. There weren't enough benches in the church for morning Mass,
so folding chairs were brought in. The new priest – also named Avedis
– had arrived, and the village had been restored to life. "It's almost historic – it's been eleven long years," the priest said. "It's important. Religion is part of our culture." Born in the city of Iskenderun, formerly
Alexandretta, still home to a small Christian community, Father
Avedis, thirty-one (born in 1980), is an affable priest with a youthful
face behind narrow-framed glasses. He has followed the traditional
path of the region's Armenian clergy: he was educated in Istanbul,
then at the Armenian theological seminary in Antelias, Lebanon, seat
of the Catholicosate of Cilicia, which was moved to Sis, near Adana,
after the genocide, and finally to Jerusalem. "I wanted to officiate here
to reopen the church's doors to the faithful. Of all the villages of Musa
Dagh, Vakıf is the last; it's completely Armenian," he said. "We must
preserve our culture and our language. The history of this village is
very important. Today, we can gradually begin to talk about that." This
young priest is breathing new life into the village, which sorely needs
it.

The older Avedis, who will soon turn one hundred, is visited by his
children only on holidays. His son Artin, a painter, lives year-round in
Istanbul. The younger generation of Musadagtsi (Musa Dagh Armenians) can't imagine a future in the village. "Organic farming is all very
well," sighs Artin. "There's a certificate, but no market."

"The village is no longer endangered by its identity," adds the priest.
"Today, young people have no reason to stay; they move to Istanbul for
economic reasons. In the end, that's the real danger."

9

Football Diplomacy

"That's really Armenia? So close?" Astonished, Abdullah Gül, president of the Turkish Republic, stood for a moment at the edge of the canyon overlooking the Akhourian River, part of the current border between Turkey and Armenia. The neighbouring country of Armenia – so near and yet so far – was just one hundred metres away. It was July 2008, and while passing through the Kars region, the Turkish president had decided to visit the ruins of Ani, the capital of the medieval Armenian kingdom, which now lies on the Turkish side of the border. Once known as the "City of 1001 Churches" and protected by thick stone walls, Ani symbolizes the splendour of medieval Armenia, although that fact is not mentioned on any sign. At its height in the eleventh century, the city had more than 100,000 inhabitants. Today, the skeletons of a few churches sit on a vast stretch of barren land. At dawn, standing amidst these ruins, the visitor feels overwhelmed by the screams of pain that seem to emanate from the gutted buildings. Barely a dozen are still standing. Since 2004, tourists have been able to visit the site, admiring the few frescos that have miraculously survived and the cathedral that, although its dome has collapsed, is as majestic as ever. Before that, Ani was strictly a military zone, the church remnants used for target practice.

Immobile in the midst of this desolate landscape, Gül eyed the remains of a collapsed bridge. On the other side of the river, a few army huts and observation towers house the Russian and Armenian soldiers who guard this accursed border, the former dividing line between the western world and the Soviet bloc. Surrounded by his learned assembly of advisors and his substantial escort, Gül looked around, soaking in the solemnity of the place. He asked about the progress of the restoration projects undertaken with the Norwegian government, then walked down the few steps to admire the remains of the Convent of the Virgins. He entered the cathedral, where time seemed to stand still. The thick morning mist covering the scorched earth added to the unreality of the scene.

So near and yet so far. Armenia and Turkey broke off diplomatic relations in 1993 following the outbreak of war for control of Nagorno-Karabakh, a province of the young Republic of Azerbaijan, primarily Armenian-populated since time immemorial but claimed by both the Azerbaijanis and the Armenians after the collapse of the Soviet Union. By intervening in this conflict, Turkey naturally revived memories of 1915. Ankara sided with Baku, the capital of Azerbaijan, through solidarity with its sister country, Turkish in both language and ethnicity. Since the 1994 ceasefire, Karabakh, the "black garden" of the Caucasus, has remained occupied by pro-Armenian forces, despite resolutions adopted by the UN Security Council calling, as it did again in 2008, for the "the full and unconditional retreat of Armenian forces from the occupied Azerbaijani territories." This tiny scrap of rugged and isolated land is now a self-declared republic with a president and a parliament, recognized only by Armenia. Serzh Sargsyan, the current Armenian president, and his predecessor, Robert Kocharian, are both former Karabakh military leaders. After twenty years of living with the status quo and fruitless diplomatic efforts, the temporary has become permanent. Refugees continue to live in squalid conditions in the outskirts of Baku, and Karabakh continues to be a grey area in the South Caucasus: a "frozen conflict" that occasionally claims a few casualties on both sides of the front lines but that would need only a spark to send the entire region up in flames again.

When this conflict with Turkey arose, the Republic of Armenia had been in existence for just three years. Like the other socialist republics, it had gained independence after the collapse of the USSR and had never really had diplomatic relations with its neighbour, aside from a few meetings of the Organization of the Black Sea Economic Cooperation.

Heir to the ephemeral Armenian Republic founded in 1918, present-day Armenia is a young country whose borders are those of the Bolshevik republic. The vast majority of Armenians are in the diaspora and, above all, have roots in the ancient Ottoman Empire and the eastern end of present-day Turkey – what the Armenians nostalgically refer to as "historic Armenia." The ruins of Ani and Mount Ararat – the national symbol, the Mount Fuji of Armenians – are both on Turkish territory. For most Armenians scattered throughout the world, their historic homeland – dream or fantasy – is on the other side of a closed border.

President Gül's visit to Ani therefore raised great hopes on both sides of the border. In Kars, Gül had discreetly added a visit to the Holy Apostles Church (Sourp Arakelots) to his itinerary. A proud, well-preserved tenth-century building with frescos and stone crosses on its walls, it symbolizes the ancient Armenian presence in the city of Kars. For once, Gül's visit did not include journalists or cameras. "What Notre Dame is to Parisians, the Arakelots church is to the people of this city," wrote the Armenian poet Yeghishe Charents (1897–1937) in 1921. Like many others, the church has been converted to a mosque several times in the wake of various invasions. In 1975, it was briefly turned into a museum before becoming home to a heating company. Finally, in 1994, it was again consecrated as a mosque and named Kümbet Cami. This was a studied insult to Armenia by the Turkish government in the midst of the Karabakh conflict.

The attention paid to this forgotten region, a geographic outpost, and to its Armenian origins gave reason to hope that there was a real political will to find an honourable exit from the trap of history. The president had shown himself to be favourable to the efforts of Naif Alibeyoğlu, the mayor of Kars, to promote reconciliation. The mayor had commissioned a giant statue – the Monument to Humanity, dedicated to friendship between peoples, to be erected on a hill outside the city. His office had also organized a great Transcaucasian Festival with artists, intellectuals, and businessmen invited from across the border. In 2004, Alibeyoğlu collected fifty thousand signatures on a petition asking that the border be reopened so as to renew historic ties between Kars and Gumri, Armenia's second-largest city, devastated by an earthquake in 1988 and left in ruins ever since. In 2007, the Kars business forum had been the inspiration for the first cross-border project: the

"Caucasus cheese initiative" by Turkish, Georgian, and Armenian cheese producers. Kars is famous for producing Turkey's best aged kashar cheese (*kaşar*) and for its *gravyer*, which resembles French gruyère. "We want to protect our common culture, which is Caucasian," explained Ilhan Koçulu, the project's promoter. "The land does not discriminate. I am deeply saddened to see these conflicts in our region. We wish to send a message to the politicians and to the people: we are all children of the Caucasus."

Commercial activity has almost completely disappeared on both sides of the border. In Akhourian, on the Armenian side, sheep graze peacefully between disused railroad tracks. The freight yard and rusty railway cars parked outside empty warehouses have not seen a train in twenty years. This was the ancient trade platform between Kars and Gumri, twin cities just sixty kilometres apart, linked by a once flourishing rail system. With the closing of the border, the trip between the two cities now takes more than twelve hours, with a detour through Georgia – enough to discourage the most enthusiastic entrepreneur. "It wouldn't take much," says a Kars business owner, one of a small group promoting this dialogue. "What would it cost to reopen the border? Why can't we get past our old quarrels?" And when he is reminded that the painful memories of the 1915 genocide are always present in the background, he answers, "Of course. So let's acknowledge it once and for all, compensate the victims, make amends for our mistakes, and move forward."

In 2008, the dialogue between Turkey and Armenia, supported financially by the US Department of State since 2001, had not yet made much progress. In 2003, when he was minister of foreign affairs, Gül had made waves by stating that reconciliation was possible "if Armenia recognizes the territorial integrity of Turkey" and gives up even symbolic claims to the western provinces of "historic Armenia." Now it was football that held out the greatest hope for rapprochement. In November 2007, in Durban, South Africa, the qualifying draw for the 2010 World Cup had placed Armenia and Turkey together in the fifth group. From a purely sports perspective, the game was not of great interest since Armenia is not a big football-playing nation but, for obvious reasons, it was still one of the most highly anticipated matches. Organizers feared the worst, however: a few months earlier, Armenia had been drawn in the same group as Azerbaijan. Since neither country's team was willing to visit the other, both Euro 2008 qualifiers had been cancelled in June for political reasons – a first for the UEFA executive committee, presided over by Michel Platini.

This time, both Ankara and Yerevan wanted to find a solution. In July 2008, secret negotiations between the two countries were launched in Berne under the aegis of Switzerland. Armenian president Serzh Sargsyan broke the ice by inviting his Turkish counterpart to watch the first match with him in September. Two weeks later, when Gül visited Kars and Ani, he still had not announced his answer. Turkish opinion did not seem to favour the visit, and the nationalist press was in an uproar. But the decision had already been made: "He really wants to go," whispered an advisor.

On the morning of 6 September, in the VIP lounge of Ankara airport, there was a palpable sense of history in the making. Journalists jostled for position at the press conference Gül held just moments before takeoff. He would be accompanied on the presidential jet by a handful of bureaucrats, Ali Babacan, the minister of foreign affairs, and a dozen Turkish and foreign journalists, some more excited about the football match than about the diplomatic mission. French reporters had been invited to attend the conference, an opportunity for the Turkish president to communicate his message of good will to the Armenian diaspora in France. It was a short flight, barely an hour and a half. As the plane flew over Lake Van and then the troublesome border, Gül sat quietly up front beside his wife, Hayrunnisa, enjoying a peaceful moment with a book. In fact, the president was engrossed in a posthumous collection of works by Hrant Dink, murdered eighteen months previously: *Two Close Peoples: Two Distant Neighbours* (published in Turkish in 2008 and translated into French and Armenian).

But the moment the plane touched down at Yerevan airport, pandemonium broke out. The delegation was swept into a convoy of vehicles that immediately headed downtown, sirens wailing. A strange honour guard greeted the visitors with placards: "Armenians demand justice," "I'm from Van," "I'm from Muş," "I'm from Erzurum," "Recognize the 1915 genocide." All along the route, demonstrators representing the Armenian Revolutionary Federation (ARF) (Dashnaktsutyun) stood behind security barriers waving signs before the Turkish president and his escort. This visit to watch a football game and promote the resumption of diplomatic ties between the two countries was clearly not enough to heal the wounds of 1915 and spare Turkey its duty to remember. Apart from these peaceful organized protests, however, Armenians generally offered a polite welcome to the Turkish president.

The arrival at Hrazdan stadium was chaotic. Colourful crowds sporting the red, blue, and orange of Armenia bordered the playing field, where odours of roast mutton and fried foods mingled just as they do in Turkish stadiums. The old Soviet stadium of Yerevan resembles a huge concave dish and holds 58,000 spectators; it sits between the downtown core and the Hrazdan River. From the main platform overhanging the field can be seen the grey spire of the Armenian genocide memorial, Tsitsernakaberd, the Armenian Yad Vashem.[50] Soaring forty-four metres into the air from the top of the highest hill, the memorial was built following the fiftieth anniversary of the genocide to symbolize the rebirth of the Armenian nation.

The Turkish players were no doubt unaware of the monument as they ran out onto the grass amid the shrill whistles of the crowd, but they could not help but be oppressed by the century of troubled history. On that momentous day in 2008, the home team was given the heavy task of defending its country's honour against its Turkish opponents. The mood in the stands was solemn, electric, but not overly aggressive. A few Turkish supporters and Turkish Armenians had made the trip to encourage "friendship between peoples." Political slogans were forbidden, but a few banners could nevertheless be seen in the stands, recalling the weight of the genocide and its denial. The words "Recognition," "Reparation," and "Restitution" were brandished by spectators while the Turkish national anthem, "March to Independence," resounded throughout the stadium. Behind thick bullet-proof glass, the two presidents, Gül and Sargsyan, stood somewhat stiffly, then shook hands. The match could begin.

When the final whistle sounded after an uneventful match, Turkey had won easily by a score of 2 to 0. The Turkish diplomats and cabinet members assembled in a corner of the distinguished visitors' gallery noisily congratulated each other amid much backslapping. Like good football fans, they had almost forgotten the purpose of the exercise. The presidents slipped away while the ministers of foreign affairs – Edward

Nalbandian and Ali Babacan – left to continue discussions on the restoration of diplomatic ties. Behind closed doors, in the basement of the stadium leading to the parking lot, the two men confirmed their desire to sign an agreement and quickly reopen embassies. The two chief diplomats continued their talks long into the night.

Karen Mirzoyan, the only Armenian diplomat in Turkey as Armenia's representative to the Organization of the Black Sea Economic Cooperation (BSEC), took Ahmet Davutoğlu, chief advisor to the Turkish prime minister, into the library of the department of foreign affairs to show him that his book, *Strategic Depth*, was indeed on a shelf there.

After spending just a few hours in Armenia, the Turkish president and his delegation returned to Ankara to celebrate their double victory. On the plane home, Gül told the journalists, "I think my visit broke a psychological barrier in the Caucasus." The next day, the international response was enthusiastic. Washington and Paris both congratulated the players on the success of their "football diplomacy." In Turkey the reaction was more cautious. "Gül's visit was a courageous act, but we shouldn't expect too much from it," warned Turkish intellectual Cengiz Aktar. "First, there is no real desire to make peace with Armenia, and, second, the atmosphere is not conducive to revolutionary decisions."

Thanks to this fruitful sports-diplomacy encounter, Turkey and Armenia had each taken a step toward each other. Fair play and good will were in the air – but this was only the beginning. The second meeting, planned for a year later, was to take place in Turkey in the brand new stadium in Kayseri, the president's hometown. In the meantime, it was important to keep things moving. The two delegations crossed paths at the World Economic Forum in Davos, Switzerland, and at the NATO security conference in Munich. In April 2009, the Berne Declaration confirmed the intention to reopen the border. And, on 31 August, the two countries unveiled a document, the results of two years of negotiation, mediated by Switzerland: two protocols on the normalizing of diplomatic ties and bilateral cooperation. On 10 October, the two chief diplomats, Ahmet Davutoğlu and Edward Nalbandian, inked the two protocols in Zurich; Hillary Clinton, the US secretary of state, and Bernard Kouchner, the French foreign affairs minister, were among the diplomats who attended the historic ceremony.

The two signatory states agreed "to respect and ensure respect for the principles of equality, sovereignty, non intervention in internal affairs of other states, territorial integrity and inviolability of frontiers." They also agreed on the importance of creating and maintaining "an atmosphere of trust and confidence between the two countries that will contribute to the strengthening of peace, security and stability of the whole region, as well as being determined to refrain from the threat or the use of force." In addition, they confirmed "the mutual recognition of the existing border between the two countries as defined by the relevant treaties of international law." This final point was a requirement of the Turkish party. Although territorial boundaries were no longer really an issue and, beginning with Levon Ter Petrosian, the first president of Armenia (1991–98), all Armenian presidents had recognized the border, Ankara was obsessed with the issue of territorial integrity. This obsession was based on a paranoid fear, referred to as the "Sèvres syndrome"[51] of the resurgence of dreams of a "Greater Armenia," as envisaged in the 1920 Treaty of Sèvres.[52] The protocols therefore entailed the de facto recognition of the Treaty of Kars, signed on 13 October 1921, between Russia and Turkey.

The two states emphasized "their decision to open the common border" and agreed to "implement a dialogue on the historical dimension with the aim of restoring mutual confidence between the two nations, including an impartial and scientific examination of the historical records and archives to define existing problems and formulate recommendations." This last section, which obviously referred to the 1915 genocide, the "historical dimension" of the conflict, worried many Armenians, who believed that the "impartial and scientific examination of the historical records and archives" would be a useless and dangerous exercise. This examination had already been done countless times and could only be a pretext for questioning the unquestionable. Did "existing problems" really need to be defined? Wasn't this just another stalling tactic on the part of Turkey?

Before coming into force, the protocols had to be ratified by the parliaments of both countries; but this never happened. The question of Nagorno Karabakh, alluded to in the protocols, remained unresolved and, encouraged this time by Prime Minister Recep Tayyip Erdoğan and his chief advisor, Ahmet Davutoğlu, Turkey quickly made this a new condition for reconciliation. According to Ankara, the principles of "territorial integrity" and "regional stability" required Armenia to make concessions in the conflict with Azerbaijan. Since 2009, the Turkish government had clearly linked the reopening of the border with the settlement of the dispute over Nagorno Karabakh and Armenia's withdrawal from the occupied territories.

Turkey began to back-pedal and split hairs over symbols. Armenia's use of Mount Ararat on official emblems was seen as an attack on Turkey's territorial sovereignty. Above all, Armenia's constitution, which refers to the "1915 Armenian Genocide in Western Armenia and the Ottoman Empire," was deemed intolerable by the Turks. The Constitutional Court of the Republic of Armenia may have determined that the protocols did not contravene the constitution, but Davutoğlu, Turkey's minister of foreign affairs since 1 May 2009, believed that Armenia "contradict[ed] the letter and spirit of the protocols." A third party soon invited itself to the rapprochement table: Azerbaijan, a close ally of Turkey and one of its main suppliers of oil and natural gas. The protocols were seen as a betrayal by Baku, which believed they "contradict[ed] its national interests."

The relationship between Azerbaijan and its "big brother" became frosty. Prime Minister Erdoğan tried in vain to assure Ilham Aliev, the president of Azerbaijan, that the border would not be reopened unless progress was made in the Nagorno Karabakh peace process. The slogan dear to nationalists on both sides of the border, "One people, two states," was forgotten. Demonstrations masterminded by the Turkish regime were held in Baku. More importantly, Azerbaijan threatened to hit Ankara where it hurt by increasing the price of the oil and natural gas it had previously supplied at preferential rates. Turkey took a giant step backward by postponing the opening of the border, which it had originally planned to coincide with the April 24th demonstrations.

Just four days after the protocols were signed, it was time for the return of "football diplomacy." Surprisingly, although a diplomatic accord had just been signed, there was less enthusiasm for the second match than for the first. For no apparent reason, the game had been moved from Kayseri to Bursa, the former imperial capital of the Ottoman Empire. Located east of Istanbul on the shores of the Sea of Marmara, the region is known for its nationalism and has a large Azerbaijani population. Clearly the choice of Bursa as host was a negative sign.

In 1912, the *vilayet* of Bursa had been home to a large Armenian community – 92,000, according to the Patriarchate – who had lived in the Kurtoğlu and Emirsultan neighbourhoods. Today, not the slightest trace of them remains. President Sargsyan, who did the travelling this time, did not receive a warm welcome. The stadium was steeped in nationalism. Thousands of police officers were stationed outside the building, where the words of anti-Armenian songs filled the air. Azerbaijani flags were everywhere. Although officially banned from the stadium – several dozen were confiscated by the police – they were still clearly visible in the stands. In one corner, members of the Genç Siviller (Young Civilians) organization, a group of pro-democracy activists, displayed a banner in Turkish and Armenian: "Welcome to the country of Hrant Dink." The stadium announcer encouraged fans to show "traditional Turkish hospitality," and white doves were released before the kickoff. But for ninety-two minutes, the Armenian players were booed and insulted. As with the first match, the Turks won 2–0.

In Baku, where the national flag is sacred (in 2010, President Aliev had the tallest flagpole in the world – 165 metres – built on the shores of the Caspian Sea[53]), the Bursa incident caused an uproar. The local press reported that Turkish police officers had seized Azerbaijani flags and tossed them in the garbage. Across from the Turkish embassy, the red and white flags bearing the star and crescent that stand in Martyrs' Lane (the cemetery, or *şehitlik*, dedicated to those killed during the 1918 liberation of Baku) were flown at half mast. In Ankara, this reaction provoked an outcry. It took a visit from Davutoğlu and several parliamentary delegations to defuse the crisis. The blackmail worked: by exerting pressure on Turkey and pulling diplomatic strings, Azerbaijan was able to sabotage the protocols. Baku simply harnessed the power inherent in its own natural resources and played the role handed to it on a silver platter by the West. The Baku-Tbilisi-Ceyhan (BTC) and Baku-Tbilisi-Erzurum (BTE) oil and gas pipeline projects had deliberately left Armenia out in the cold. In fact, the bypassing of its territory had been a key condition when the pipeline route was planned.

There would be no rematch, and the protocols appeared to be dead in the water. It quickly became clear that major obstacles stood in the way of the reconciliation for which the world had had such high hopes. On 9 February 2010, Sargsyan wrote to Gül, "A situation where words are not backed up by actions leads to mistrust and scepticism, giving convincing arguments to those who oppose the process." The next day, he confirmed that "the Armenian parliament will ratify the protocols if the Turkish government does so." But the process was stalled, and Armenia was looking for a way out.

After the policy of openness initiated by Abdullah Gül and Ali Babacan, the Erdoğan-Davutoğlu team had adopted a more nationalist line and was far less forward-thinking about the idea of rapprochement with its Armenian neighbour. Two very different visions with diverging national discourses had taken shape around the Armenian question. The first, realistic and confident, took into account the need to deal with the realities of the 1915 genocide. "Going to Yerevan was risky, but it was the right decision," confirmed the Turkish president in 2012. The second, more traditional and defensive, relied on force to impose a Turk-centric interpretation of history. In mid-March 2010, things came to a head when Prime Minister Erdoğan reacted angrily in an interview with the BBC's Turkish service:[54] "We are tolerating the 100,000 Armenians living illegally in Turkey. If necessary, I could ask those 100,000 people to return to their own countries," he threatened in one of his trademark outbursts. Erdoğan's slip horrified Armenians in Istanbul, who could not help but be reminded of the 1915 deportations. Edward Nalbandian, Armenia's minister of foreign affairs, reacted immediately: "This declaration shocked everyone. The Armenian genocide began in exactly the same way … It is regrettable that the leaders of modern Turkey have not abandoned the racist and discriminatory practices of the Ottoman period." Erdoğan tried to smooth things over, while Egemen Bağis, minister for EU affairs, just added fuel to the fire: "Some seventy thousand Armenian citizens work illegally in Turkey, and we close our eyes to that fact."

Ninety per cent of those "Armenians from Armenia," whose numbers are in fact closer to fifty thousand than one hundred thousand, are women between thirty and sixty who work as nannies and caretakers for children and the elderly in upper-middle-class Istanbul homes. A smaller number of men have been hired by leather and shoe factories in the Laleli and Kumkapı districts. As in most neighbouring countries, this economic immigration is a recent phenomenon that arose with Turkey's rapid economic expansion and the opening of new air routes.

If you happen to be taking an Istanbul-Yerevan flight, you'd be well advised to travel light. Seats are booked weeks in advance since Armenian workers must leave the country every three months so as not to overstay their tourist visa. To help pay for their tickets, they stuff their bags with cheap goods purchased from Istanbul wholesalers to be sold in Armenia: leopard-skin coats, blue jeans, and high-heeled shoes.

The prime minister's xenophobic blunder and the stigmatization of Armenians working in Turkey were enough to convince the public of the negative implications of the protocols, effectively taking them off the table. Worse, a climate of fear returned to Istanbul neighbourhoods frequented by Armenians. "We're worried," admits Shusha, who sells leather jackets in a shop in the city. "My family comes from Gumri, and we lost our house in the earthquake in 1988. I studied philology and, until 2004, I worked as a teacher for $50 per month. After that, I decided to come here." Donara, fifty-three, says, "The genocide? We can never forget it, that's for sure. My family was originally from Muş and Kars, and it's something that's always with us."

The following Sunday, tensions ran high at the Gedikpacha church in the Armenian district of Kumkapı. Recep, who sells Bibles in front of the evangelical church, recounts, "Yesterday, while a TV crew was here filming us, neighbourhood kids showed up, and someone threw a lighter. They were shouting, "We'll burn you down! We'll blow you up!" Wire mesh has since been installed on the church windows. "We were tired of replacing the window panes. They kept throwing stones and bottles."

Many Armenians attend Sunday services here in four languages: Turkish, Armenian, Russian, and Farsi, for people from Iran. "The Armenians here feel threatened," Recep says. "They go directly from home to work and back again. They don't hang around outside. They're just trying to survive. But Armenian citizens should be able to work here, shouldn't they? Like Turks do in Germany. If Germany said they were going to expel all the Turks, how would they feel about that?"

Seated in his office in the basement of the church, Reverend Krikor rages against this government-sponsored campaign. "The state is already causing enough problems for Turkish Armenians – its own citizens. All the property belonging to churches and foundations has been confiscated. How can a government that steals from its own citizens claim to protect Armenians from Armenia? This concerns us as well: they are hurting, despised, mistreated; they work like animals. Help like that they don't need."

For Krikor, the root of the problem is the memory of the genocide and its denial. A simple reminder of this history by the Armenian Constitutional Court caused a brutal backlash. "They threaten us because they are frightened. Turkey knows full well that the genocide happened; it's just trying to figure out how to silence the demands. It's like a child who can't fight the bigger kids in the neighbourhood, so it beats up its little brother. The Turkish state has not changed since 1915."

In fact old prejudices die hard, and politicians often fall back on traditional anti-Armenian rhetoric. "Son of an Armenian!" is an insult synonymous with "Traitor!" In late August 2012, during a parliamentary debate on attacks by the Kurdistan Workers' Party (PKK), Erzurum's JDP deputy Muhyettin Aksak declared, "Our Kurdish brothers should not be equated with PKK members. We must make a distinction. They are nothing more than the children of Armenian apostates." The declarations of Idris Naïm Şahin, minister of the interior, run along the same lines. Football diplomacy and other attempts at rapprochement have done little to tone down the nationalist, anti-Armenian, almost atavistic reflexes of Turkish leaders, beginning with those at the top.

In January 2011, during a visit to Kars, the prime minister's words directly contradicted those of the president three years earlier. Far from calling for reconciliation, Erdoğan referred to the unfinished Monument to Humanity that stood above the city as a "monstrosity," demanding it be torn down immediately. Commissioned in 2006 by the former mayor of Kars, the statue by artist Mehmet Aksoy symbolized friendship between Turkey and Armenia. Objecting strenuously to the fact that the "monstrosity" stood near tenth-century Islamic ruins, Erdoğan demanded that it be destroyed before his next visit. Without hesitation, the administration carried out his wishes, sending bulldozers to accomplish the grim task – on 24 April.

10

An Obsession with Denial

Stairs lead to the top of a mound from where the curved blades of four gigantic swords carved of Chinese granite rise into the sky above Iğdir, their tips meeting at the top. In the background can be seen the snowy foothills of Mount Ararat. From a distance, this aggressive structure resembles a missile targeting the neighbouring country of Armenia: the border, closed by Turkey since 1993, is just a few kilometres away. Surrounded by a few dusty Turkish flags bleached by the sun, the Iğdir Monument, some forty metres high, was placed so that it could be seen from the enemy camp. Inaugurated in 1999 by Ramazan Mirzaoğlu, Turkey's minister of state, it was erected to honour the memory of the genocide victims. Not the 1915 genocide, not the Armenian genocide, but the "genocide of Turks by Armenians," explains Göksel Gülbey, formerly a local official of the Grey Wolves and now president of the "Association to Fight False Armenian Accusations." The official state version of history, that Armenians carried out a genocide against Turks and Azerbaijanis between 1918 and 1921, is supported here by collections of yellowed photographs of mutilated bodies and common graves and by mouldy works of propaganda.

The decision to build the memorial was made in 1965 during the so-called International Symposium on Historical Realities and Armenians, held in Igdir to counter Armenian claims on the fiftieth anniversary of the genocide. The symposium resolved that "a monument to the martyrs should be erected in memory of the more than one million Turks who fell in Eastern Anatolia and to respond point by point to those celebrating 24 April as the anniversary of the genocide and who erect monuments around the world to commemorate the genocide allegedly perpetrated against the Armenians."

In this region, at the eastern edge of Turkey, where a significant minority of Azerbaijanis moved to escape Armenian reprisals at the end of the First World War, the memories of those days are still fresh. Here, the ultranationalist MHP (Nationalist Movement Party), and its youth wing, the Grey Wolves, are on firm ground.

The monument was built along the road leading to the Alican border crossing, guarded by a few sleepy Turkish soldiers in the middle of a grassy field. In 2009, when Turkey and Armenia were attempting to reconcile, it was this crossing they considered reopening. To enter Turkey, Armenians coming from Yerevan would have had to drive by this massive symbol of denial – a strange approach to reconciliation.

The Iğdir genocide monument is the ultimate caricature of the Turkish government's policy of denying the 1915 genocide by rewriting history and transforming victims into guilty parties. But Turkish revisionism takes other forms as well, starting with the glorification of the masterminds of the massacres, whose names are omnipresent in the country today. Dozens of high-ranking officials, all players in the 1915 genocide, were recycled into government administration and have given their names to streets, airports, and stadiums. Take, for example, Talaat Pasha,[55] minister of the interior of the Committee of Union and Progress (CUP) and chief architect of the genocide. Using telegraph equipment that he had installed in his own home, Talaat sent orders for the roundup of Armenians to governors and sub-prefects throughout the empire. He is still celebrated as a hero by the republic, and his name is omnipresent: it has been given to a boulevard running through the centre of the capital city of Ankara, to an avenue in Istanbul, and to districts (*mahalle*), schools, and parks. Every new wave of nationalism brings more examples. This was particularly true after the 1971 and 1980 coups d'état.

During the First World War, the CUP established its headquarters at the University of Istanbul, the country's largest and oldest seat of learning. Behind the monumental gateway through which students pass today, one wing, a small late-nineteenth century pavilion with high painted ceilings and varnished parquet floors, was taken over by Talaat Pasha, who installed his office there. Today, the space is used as a dining hall by university professors and their guests. So, every day at noon, unsuspecting visitors may be invited to sit at the murderer's table in an old-world setting and be served tasty Turkish dishes by waiters in crisp white shirts.

Talaat's body was laid to rest in the heart of Istanbul on the Hill of Eternal Freedom (Abide-i-Hürriyet Tepesi). That hill lies within a triangular area bordered by three major highways, a hospital, and the gigantic Çağlayan Justice Palace, built in the shape of a flying saucer. The cemetery gate creaks open, waking the bearded guard slumped before a television set in his hut near the entrance. A murder of crows takes flight, cawing angrily. Two mangy dogs disappear behind bare pine trees.

The cemetery holds a few government dignitaries, heroes of Turkish modernism, and the seventy-four soldiers killed in the 1909 attack on parliament in the name of Islam. This was a significant battle in the war between the heirs to the original Tanzimat reforms,[56] modernist Ottoman intellectuals influenced by the Enlightenment and Bonapartism, and supporters of the absolute sovereignty of the sultan. A monument at the top of the hill in the form of a cannon pointing skyward is seen today as a symbol of modernism, positivism, secularism, and resistance to reactionary forces. In April 2007, huge Kemalist demonstrations, secretly organized by the military to oppose the election to the presidency of an Islamist, Abdullah Gül, set out from here.

This was also the place chosen by the Kemalist government to bury Talaat Pasha with full honours after his ashes were returned to his homeland in 1943. To gain Turkey's favour, Hitler had decided to return the remains of its hero to Istanbul. At the end of the First World War, many of the most senior Young Turks, Talaat among them, had fled to Germany, their ally. Some were tracked by "genocide hunters." Talaat, who believed he was safe there, was assassinated in 1921 by Soghomon Tehlirian, a young Armenian whose entire family had been massacred a few years earlier. This act of vengeance was the masterstroke of Operation Nemesis.[57]

The decision to bury Talaat on the Hill of Eternal Freedom was ideologically significant. After all, the Armenian genocide was carried out in the name of a kind of modernism. The decision to bury Enver Pasha, former minister of war, in the same location was more recent.

In August 1996, Enver's body was repatriated from Tajikistan by the Turkish government, headed at that time by the Islamist Prime Minister Necmettin Erbakan. At the end of the First World War, Enver, the champion of pan-Turkism, had dreamed of unifying all Turkic peoples in central Asia. In 1922, he was killed in a skirmish with the Red Army – by Armenian soldiers, legend has it. Reunited in death, the two Pashas receive few visits, according to the cemetery guard. Their grey gravestones covered with dead leaves seem lost in the midst of the urban chaos. The Hill of Eternal Freedom is now neglected and is no longer honoured on ceremonial occasions.

The adulation of Talaat Pasha is nevertheless very much alive in the highest nationalist circles. In 2006, the Islamic-conservative government of Recep Tayyip Erdoğan did not oppose the striking of a Talaat Pasha Committee to glorify the Grand Vizier of the Armenian genocide. Committee members have included such high-ranking officials as Süleyman Demirel, the grand old man of Turkish politics, a former president of the republic who served as prime minister seven times; Rauf Denktaş, founding president of the self-proclaimed Turkish Republic of Northern Cyprus, who died in January 2012; and Doğu Perinçek, a former Maoist who converted to ultranationalism and leads the Workers' Party. Perinçek was imprisoned in 2007, accused of being one of the linchpins of the so-called Ergenekon "deep state" military-backed plot to overthrow the government.[58] All of these men have been involved in organizing revisionist demonstrations in Lausanne, Switzerland, where Perinçek was convicted in 2007 of publicly denying the Armenian genocide. They have also been active in France where, in May 2011, the government authorized the Talaat Pasha Committee to hold a parade on Paris's Place de la Bastille. The same committee, closely linked to Turkish political and civic networks, played a highly visible role in the "pro-denial" demonstrations in front of the National Assembly and the Senate prior to the vote on the Boyer law criminalizing denial of the genocide. Worse still, on the ninetieth anniversary of Talaat's death, a torchlight ceremony was held in his honour in Berlin.

The celebration of the guilty parties is just one aspect of Turkish revisionism that over the years has become increasingly sophisticated, answering point for point the demands for justice of Armenian communities. Almost a century later, Turkey still refuses to use the word "genocide" to describe the systematic deportation and massacre of 1 to 1.5 million Armenians. In recent years, it has begun to refer discreetly to the "events of 1915." Ankara will admit that there were "population displacements" and reciprocal massacres. It acknowledges that 300,000 to 500,000 Armenians died, but attributes those deaths to the troubled context of the First World War. For Turkey, the deportation of Armenians was justified by their supposed support of its Russian enemy, even though the majority fought in the Ottoman army. "There has been no genocide in our history," declared Erdoğan, toeing the party line, when the debate over the French legislation was raging. "Just how many Muslims have been killed in the Balkans?" demanded Ibrahim Kalım, advisor to the prime minister, during a meeting of a specially constituted parliamentary committee. This is the official state historiography, against which there can be no argument.

For a better understanding of the mechanisms of revisionism, we refer again to *Assassins of Memory*, by Pierre Vidal-Naquet:

The worst of all historiographies is plainly state historiography, and governments rarely confess to criminal activity. Perhaps the most painful case of this sort is that of Turkish historiography concerning the Armenian genocide of 1915. What could be more natural than for the Turks to insist on the wartime situation, on the support many Armenians voiced for the Russian offensive, and on the local conflicts between Armenians and their neighbors, in which Armenians did not always behave like the lamb in La Fontaine's fable. But the Turks do not stop there: they offer the very exemplar of a historiography of denial. Let us put ourselves in the position of Armenian minorities throughout the world. Imagine now Faurisson[59] as a minister, Faurisson as a general, an ambassador, or an influential member of the United Nations; imagine Faurisson responding to the press each time it is a question of the genocide of the Jews, in short, a state-sponsored Faurisson combined with an international Faurisson.[60]

Vidal-Naquet later used the term "negationism," coined by French historian Henry Rousso in 1987 to refer to the denial of the Holocaust, to refer to the Armenian genocide.[61] The denial by the Turkish state and by all those who defend its official position follows the same pattern as the negation of the Holocaust. The methodology and the rhetoric are identical: eye-witness accounts of survivors are systematically discredited or ridiculed. The testimony of foreigners and others is said to be the work of an international anti-Turk conspiracy. Historic documents and physical evidence are dismissed as forgeries. As Faurisson did with the gas chambers, deniers of the Armenian genocide twist the facts to the point of suggesting that the systematic deportation and massacre of Armenians is "theory" or "opinion" – not historic fact. Just as it was supposedly typhus that killed the Jews deported to Auschwitz, it was hunger and thirst that killed Armenians on the road to Deir ez-Zor. Like denial of the Holocaust, the denial of the 1915 genocide exploits widespread ignorance about a historic event that is not taught in schools. Just think of the explanations that have been put forward in France, even by elected representatives and eminent lawyers and historians, to justify or minimize negationism. As Vidal-Naquet says, responding "on paper" to negationists and their often huge distortions of the facts does require at least a minimal understanding of the issue. But in this type of debate, the form and the force of the affirmation take precedence over the substance.

"The denial of the Armenian genocide is an industry," declared Turkish historian and sociologist Taner Akçam in an interview in *Le Monde* in January 2012.[62] The author of *A Shameful Act: Armenian Genocide and the Question of Turkish Responsibility*[63] and a professor at Clark University in Worcester, Massachusetts, Akçam began in the early 1990s to question the official version of history, one of the first Turkish intellectuals to do so. "By denying what happened in 1915, Turkey reproduces the institutions, social relations, and mindset that lead to the genocide. Genocide denial goes beyond the defence of a former regime whose mindset resulted in genocide in the past. Denial also fuels a policy of on-going aggression, both inside and outside Turkey, against anyone who opposes the denialist mentality. This is why Hrant Dink's true murderers are still at large. This is why attacks are organized against Armenians and their memorials in Europe. This is why, in the US, campaigns of hate and hostility are organized against me and other intellectuals." Akçam has spoken in favour of the proposed law to criminalize denial in France. "What should be clear to everyone is this: In Turkey, genocide denial is an industry. It is also a state policy of primary importance. In 2001, the National Security Council, Turkey's highest constitutional authority, established a coordinating committee for the fight against baseless claims of genocide. I repeat: Denying the genocide is one of the most important national policies of the Turkish state. You need to realize that you aren't just confronting a simple denial: you're up against a denialist regime."[64]

Indeed, the Turkish government deploys enormous resources to discredit what it commonly refers to as "Armenian allegations of a so-called genocide." A quick perusal of government websites is enough to reveal the lengths to which it goes. Very few do not contain the standard spiel about the "so-called" genocide and Armenian "lies." The Department of Culture is the most verbose on the subject, devoting half of its historical documents to the issue. The website of the Department of Foreign Affairs honours its "martyred diplomats," killed by terrorist members of the Armenian Secret Army for the Liberation of Armenia (ASALA), with no mention of the organization's goals or intentions, which are closely linked to the genocide.[65] The National Intelligence Agency (Milli İstihbarat Teşkilatı, or MIT) itself claims to be a direct descendant of the Special Organization (Teşkilât-ı Mahsusa), founded in 1914, which played a central role in the massacres. Turkey's version of history is promoted with expensive brochures, pamphlets, and CD-ROMs distributed at tourism offices, international trade shows, and exhibitions such as the 2010 Season of Turkish Culture in France. For this type of event, Turkey's Promotion Fund can be counted on for support. The country is obsessed with denial.

As Akçam reminds us, the Committee to Coordinate the Struggle with the Baseless Genocide Claims (ASIMKK), chaired by the deputy prime minister, is composed of representatives of key government departments (defence, justice, interior, foreign affairs, education, culture), the chair of the Council of Higher Education (YÖK), the director of the National Intelligence Agency (MIT), representatives of the National Archives and the Promotion Fund of the Prime Ministry, the president of the Turkish Historical Society (TTK), and – of course – the military. It's the last word in the institutionalization of denial. The committee was struck by a government uniting the Kemalist left of Bülent Ecevit and the Grey Wolves of Devlet Bahçeli when the French were voting on the law recognizing the Armenian genocide. If there is one subject on which all Turkish parties (aside from the pro-Kurdish party) agree, it is the denial of the genocide. The ASIMKK had been inactive for years but, in response to new legislative rumblings in France, it was reactivated. In 2007, it was also mobilized for the production of a six-part documentary on Turkish-Armenian relations, *Sarı Gelin* (The fair-haired maiden), named after an old Armenian folk song. The propaganda DVD was distributed by the department of education to primary schools throughout Turkey – including Armenian schools – with orders that they show it to classes and report back to the department that they had done so.

The best example of state-sponsored denial is that of the Turkish Historical Society (TTK), an institution founded by Kemal Atatürk with a mandate to promote the official version of history. Long run by historian Yusuf Halaçoğlu, the master denier, now a deputy for the ultranationalist MHP, the TTK has a well-funded "department of Armenian research." The head of that department, historian Kemal Çiçek, is the go-to person for television and newspaper journalists needing sound bites on Armenian issues. In reports and documents published by the state's historical-political mouthpiece, Armenians are lumped together as "traitors" or "terrorists" allied with Russian troops. This is the version of history that is still found today in school textbooks and that shapes the minds of Turkish students from kindergarten through university. Says Taner Akçam, "Turkey has pursued a policy of voluntary amnesia and stall tactics, sweeping the subject under the rug, pretending that it doesn't exist, and hoping it will eventually be forgotten. That's why it is so angry with France: Turkey doesn't like to have its memory refreshed."

But the centennial of the genocide is fast approaching, and Turkey is worried about the international campaign that is on the drawing board. After France and the twenty-odd other countries that have already done so, more could officially recognize the 1915 genocide. In the United States, Turkey's biggest ally on the international stage, the question is raised during every election campaign: by the Democrats when the majority in the House of Representatives or the Senate is Republican, and by the Republicans when it is Democratic. Before being elected to his first term of office, President Barack Obama promised to recognize the Armenian genocide, but he has repeatedly broken that promise. On 24 April, the White House traditionally issues a statement in memory of the victims, and its words are carefully weighed. Each year, more than one million Armenian-Americans wait to hear the president say the word "genocide." But since 2008, Obama has spoken only of a "Meds Yeghern," or "great catastrophe."

"Every year, on April 25, newspapers across Turkey breathe a collective sigh of relief: 'Phew! We made it through another year!'" notes Akçam ruefully. "As we approach 2015, the strategy will remain unchanged. Turkish leaders know that the subject will arise, especially overseas. So, in preparation, they're doing as much damage control as possible. The memory of the genocide is like a ghost that haunts them." Turkey is sparing no effort to counter claims in countries with large Armenian communities. "The government is devoting enormous resources to avoiding accusations of genocide," says historian Samim Akgönül, professor in the department of Turkish studies at the University of Strasbourg. In France, for example, pressure groups and websites have been created to promote Turkey's official version of history and policy of negationism. To achieve these goals, Turkey's Promotion Fund of the Prime Ministry has been given an almost unlimited budget. Even more impressive, the US-based Turkish Coalition of America (TCA), with an annual budget of several million dollars, lobbies elected representatives in both chambers, some of whose campaigns are financed by Turkey. Ankara sponsors university chairs and runs media campaigns. With its 6 June 2005 edition, *Time* magazine distributed a CD-ROM of Turkish denialist propaganda.

But in the run-up to 2015, the Turkish government is switching tactics. A shrewd strategist, Ahmet Davutoğlu, the minister of foreign affairs, understands that over-the-top denial will be counterproductive in the long run. In spring 2012, once the matter of the French genocide law had been settled, Turkey decided to group all of its institutions charged with fighting "baseless claims of genocide" under the authority of the prime minister's office. Columnist Murat Bardakçı applauded the move in a

June 2012 issue of the Turkish daily *Habertürk*: "As of now, one single institution will be responsible for dealing with all claims related to the genocide," he wrote. "In Turkey, there is now a wide range of government and university institutions and foundations dealing with Armenian claims. And what have we accomplished with all that effort? Absolutely nothing. The Armenian diaspora has been effective at European and American universities and research centres. It has produced professional, high-quality documents, including numerous attractive publications and hundreds of websites." Bardakçı, the author of several books on the genocide, also edited the notebooks of Talaat Pasha.[66] He questions the Turkish strategy to date: "Since most of our publications target only our own citizens and do little more than promote ourselves to ourselves, little attention is paid to those publications outside our borders ... Nobody reads the books and brochures that our ambassadors try to distribute in other countries because they are written in the boring style of 1960s propaganda." Despite recent efforts by certain think tanks to recruit foreign genocide deniers – particularly in France – Bardakçı is concerned about the lack of credibility of government efforts on the eve of the centennial. "We don't have one single publication that is taken seriously in foreign academic circles ... Our disastrous inability to understand that you can't reduce the events of 1915 to a body count must be overcome. Otherwise, Turkey's headaches are going to become more painful than ever."

11

Sevag Balıkçı: 1,500,000 + 2

The Balıkçı family won't be celebrating Easter any more – or anything else, for that matter. Under a grey sky, his collar raised against the wind and gaze fixed on the waves crashing against the docks, Garabet Balıkçı chain-smokes mechanically. In his free hand he holds a small bouquet of white flowers. On this Easter Sunday, when Istanbul Armenians are celebrating the resurrection of Christ around a family meal and children are painting Easter eggs, Garabet is crossing the Bosphorus to lay flowers on the grave of his son in the Şişli Armenian Cemetery.

Facing the headstone is a small stool made of the same marble. "They put this stool here so I could sit and talk to him," Garabet says sadly. "But I no longer hear his voice. He's dead." His handsome son won't ever be coming home. Every Sunday, his father visits his grave, replaces the wilted flowers, burns a little incense, and sits for a few minutes to speak to his son, murdered one year ago, on the Thursday before Easter.

Sevag Şahin Balıkçı, born 1 April 1986, died on 24 April 2011. "Every Armenian knows what that means," says a family friend, who has come with his wife and children to pay his respects. April 24th is the anniversary of the beginning of the 1915 genocide. On that day, hundreds of Armenian leaders and intellectuals – doctors, lawyers, journalists, politicians – were arrested, held at Sultanahmet prison, and then deported to Anatolia from the Haydarpaşa train station. The Armenians of Turkey have long commemorated that date in silence, but the Balıkçı family is no longer holding their tongues. "They said that, with Hrant Dink, there were 1.5 million+1 victims. Now, with my

son, there are 1.5 million+2," says Ani, still reeling from this double
blow.

The news of Sevag Balıkçı's death was first met with incredulity by
the Armenian community. Then it had to face the hard fact: Sevag was
the most recent victim of the Armenian genocide, the latest casualty of
24 April. The young man was doing his military service in the Kozluk
district of Batman Province, a Kurdish region in southeastern Turkey.
Dominated by the guerrilla movement of the Kurdistan Workers' Party
(PKK), the region is hostile to the Turkish army and its conscripts. Sevag
would have been demobilized in just twenty-three days: less than a
month to go before returning home to his parents, his sister, and his
small bedroom in the family's new apartment in Moda, on the Asian
side of the Bosphorus. "He was looking forward to returning home to
work with me," says Garabet, a goldsmith in a jewellery store near
Istanbul's Grand Bazaar. It had been a difficult winter for Sevag, far
from his home: the army, the violence, the isolation, life in a barracks
sixteen hundred kilometres from Istanbul. The ordeal had shaken him.
Yet in the last pictures the family has of him, the harshness of his
shaved head is softened by his round, smiling face. Military service is
compulsory for all Turkish citizens, including "non-Muslim minorities" – *gayrimuslim*. And Sevag had done his duty.

Like all good Turkish families, the Balıkçı family had made a small
photo album devoted to their son's military service. It stands in a place
of honour on a shelf in their living room. Garabet slowly turns the
pages, revealing photos of Sevag in his combat uniform and khaki T-
shirt, in the mountains or lounging around the barracks. Unlike many
other conscripts, he is always smiling in the photos, never armed or
adopting a warlike posture. In many group photos, he stands in the
middle of a dozen young soldiers in his company. Everyone seems
relaxed and friendly. And yet … Garabet points to a face: "That's the
killer." The young man he points to, Kıvanç Ağaoğlu, looks like any
other soldier. In one photo he poses proudly in the centre of the group,
brandishing an assault rifle. In another, he stands arm-in-arm with his
future victim, staring at the camera with bulging eyes.

On the morning of 24 April, the commander of the Kozluk army
barracks assigned part of the garrison to repair the fence surrounding
it. Every spring when the snow melts, military operations and am-

bushes by PKK rebels resume in full force, and the region is on high alert. Military posts are sometimes attacked, so it was time to beef up security around the barracks, adding a few rolls of razor wire. Half a dozen soldiers, including Sevag, were happy to grab picks and shovels and spend a few hours working in the fresh air. An armed soldier stood guard: Kıvanç Ağaoğlu. Suddenly, a shot was fired. The bullet tore through Sevag's T-shirt, hitting him in the abdomen. He died instantly.

This tragic event cast a dark shadow over the annual commemoration of the genocide. ("Every Armenian knows what that means...") Istanbul's Armenian community was in shock. The funeral was held three days later at the Armenian church in Feriköy. The atmosphere was heavy, anger drowned by fear and grief. Sevag's coffin was draped with a Turkish flag bearing the crescent moon, symbol of Islam, as is traditional for armed forces "martyrs." Many officials were in attendance. In the front row, Egemen Bağış, minister for European affairs, rubbed salt in the wound. For him, Sevag's death during his military service was evidence of the harmonious integration of the Armenian community in Turkish society.

The military was represented by Third Army Corps Commander General Hulusi Akar and Gendarmerie Regional Commander General Ibrahim Yaşar. Yaşar held out the Turkish flag to Sevag's father, Garabet, who leaned over and kissed it. Neither the general public nor Sevag's family, accustomed to this extreme idolization of republican emblems, saw the symbolic violence of this act, which somehow embodied the submission of the victims to their murderers. Hundreds of mourners, many of them strangers – ordinary citizens of Armenian descent affected by the death of Sevag Balıkçı – attended the funeral and offered their condolences. Among them was Rakel Dink, the widow of Hrant Dink, murdered four years earlier – also because of his Armenian origins. After the service, the coffin was taken to the Şişli Armenian Cemetery. Garabet, distraught and still unable to fathom the death of his son, climbed into the front of the vehicle as the church bells rang to signal Sevag's passing.

Immediately following the young soldier's death, the army set to work promoting the theory that it had been an accident. Before the inquiry was even finished, its conclusions were known. "A delegation of officers came to the house to explain that it was an accident and that, in reality, Sevat and Kıvanç had been friends," says Garabet. But the family did not believe it. One week later, the army invited them to visit the fateful spot where their son had died, to tour the Kozluk barracks, and to grieve. Ani and Garabet Balıkçı flew to Diyarbakir and were taken by helicopter to the army base. There, they visited the scene of the crime, were welcomed by the officers, and were even introduced to the soldiers who had witnessed Sevag's death. "Kıvanç Ağaoğlu was walking around, free as a bird and still armed, as if nothing had happened," says Ani, disgusted. He told them that "the rifle had gone off by itself while he was returning it to position." They also met the six young conscripts who had been present on the day of the shooting. "One of them was trembling," recalls Ani. "I went up to him quietly and asked what was wrong." Visibly upset, the young man told her that he was the one who had taken Sevag's body to the hospital, where he had been declared clinically dead. And, above all, that there had been nothing accidental about the shooting. He told her that Kıvanç had deliberately taken aim and shot Sevag.

But the young soldier would change his story by the time of his first court appearance. For a trial was indeed held at the Diyarbakır Military Court to investigate the circumstances surrounding Sevag's death and determine whether or not it had been an accident. Every one of the hearings held in the large Kurdish city, all attended by Sevag's parents and his older sister, Lena, was a nightmare for the family. The killer was still free and able to look them in the eye. Over and over again, he claimed that the shooting had been accidental. "It wasn't an accident," whispers Garabet, shaking his head. Ani adds, "It was obviously related to the date, April 24th. I told the court that. His friends knew Sevag was Armenian. He even made the traditional Easter pastry – that came out during the trial." She sighs. "My son was killed because he was Armenian. He was chosen to be sacrificed. All I want is for this to be recognized as a hate crime and for the murderer to spend twenty years in prison."

Many troubling details emerged during the legal proceedings. The burgundy T-shirt worn by Sevag on the day of his death – an essential piece of evidence – appeared to have disappeared from the case file. "They showed us a different T-shirt that wasn't even his size," says his mother. "And there was confusion about the trajectory of the bullet."

The crime scene was tampered with, and there was more than enough time to move the evidence, according to attorney Ismail Alavut. The testimony of the Kozluk soldiers almost all corroborates the official version of their superiors, but if you look closely, many discrepancies emerge. "They are all lying, out of fear. None of their stories seems credible. It's clear that pressure is being exerted on the witnesses," says Alavut. The family of the killer, Kıvanç Ağaoğlu, itself threatened one of the witnesses. "They phoned to intimidate him and contacted him through a post office employee who lived in the same city," Alavut says, consulting the thick file. "One of the young soldiers even talks about how the officers pressured them about their testimony." On the day of the reconstruction, all of the witnesses asked to be excused. They all sent the judge the identical letter, down to the last comma.

But it is mainly the character of the shooter that fuels suspicion. Originally from Elazığ, the former Armenian city of Kharpert, now a Turkish nationalist stronghold, Ağaoğlu did not hide his support for the far-right nationalistic youth group Alperen Ocakları (roughly translated as Hero-Saint Hearths), linked to the Great Union Party (BBP) (Büyük Birlik Partisi), a nationalist Islamist party that is an offshoot of the MHP. In fact, Ağaoğlu's father was head of the local branch. On his Facebook page, Ağaoğlu declared his enthusiastic support for this racist organization, which is hostile to minorities. "The soldiers who don't dare testify are afraid of this ideology and the network that likely stands behind it," says Alavut.

Despite the army's efforts to cover up this anti-Armenian crime, tongues eventually began to wag. Sevag's Armenian girlfriend, Melani, was the first to speak. Several weeks after the shooting, she finally began telling what she knew. During his year of compulsory military service, Sevag would call her, feeling freer to confide his feelings of fear and isolation to her than to his parents. He had received death threats. One day, in front of several witnesses, one of the soldiers in his regiment had pulled him aside. "If war ever breaks out between Turkey and Armenia, you'll be the first to die," he had said to Sevag, according to Melani. Sevag had been deeply shocked by these threats. His parents had known nothing about the terror that haunted their son.

A year after the tragedy, the family's agony was prolonged by the wait for a court ruling. The case was dragging on, and Sevag's autopsy report had still not been added to the case file. "I get the impression that the judge is being very lenient," says Ani. "He told us the verdict has to allow him to look both families in the eye. But, at the same time, as the Turkish proverb says, they 'watch you with their left eye and strike you with their right.'" A "Justice for Sevag" committee was created to support the family. Its members include Rakel Dink and her son Arat, choreographer Zeynep Tanbay, and young Armenian community leaders Hayko Bağdat and Garo Paylan. But, as has been true since 1915, impunity is the rule. Despite the support of Turkish democrats, international pressure, and media attention, the trial of the murderers of Hrant Dink concluded in January 2012 with the conviction of just Ogün Samast and Yasin Hayal, the final links in the criminal chain that planned the murder of the journalist and spokesperson for Turkish Armenians. The senior police officers in Trabzon and Istanbul who had been in contact with the killers were simply transferred. The government was cleared of all suspicion. "Ağaoğlu's profile is very similar to that of Samast," observes Alavut, who has worked on both cases.

As long as such acts go unpunished, the small Armenian community must live with the paralyzing fear that more will be committed. In April 2012, Ani, Garabet, and a few close friends met at the Jash restaurant in the Beyoğlu district of Istanbul for the opening of an exhibition of Sevag's art. Although the fact is not mentioned in the window, Jash is one of the city's few Armenian restaurants. The name means "meal" in Armenian, "something everyone needs to live," says Dayk Miridjanian, the restaurant's owner, with a smile. He comes from a long line of Istanbul residents, some of whom survived the 1915 massacres; his grandfather ran a delicatessen in the city's Kurtuluş neighbourhood.

On the ground floor of the restaurant, Miridjanian has pushed the tables aside to make room for Sevag's sculptures. The young goldsmith was skilful with his hands, and he loved to give free rein to his imagination by playing with clay. In the presence of these childlike sculptures, tears roll down cheeks and mascara runs. Ani Setyan, Sevag's high-school art teacher, murmurs as she examines the sculptures, "Why did they have to kill him? Why him? He was so sweet. He was just a child." In the small room are friends of Sevag's parents, their faces grim, and Sevag's former classmates, including three young women, dressed up as though for their first date, who break down in tears. Former Turkish deputy Ufuk Uras drops by as a neighbourly gesture.

Ani Balıkçı stands at the door, dressed in black as she has been since the death of her son, accepting condolences. Solid as a rock, head held high and refusing to cry, she smiles and thanks each guest for coming, her voice raspy from too many cigarettes. Behind her, Garabet is grief-stricken. He too has started smoking again, despite his bad heart. His face and body, everything about him, express his pain. Taking refuge in silence, he generally responds with a sigh or a shrug. He has wrestled with his feelings for months, especially when alone in his shop. Next to him, his daughter Lena, Sevag's older sister, a young woman with chestnut hair and large brown eyes, is proving herself to be both tough and determined.

One year after Sevag's death, on 24 April 2012 – the ninety-seventh anniversary of the Armenian genocide – it is Lena who speaks at the cemetery, standing on the marble pedestal of her brother's flower-strewn headstone. "We were a close-knit family. There were four of us. Now, there are three. We miss Sevag. We sent him to do his military service. We gave everything to this country. And you?" She glares into the camera of a Turkish television station that is filming the event. "What did you do to protect him?" The time is clearly past for mollifying speeches and fantasies of Turks and Armenians living together harmoniously. Speaking coldly and deliberately for ten long minutes, Lena gives free rein to her anger. Few people have come to pray in the Şişli cemetery – just a handful of familiar faces and a few unknown Armenians. The Turkish intellectuals and democrats who, when in the media spotlight, claim to be defenders of the Armenian community, are conspicuous by their absence. Only activists from the Istanbul branch of the Turkish Human Rights Association (IHD) have come with their leader, attorney Eren Keskin, to pay their respects.

"In any case, in this country, they will never understand," says Ani. "They can't get past their meaningless platitudes, like 'we share your pain.' Basically, we've always felt we were different."

On this day of remembrance, the commemorations are mixed: those for 1915, the anniversary of the Armenian genocide, and those for Sevag, the latest victim of a crime that will never be put to rest as long it goes unpunished and unrecognized. The lack of justice for the Balı-kçı family is an incitement, an encouragement, to the most nationalist elements of Turkish society, who regularly threaten to "finish the job" – to finalize the extermination of the Armenians. On the esplanade of the ancient Byzantine Hippodrome, just across from the famous Blue Mosque, the activities begin at about 1 pm. The IHD displays a banner and lights candles in front of the Turkish and Islamic Arts Museum – the former prison where, on 24 April 1915, Armenian leaders and intellectuals were rounded up before being deported. The demon-strators brandish photos of these men, the first victims of the genocide. One of them is of Daniel Varoujan, a brilliant poet, who, during his captivity, continued to write *The Songs of Bread*, published posthumously in 1921. Varoujan's work contains some of the most beautiful imagery in Armenian literature. A few months after their capture, he and four others were tied to trees, tortured, and killed. Varoujan was thirty-one. Among the signs depicting yellowed photo-graphs of the long-dead intellectuals is a colour photo of Sevag, the most recent victim. For his father, Garabet Balıkçı, attending this event for the first time, the support is comforting.

In front of the former prison, visited daily by hundreds of tourists oblivious of its tragic history, Eren Keskin reads a message, a symbolic letter to Aram I, Catholicos of the Holy See of Cilicia, forced to take refuge in Antelias, Lebanon, after his predecessor was expelled from Sis, near Adana, in 1915. "With shame and respect, we honour the memory of the Ottoman Armenians who were massacred and stripped of all their wealth, even of vestiges of their past ... On 24 April 2011, while we stood here commemorating the arrest of Armenian intellectuals, Sevag Şahin Balıkçı was gunned down in Batman Province while doing his compulsory military service in the Turkish army. Officials distorted the facts and manipulated witnesses to ensure a verdict of accidental death. More in-depth inquiries have since revealed that this was, in fact, a premeditated murder. The death of Sevag Balıkçı is proof that, since 1915, Armenians have never been able to live in safety, that the genocide continues, and that its denial for the past ninety-seven years has only perpetuated the suffering."

The wall of denial is still far from crumbling.

12

Çankaya Palace:
The Republic's Original Sin

In 2007, when he took possession of Çankaya Palace – official residence of the president of the Republic of Turkey – Abdullah Gül redecorated it to his taste, bringing paintings by Ivan Aivazovsky up from the basement to hang in his office. Since the late nineteenth century, the Turkish state has been in possession of an impressive collection of landscapes and seascapes by the Russian master, considered to be one of the greatest marine artists of all time. In 1874, Sultan Abdülaziz, the thirty-second sultan of the Ottoman Empire, had commissioned some forty paintings from Aivazovsky, inviting him to Constantinople to receive the honorary badge of the Order of Osmanieh.[67] But after the empire's admiration came republican disgrace. Ivan Aivazovsky was born into an Armenian family, so his identity had not been ideologically compatible with that of the previous president of the republic, Ahmet Necdet Sezer, a staunch Kemalist. The incumbent, on the other hand, who was personally invested in the failed reconciliation efforts with Armenia, takes great pleasure in showing the paintings to his guests. His esthetic choices harmonize perfectly with his feelings about the "Armenian question." Still, there are limits. As the head of a denialist state,[68] Gül keeps another aspect of his home under wraps.

Çankaya Palace, the official residence of the head of state since Mustafa Kemal, was built on a hill in the heart of the capital city of Ankara. This grandiose symbol of the republic stands on stolen property that, before the First World War, belonged to a wealthy Armenian jeweller and merchant named Ohannes Kasapyan. What an indiscretion on the part of a state founded largely on property confiscated from Armenians and other non-Muslim minorities! It is tempting to see this as the confession of a crime – or even evidence of a sense of total impunity. This embarrassing fact is not advertised, of course; it is known only to the inner circle. There seems to be a tacit agreement among nationalists to keep this information hidden from the public. Every once in a while, however, it bubbles to the surface – but only in the form of a threat. In August 2010, the publication of a book by Turkish journalist Nevzat Onaran on the confiscation of Greek and Armenian property briefly focused media attention on the building's past. "Armenians eye Çankaya Palace," screamed the *Vatan* (Homeland) newspaper. "The Armenians want Çankaya'" was the version printed by many others. Among readers, these ominous words recalled images of those dangerous Armenians who threaten the very existence of Turks. But, aside from these occasional reminders, quickly sucked back into the black hole of national oblivion, it is the official version that prevails – along with its significant gaps.

The website of the Presidency of the Republic of Turkey offers a prime example of such gaps. A large section is devoted to explaining the history of the Çankaya köşkü – the Çankaya Villa. The story, it says, began in 1921, at the start of the "war of independence." In Europe, the First World War was over, but in the Ottoman Empire, on the losing side and now in its death throes, Istanbul was occupied by French and British troops. The Allies were plotting to carve up what remained of the empire and fighting over territory. Ankara, the future capital of the republic, was nothing more than a large agricultural town with a population of fifteen thousand. In Anatolia, General Mustafa Kemal took over the leadership of the Turkish nationalist movement in an attempt to save what he could from the greedy Western powers. According to the website, "Mustafa Kemal, who came to Ankara on 27 December 1919, first of all stayed at the Agricultural School and later at the Train Station Chief's Villa and used them both as a residence and as a place of work. Since these buildings were inadequate for the work and relaxation of Ata (Atatürk), a search was entered for a suitable residence. A vineyard house, located in the vineyard region at Çankaya, was given as a gift to Mustafa Kemal on 30 May 1921 by the Ankara Municipality with the objective of his living in a quieter and more peaceful environment." The previous owners, the Kasapyan family, and the reasons for their departure are never mentioned.

The official story of the construction of the Turkish state thus commandeered the two-storey, half-timbered home in its bucolic setting, as it can be seen in a black-and-white photo published in *Agos* – just another element in a national history where the Armenian genocide did not take place. According to the authorized version, "This house of Ata's, which was the witness of very important events during the War of Independence and the first years of the Republic, was where Mustafa Kemal Atatürk planned the founding of the Republic." Over the years, the modest home was expanded several times, then finally abandoned by the president's successors, who preferred the comfort of more modern surroundings. Converted into a museum, the Çankaya Villa remains the heart of the presidential compound. Visitors stroll reverently from room to room as if visiting a shrine. In the "Green Room," they picture the tea parties given there by Latife Hanım (Madame Latife), Atatürk's first wife. In the "Smoking Room," they imagine the weighty discussions of the country's future taking place in tufted morocco leather armchairs, the crackling of the radio discernible in the background.

In 2007, Soner Yalçin, then a columnist at the *Hürriyet* newspaper, briefly rescued the Kasapyans from their historic obscurity. He happened to mention that "the first owner of Çankaya was an Armenian." Displaying an impressive mastery of euphemism and omission, Yalçin reported that "when he left the city during the war, the wealthy merchant sold the house with its furnishings to the Bulgurzades, a prominent Ankara family." The house then passed into the hands of Rifat Börekçi, the *mufti*[69] of Ankara and local head of the Committee of National Defence, who is said to have given the house to Atatürk after he admired it one day while out riding.

Only a well-informed reader could have read between the lines of this ambiguous piece of reporting – unless, that is, they had read the article on *Hürriyet*'s website and been curious enough to peruse the comments. Normally, articles mentioning Armenians arouse the anger of readers, who respond by hurling insults at those "traitors of our homeland." But,

amazingly, at the bottom of the page, a certain Edward J. Cuhaci, an
architect who has been living in Ottawa, Canada, since 1957, felt it was
important to "add the following clarification": "My mother's name was
Rose Kasapyan. Born in Ankara, 1896–2001. The name of her father (my
grandfather) was Ohannes Kasapyan. Born in Ankara, 1857–1944. The
Kasapyan family never sold the Çankaya residence to anyone. It was the
government that confiscated not just the house, but all the family's
property, and ordered the entire family to be deported in August 1915.
Since, at the time, my father (born in Ankara, 1887–1930) was working
for a foreign company that owned the railroad, he was able to save the
family by moving from Ankara to Istanbul, via Konya."

Cuhaci's grandfather and the grandfather's brothers may have been
forced to abandon their prosperous business exporting Angora wool to
England (Ankara was known as Angora under the Ottoman Empire),
but they escaped with their lives. According to historian Raymond
Kévorkian,[70] between 14 and 20 August, 1,200 Armenian men, "tied up
in twos," were taken outside the city and massacred. On 29 August,
1,500 more were deported to Syria. "Two hundred of them, including
the bishop, made it as far as Aleppo," he says. Thirty-four survived in the
camp on the plain of Meskené, an open grave on the shores of the
Euphrates, northeast of what is now Syria.

Edward Cuhaci is an extraordinary witness to the history of the
Çankaya Villa and its original owners, middle-class members of the
Catholic Armenian community caught up in the horrors of the First
World War. A member of the first post-genocide generation, he is now
an elderly man, but his lucid response to Yalçin's article proved that his
memory was intact. Our hopes therefore turned to Ottawa, and we
contacted him. Weary of the whole business, he was polite but firm. He
believes that our plans to follow the trail of the genocide have "no
constructive value for future generations" and that "investigating the
unfortunate events of the last century" will not lead to reconciliation
between the Turkish and Armenian peoples. The Canadian trail thus
dried up as quickly as it had appeared, a frustrating dead end.

It was Sevan Nişanyan who put us back on the trail. Few people
know that a descendant of the Kasapyans still lives in Istanbul: one of
Sevan's childhood friends, Verkin Kasapoğlu, an eccentric upper-

middle-class woman who once hobnobbed with wealthy young Turks at the wheel of her white Cadillac.

In those carefree years, her family background did not concern the young woman, who had received a cosmopolitan education at a posh boarding school in Switzerland. She was completely unaware of it. Surprised by our phone call, she nevertheless extended a gracious invitation to come for tea at her private mansion, inherited from her father. It is located on Bank Street in the old European district of Pera, once the financial heart of the empire, controlled by minorities and foreign powers. Kasapoğlu's living room offers a splendid view of the minarets of the historic peninsula on the other side of the Golden Horn. On the wall are an Andy Warhol painting and a pipe that belonged to John Lennon, "gifts from Sam Green," the former director of Philadelphia's Institute of Contemporary Art, she said coyly. Between the uncontested king of pop art and the former Beatle hangs an old family photograph. In the centre is a stern-looking woman with a stately air, Verkin's grandmother, after whom she was named. Next to the family matriarch is her husband, Rokos, a small man with a moustache. It was Rokos who brought the Çankaya house into the family. "When she was fourteen or fifteen," says Kasapoğlu, "my grandmother was sent to the Kasapyans, also Catholic, in Ankara, to marry their second-oldest son." Unimpressed with her intended, the rebellious teenager scampered back to Istanbul. Already smitten, however, he followed her, and the union was eventually sealed.

For many years, Kasapoğlu had heard nothing about Ankara but the romantic misadventures of her grandparents. The national taboo concerning the origins of the Çankaya Presidential Palace was so powerful that even its former owners did not mention it. "In 2001, the Patriarch told me about my family's history, and that's when he said 'Çankaya belonged to you.' It came as a shock," she recalls. It also brought back a memory of the only time her father, Antoine, had hinted to her about the property her family had lost during the First World War. "I must have been about four. My father took me to Ankara by train, and we visited a place where I ran around in a garden. It wasn't the Çankaya Villa, but a different summer resort. He told me it used to belong to a cousin, nothing more."

Antoine Kasapoğlu took the secret with him to his grave. "He wanted me to remain in Turkey and to be a fighter. In hindsight, I think he must have thought Çankaya would have been too heavy a burden to bear," says his daughter. Throughout the twentieth century, non-Muslims who escaped the massacres and did not flee the country had to submit to the hostility of the Turkish Republic, which was officially secular. In 1942, her father had been unable to pay the *varlık vergisi*, a wealth tax imposed by Ankara on minority communities. The tax was so heavy that many who could not pay it were forced to sell their homes and businesses at discount prices. That was the whole point, of course: the tax was a disguised land grab, enabling the Turkish state and its citizens to acquire properties that had so far escaped their grasp. So Antoine lost his property, but that was not all: he was also sent to a forced labour camp in the Erzurum region in eastern Turkey. In that poisonous environment, it's understandable that he avoided burdening his daughter with the story of the presidential palace. She has spent much of her life in Turkey and has never wanted to spend much time away from her homeland. But "to be on the safe side" and to protect her two children's future, she made sure they had dual citizenship. They are Turkish Americans – because "you never know."

Perhaps the person most troubled by this family history is her son, Süreyya. Rokos's great-grandson is writing a thesis on the history of the Patriarchate of Constantinople. His bookshelves contain every title published on the plundering of minorities under the empire and the republic. He is familiar with all twentieth-century laws discriminating against non-Muslims, and he has visited Çankaya. "The official guide explained that the house had been owned by a Bulgarian compatriot," he says. He had not contradicted the guide, and he also avoids mentioning the subject to his friends: "They wouldn't believe me. They'd think I was bragging." Neither has he told his professor, sociologist Ayhan Aktar, a recognized authority on the Turkification of minority properties. Turkey may be relaxing somewhat on the "Armenian question," but discretion is the better part of valour. Self-protection reflexes are passed down from generation to generation – instinctively.

Süreyya has also wondered about his grandfather's silence. "It was a wise decision," he concludes thoughtfully. "What good would it have done us to know? We couldn't have done anything about it in any case. And it might have made us resent Turkey or, worse, put our lives in danger. Since we didn't know about it, we were free to live our lives." Without being a prisoner of the past, Süreyya admits that, since his mother told him the family secret, he has become "more and more emotional" about Çankaya.

In the decades following the genocide, the Kasapyans began to put down roots overseas. Beginning in 1922, "the majority left the country with a foreign passport, giving up their right to return," Süreyya explains. "And along with their nationality, they also surrendered the right to file claims." Only his mother and uncle remained in Turkey, so they are the only descendants who may have legal rights to Çankaya. But while Article 65 of the Treaty of Lausanne, signed in 1923, stipulates that confiscated property must be "immediately restored to the owners," they would face a legislative arsenal designed to strip Armenians of their possessions. When asked whether he has ever thought of seeking financial or moral reparations, Süreyya smiles. According to his research, "Çankaya is administered by the presidency, but its owner is the Grand National Assembly of Turkey. Taking the case to court would mean suing parliament, the representative of the people." Unless they were feeling suicidal, no Armenian living in Turkey today would consider such a thing.

13

"If You Destroy a Nest, You Can't Make It Your Own"

"Draw two maps and put them side by side. On one of the maps, mark out where the Armenians were located before they were driven out of Anatolia. On the other, mark out the origins of the richest families in Turkey. These cities will appear on both maps: Adana, Kayseri, and Malatya. So, while the Armenians were disappearing from the surface of Anatolia, at the same time a 'new Turkish bourgeoisie' was emerging. The disappearance of the Armenians was just the beginning of this story."

In a column published in *Today's Zaman* on 28 August 2012, human rights lawyer Orhan Kemal Cengiz did not mince words. His pen struck directly at the Turkish Achilles heel: not satisfied with merely killing their victims, the criminals had also stolen all their worldly possessions. The state, the local leaders of the Young Turks party, the police, dignitaries, neighbours – all scrambled to get their hands on the "abandoned" property. Of course, greed may have been the starter's pistol in this race to plunder Armenian belongings, but, beyond that, it was all part of a master plan set in motion at the highest government levels. The goal of the plan, formulated by the minister of the interior, was to accomplish an economic shift. In just a few months, industry, trade, and crafts traditionally in the hands of Armenians became the responsibility of Turks who, until then, had primarily been government officials, soldiers, and farmers.

In southern Turkey, thirty kilometres from the Mediterranean Sea, the city of Adana evokes images of spicy Adana *kebab* and refreshing *şalgan* (a popular beverage flavoured with aromatic turnip), two regional specialties. But don't let the idyllic image of lazy hours in the shade of a palm tree lull you into a false sense of complacency. The fifth-largest city in Turkey, Adana is an "Anatolian tiger," one of those vibrant inland cities that have built their economic success on exports. Textiles, machinery, and agriculture are the chief economic engines of this city of 1.5 million. Under a sky full of sand, Adana stretches its industrial zone into the fertile plain of Çukurova (ancient Cilicia), the inspiration for the stories of Anatolia's poor tenant farmers penned by Yaşar Kemal. This generous land is drenched in the blood of Armenians who once grew cotton and cereal grains here. On the eve of the First World War, Adana was already the region's economic hub. Cotton production had led to industrialization, fuelled by the export of textiles to Europe. The some eighty thousand Armenians in the province made up the core of this new class of Ottoman entrepreneurs, but they could also be found in trade and in the handicraft shops at the bazaar.

Of these eighty thousand, only a handful of crypto-Armenians are left; invisible, they keep a low profile in the few remaining downtown houses inherited from their ancestors. The largest of these, described only as "a traditional nineteenth-century home," now houses the Atatürk Museum, explains a lawyer from Adana, a local history buff who is giving us a guided tour of the city. The founder of the republic spent a few nights there in 1923. A little further along, half-timbered houses have fallen into a state of disrepair. They appear to have been abandoned, as if no one dares touch these silent witnesses to the crime. On a wall, a defiant piece of graffiti has been scribbled: *Ne mutlu Türküm diyene* (How happy is the one who says "I am Turkish"). No passerby has thought to erase these words, attributed to Mustafa Kemal, for an obvious reason: no one questions the truth of this racist sentiment, establishing the superiority of Turks over all other peoples, including, of course, Armenians. Every morning, they are recited by students throughout the country, including those of the nearby Gazipacha (heroic commander) primary school. This imposing building was once just one of the community's twenty-five schools. Armenian *konaks* (homes) are still in the hands of wealthy Turkish families. One has been converted to a Koranic school; another is used as the set for a popular television program, *Hanımın Çiftliği* (Lady's Farm), according to our guide.

As in the rest of Anatolia, these widespread property seizures began in 1915 and occurred simultaneously with the deportations. Officially, the Abandoned Properties Commissions guaranteed Armenians that their homes would be protected and their belongings given back to them when they returned. Such hypocrisy! The raids were organized by Talaat Pasha and "legalized" by a series of laws, decrees, and regulations. The deportees were prohibited from selling their homes (except at rock-bottom prices), leasing their farms to tenant farmers, or transferring ownership of their businesses to family members living outside the country. Their bank accounts were frozen, then seized.

Instead of protecting them, local offices of the Abandoned Properties Commissions evaluated and liquidated the possessions of Armenians. Their empty houses were given to the thousands of Muslim refugees from the Balkans and the Caucasus who had settled in Anatolia.[71] In the cities, members of the Muslim elite, civil servants, and leaders of the Young Turks government appropriated the most beautiful homes or bought them for a song. In August 1915, a telegram sent to the provinces by the Ministry of the Interior ordered that only Turkish bidders could buy Armenian goods sold at auction. The money raised by the auctions was pocketed by the state and deposited in the Ottoman Bank. The survivors would never receive a penny of it.

According to the meticulous notebooks kept by Talaat Pasha, 696 properties were confiscated in Adana Province. These included churches, schools, houses, farms, warehouses, office buildings, and factories. The government used these "spoils of war" to support Turkish activity, and the republic adopted the same policy: there was no question of returning the tiniest plot of land to its rightful owner. In Uğur Ümit Üngör and Mehmet Polatel's *Confiscation and Destruction: The Young Turk Seizure of Armenian Property*, the authors report the following excerpt from a 1923 speech given by Mustafa Kemal to the Association of Artisans in Adana: "The Armenians have no right to this fertile land. The country belongs to you Turks ... This country is historically Turkish, so it is Turkish and will always remain so ... These fertile lands are the fundamental essence of Turkey."[72]

And those fertile lands continued to be productive. In 2011, Turkey was the seventh-largest cotton producer in the world. In Çukurova, endless fields of fluffy white bolls stretch to the misty horizon. Yesterday's cotton mills have given way to modern factories that line the highway crossing the plain to Karataş. In 1934, the Cotton Research Institute was founded, helping to boost production. Its current director has little to say about this history, however, acknowledging only that "the region has been producing cotton for more than a hundred years." Yet the reason for its creation is not without interest. In the years following the First World War, agricultural production declined dramatically. In 1921, Adana Province produced just 15,000 bales of cotton, compared to 135,000 in 1914. The new "owners" did not understand the technology, and there were labour shortages. A similar chaos reigned in those factories that had not simply been abandoned. The founding of the Cotton Research Institute was just one of many steps taken by the government in response to this economic disaster. Writes Üngör, "The government took over the abandoned office buildings. The land and the warehouses were reserved for cotton producers."[73]

The ravages of the genocide made the fortune of the Sabancı family, now head of the country's second-largest conglomerate. In 1921, its founder, Haci Ömer, then fourteen, left home on foot, heading from Akçakaya, in the province of Kayseri, to Adana, 450 kilometres to the south. "At that time, there were many workers from Kayseri who, like Ömer, were attracted by opportunities in cotton farming and industry," writes economist Ayşe Buğra in *State and Business in Modern Turkey*. "Among them were rich merchants from Kayseri who arrived to take over the properties of Greeks and Armenians along with the commercial and industrial establishments left idle after their departure. Such takeovers were encouraged by the government, and those who had connections with the authorities could benefit greatly from such opportunities."[74] An orphan who could barely read or write, Ömer lacked such connections, but he "benefited from the same situation indirectly through the ties of 'fellow townsmenship,' which can be very important in Turkey … Through acquaintanceship with families from Kayseri, he took some part in the takeover of old minority-run businesses in Adana."[75]

The young man began at the bottom of the ladder as a planter, but by 1932 he was co-owner of a cotton-ginning plant. He went on to acquire two factories producing cotton-based vegetable oil and a thousand-hectare farm in the Çukurova Plain (the first of four farms he eventually owned). According to Üngör, during his lifetime, this "self-made man" acknowledged being given cotton fields by the state. He also founded BOSSA, now Turkey's largest integrated textile manufacturer. The last two letters of the name (SA), refer to Sabancı, and the first three (BOS) to his partner, Salih Boşnak. Boşnak was born in 1865 in Mostar, now in Bosnia but then part of the Ottoman Empire. "A refugee from the Balkans, he was one of the leaders of the Armenian massacres in Adana in 1909," says Saït Çetinoğlu, who has researched the origins of fortunes of Turkish and Muslim families.

Almost a century later, these humble beginnings have blossomed into a financial and industrial empire: Sabancı Group has 57,000 employees, operates in eighteen countries, and is active in a wide range of markets, including energy, banking, distribution, textiles, and cement. The conglomerate's multinational business partners include such prominent companies as Carrefour, Mitsubishi, Bridgestone, and Philip Morris. In 2011, the group's consolidated net revenues were €808 million ($US1.1 billion). Sabancı knows what it owes to Adana, and has not been stingy in repaying its debt. It generously funded the country's largest mosque, which stands in the centre of town on the banks of the Seyhan River. On the other side of the river is the Hilton Hotel, also owned by the Sabancıs. Among other things, the Sabancı Foundation has built schools, dormitories, a cultural centre, a swimming pool, and a language laboratory. Adana's organized industrial zone is named after the family patriarch.

Somewhat surprisingly, but perhaps under the influence of Güler Sabancı, the enlightened chair of Sabancı Holding, the Armenian question is often addressed by its offshoots. The Sabancı Museum has exhibited the art collection of the Lisbon-based Calouste Gulbenkian Foundation, named after its founder, a wealthy Armenian businessman born on the Asian side of Istanbul. And Istanbul's Sabancı University has supported research on the genocide and the Armenians. In particular, it organized a conference on the 1909 Adana massacres, thus breaking the code of silence surrounding the anti-Armenian pogroms that preceded the genocide.

The story of Sabancı's success offers insights into the machinations behind the rise of some sections of the Turkish bourgeoisie. Some entrepreneurs had blood on their hands. Others simply exploited the opportunities generated by the crimes, without shame and with the blessings and assistance of the state. The government's goal was not to fill the coffers of an empire at war and on the verge of bankruptcy: it was more ideological – to build an ethnically Turkish economy. Talaat Pasha issued the following empire-wide decree concerning confiscated businesses:

> Movable property left by the Armenians should be conserved for long-term objectives. To increase the number of businesses run by Muslims in our country, companies must be founded only by Muslims. Movable property must be allocated to them under favourable conditions to ensure their long-term sustainability. Company founders, managers, and representatives must be chosen from among respectable leaders and the elite. To enable merchants and farmers to participate in their profits, vouchers should be half a lira or one lira and registered in their names to ensure capital does not fall into foreign [read non-Muslim] hands. The development of entrepreneurship among Muslims must be supported. This endeavor and its results will be communicated to the Ministry step by step.[76]

For historian Uğur Ümit Üngör, "This order constitutes perhaps the most unequivocal document attesting to the intentions and policies of the Committee of Union and Progress. It encapsulates the ideology of 'Turkification' and 'National Economy' in a single, explicit, incontrovertible formulation.[77]

The real question is just how vital this looting was to the economy of the new state, established in 1923. "When we look at the long list of stolen property," says Üngör, "we cannot but suggest that all of this property must have had a very significant, traceable impact on the economic development of the Turkish Republic. There is hardly a diplomatic way of phrasing these facts: the modern Turkish economy was for a large part established, quite fundamentally, on the Young Turk seizure of Ottoman Armenian property."[78] A good example is the production of hazelnuts cultivated in the Black Sea region: "According to 1914 Ottoman statistics," Üngör continues, "of the some one hundred hazelnut producers, more than half were Armenian. During the genocide, this industry was confiscated and transferred to Turks in just a few weeks. In 2010, 688 hectares of hazelnut trees produced 600,000 tons of nuts and monthly revenues of US$860 million. Turkey accounts for 75 per cent of the global production of hazelnuts, so exports bring in a lot of cash. Even Ferrero imports hazelnuts for its Nutella products."[79]

As we have seen with the Çankaya residence, the republic did not hesitate to help itself to the spoils. Government ministries and municipalities also took their share, reserving choice bits for themselves. A complete inventory would fill many pages. From Thrace to the Iranian border, no town was spared. To name just a few: the prison in Gaziantep, the Numone Hospital in Konya, the public hamam in Erzincan, the Atatürk Museum in Trabzon, the prefecture in Elazığ, and the Ziya Gökalp school in Diyarbakir. The Armenian Sanasarian College, founded in 1881 in the eastern province of Erzurum by Meguerditch Sanasarian, an Armenian merchant and philanthropist, had until the First World War been a prestigious educational institution that rivalled the Armenian high schools in the capital. But the large, austere building was not only plundered but also entirely recycled as the location of a pivotal event in the nation's history: the Erzerum Congress, which, in the summer of 1919, played a fundamental role in the founding of the Turkish Republic. The Ottoman Empire was under Allied occupation, its back to the wall, when Mustafa Kemal began to lay the groundwork for the nationalist struggle that led to the creation of modern Turkey.

The Armenian Patriarchate of Istanbul, owner of the Sanasarian Foundation, has not yet dared lay claim to the former college,[80] fearing that to do so would stir up hatred for Armenians – those infamous traitors to the homeland. The Patriarchate has, however, begun legal proceedings to recover a large commercial building, or *han*, built by Sanasarian in the Sirkeci district of Istanbul near the Sirkeci train station – once the last stop of the famed Orient Express. The rental income from this property once financed the school in Erzurum. This building is also known to Turks, not because it was confiscated but because it was converted into the General Security and Police Headquarters of Istanbul and became notorious for the imprisonment and torture of political prisoners, including the famous poet Nazim Hikmet.

The restitution of stolen property and the payment of compensation are fundamental aspects of genocide recognition. These are demands of the diaspora, and they keep Turks awake at night. This material dimension of the events of 1915 is a major reason for Turkey's continued refusal to acknowledge its crimes. The amounts involved are huge. In 1926, the British Liberal Party leader H.H. Asquith and Conservative Party leader Stanley Baldwin sent a memorandum to Prime Minister Ramsay MacDonald declaring that "the sum of 5 million pounds (Turkish gold) deposited by the Turkish Government in Berlin in 1916, and taken over by the Allies after the Armistice, was in large part (perhaps wholly) Armenian money. After the enforced deportation of the Armenians in 1915, their bank accounts, both current and deposit, were transferred by order to the State Treasury at Constantinople."[81] The defeated Germans used this money to make war reparations, transferring the funds to France and Britain, which did not turn up their noses at it. This was only a small percentage of the stolen property, of course. But, almost a century later, how could the market value of tens of thousands of homes, shops, barns, looms, forges, fields, companies, and businesses possibly be assessed? The thought that the spoils of those crimes have led to the ease and prosperity of business people, landowners, and craft workers in Turkey today is unbearable to the victims, adding insult to injury.

Turks avoid the subject by hiding behind the usual arguments. After all, the republic cannot be held responsible for events that occurred before it even existed, can it? Except that, since its creation, modern Turkey has followed the trail blazed by the Ottoman Empire. The Grand National Assembly continues to pass laws ensuring that what has been done cannot be undone and protecting its loot from legal redress. In 1922, a directive ordered the confiscation of property in the province of Adana left by Armenians who had fled the country; in 1923, this measure was extended to the entire country. That same year, another directive prohibited Armenians from eastern *vilayet* and Adana from returning to Turkey. Not only did the republic give nothing back but it continued to seize the money and assets of minority populations. In 1942, a crushing wealth tax forced non-Muslims to sell their property to pay the tax. Those who were unable to pay it were sent to forced labour camps in the east. In 1974, using the pretext of the attempt by the Greek military junta to annex Cyprus to Greece, the state confiscated 1,410 additional properties owned by Greek, Armenian, and Jewish foundations – a continuation of the work begun sixty years earlier.

It was the launch of negotiations to join the European Union that finally forced Turkey to rethink its position. In 2008, pressured by Brussels and the European Court of Human Rights, the Islamic-conservative government of Recep Tayyip Erdoğan passed a law regarding the possessions confiscated from non-Muslim religious groups. This law was followed in 2011 by a decree concerning the properties seized following the 1936 census, primarily in 1974. The decree provides for the restitution of these properties or the payment of compensation, if they have been sold or disposed of. The decree is of symbolic importance since it flies in the face of judicial practices implemented throughout the twentieth century – and that hold sway to this day! On 26 January 2011, for example, the Turkish Supreme Court granted substantial parts of the Syriac Mor Gabriel (Saint Gabriel) Monastery to the Turkish Treasury.[82]

Interested parties were given just one year, until August 2012, to reclaim their properties. Armenian groups managed to submit three hundred applications, but, for other properties, had insufficient time to locate documents needed to prove the identity of the original owners. The legislation did not reach back as far as the First World War; in fact, it disregarded all seizures prior to 1936, the year for which the groups had to list all of their possessions. These included, for example, that of the Armenian cemetery located on a vast expanse of land donated by Suleiman the Magnificent, north of what is now Taksim Square in the heart of Istanbul. Known as Elmadağ, "Apple Hill," it was officially declared an "abandoned property" in 1939. The gravestones, some dating back four centuries, are gone now, replaced by the luxury Divan Hotel (property of the Koç family, one of Istanbul's wealthiest families), a Hilton Hotel, a part of the Military Museum, and the home of the TRT, Turkey's national public broadcaster.

Three descendants of genocide survivors now living in the United States have tried to take Turkey to court, seeking compensation for the seizure of fifty hectares of land fifteen kilometres from Adana in a place known as Incirlik (fig-tree grove). This fertile land was once known for its orchards, but since 1953 a US air base has occupied part of the property, rented from the Turkish government. During the Cold War, it played a key role in monitoring the activities of the Soviet Union. Strategically placed at the gateway to the Orient, it was also on the front lines during the Gulf and Iraq wars and still provides logistical support to troops in Afghanistan. The large village of Incirlik has become a garrison town with Internet cafes, pubs, barbers, and fast-food joints frequented by soldiers.

The three Armenian-American plaintiffs are seeking compensation of about US$61 million for confiscated properties and loss of income from the Republic of Turkey and its two major banks, the Central Bank and the Ziraat Bankası (Agricultural Bank). In 2011, at the request of the Federal District Court of Los Angeles, the banks provided their defence. It was the same old story: they couldn't be held accountable for the actions of the Ottoman Empire. The Turkish government did not even bother to respond. The outcome of the trial is uncertain, the ability to enforce a court ruling even more so. In this particular case, the plaintiffs have eleven property deeds in their possession, so they can prove that their families were dispossessed. Very often, however, documents have been lost or destroyed; in their haste to leave, deportees did not always pack them. After so much time has passed, how can they hope to find those deeds, even if they still exist? Once again, time is on the side of the Turks, who are careful to keep hidden any papers that would establish the ownership of confiscated properties. They know such documents could serve as valuable ammunition in the fight for reclamation.

Ankara has opened whole sections of its archives concerning the Armenians, so historians are finding it increasingly easy to access records documenting the genocide. A glaring exception, however, is sources that would help make an accurate inventory of confiscated properties. These include the registers of the thirty-three regional commissions created to seize and liquidate properties, which remain hidden, as well as the Ottoman land registry and property deed records. As part of reforms undertaken by the Erdoğan government in its bid to join the European Union, this second set of documents was translated into modern Turkish and digitized. But on 26 August 2005, the National Security Committee of the Turkish Armed Forces ordered that they remain closed to the public: "The Ottoman records kept at the Land Register and Cadaster Surveys General Directorate offices must be kept sealed and unavailable to the public as they have the potential to be exploited by alleged genocide and property claims ... Opening them to general public use is against state interests." This was a shameless admission of both weakness and guilt.

Turkey would do well to heed the words of Yaşar Kemal, a renowned Turkish author of Kurdish origin, in his novel *Salman the Solitary*.[83] The book tells the story of a family forced to flee to Cilicia during the First World War. The main character, Ismaïl Ağa, receives the following warning from his mother: "My son, if you go to that village, I expect you to refuse to accept either a house or a field left by Armenians. When a nest has been abandoned by its owner, no other bird may find refuge there. If you destroy a nest, you can't make it your own. When you sow misfortune, you reap only misfortune."

14

The Soul of the Resistance Movement

"*Barev*!" (Hello!) cries a young man in Armenian as he strides toward us, leaping over puddles in the dirt road rutted by tractor tires. He is a tall, fit, blue-eyed man in his thirties with a handsome face. We are in a former Armenian village near Ovacık, in the foothills of the Dersim Mountains, during the spring thaw. An encounter in Istanbul leads us to this meeting with Cem (not his real name), and he can't wait to tell us his story. He guides us away from the other villagers, Kurdish Alevis who cast curious glances in our direction. Cem is the only son of an Armenian, the last in his village. His father, a farmer with the build of a lumberjack, lives in a small house, isolated from the rest by fear and poverty, with his loving wife, a Kurdish Alevi from a neighbouring village. Long after the genocide, which the village survived, the family was dispossessed of its business and its property by the local clans. In the end, Cem's father lost everything. Since the identity he has long hidden has brought him nothing but problems, it's something he prefers not to talk about.

Cem began by converting to Christianity, the heart, for him, of the Armenian identity, even though he has no idea how it is practised. Then he began to study the language. During the long winter, when the village is buried under several metres of snow, he lives in Istanbul, where he works ten-to-twelve-hour days as a textile worker along with Armenian immigrants in a basement in the Laleli district. Next, he plans to change the first name on his ID card to Varoujan, an Armenian name. Finally, to complete the picture, he has declared himself to be a "partisan," a member of TIKKO (Türkiye İşci ve Köylü Kurtuluş Ordusu), the Liberation Army of the Workers and Peasants of Turkey. This is the armed wing of an obscure far-left group that emerged in Turkey in the early 1970s.

"We are the partisans, the descendants of the Armenian resistance fighters, the successors of the Komitadjus, the Tachnak and the ASALA fighters," he declares. This profession of faith astonishes everyone. Is this his way of reclaiming his long-denied identity? Of furthering a misguided political agenda? Whatever the case may be, Cem has opened a window, unwittingly putting us on the trail of a secret that is carefully guarded in these mountains. Radical movements inspired by Marxist ideology or Kurdish nationalism and employing armed struggle, even terrorism, provided a channel for the Armenian rebellion – a struggle that was at the core of some of these political movements. Cem is a revolutionary, and his family history is that of thousands of genocide survivors. After the generation of fear, that of his father, came the generation of revolt. Imbued with the spirit of its rebellious forebears, his own has chosen the path of guerrilla warfare.

Just as the ideology of the Young Turks, the cult of Talaat Pasha, and the mechanics of the 1915 genocide have been perpetuated to this day, so the spirit of sedition and resistance has never been completely crushed. The soul of the Armenian resistance has been passed down, more or less consciously, throughout the past century. This reality has often been distorted by the nationalist discourse of the Turkish State, for whom the PKK is basically no more than a secret Armenian organization. Yusuf Halaçoğlu, past president of the Turkish Historical Society (TTK), loved to say that the Kurdish rebellion led by Abdullah Öcalan was in fact the work of a pack of Armenians. Such myths die hard. Labouring under this illusion, nationalists are convinced that the members of this "terrorist organization" "eat pork" and "are not circumcised." These arguments are presented as proof of the connections between the two groups and regularly trotted out by the military after encounters with the rebels. After the truck bombing on 18 August 2012 in Gaziantep that killed ten people and for which the PKK denied all responsibility, the Erzurum deputy for the governing party declared that the attack could only have been carried out by "sons of Armenians."

In the minds of Turks, Armenians are still "the usual traitors." And, indeed, for some Armenians, the PKK rebellion is seen as the best way to express their rebellion against the Turkish state, which has been oppressing them for more than a century. But while these ties are real, they are far from universal. "About 8 per cent of PKK members are Armenian," says Mehmet, a former officer in the guerrilla forces, himself a descendant of an Armenian family from Dersim. In the small cemeteries reserved for "martyrs" in the Qandil Mountains of northern Iraq, an area controlled by the PKK, some family names painted on gravestones end in "ian," revealing Armenian ancestry. At the highest levels of the organization, it is even said that Cemil Bayık, one of the principal leaders and a founder of the PKK, is also of Armenian descent. For a time the PKK's second in command (below Abdullah Öcalan), Bayık was born in 1951 in a village near Keban, where Turkey built the enormous Atatürk Dam on the Euphrates River. Before the genocide, that region was home to a large Armenian population.

The physical proximity between the Armenians and "the mountain," a word often used in Turkey to refer to the resistance and thus to the PKK, is grounded in history. Mirhan Pırgiç Gültekin, president of the Dersim Armenian Association, explains that "when they felt threatened – particularly in 1915 – Armenians who fled the massacres and deportation hid in the mountains." The mountain was primarily a refuge. Afterward, the survivors settled in high-altitude villages, ready to flee if the Turkish soldiers returned. As close as possible to the summits, it was in these eagles' nests that the resistance fighters were kept hidden and fed. It was also on these steep slopes, now the domain of Kurdish guerrillas, that groups of armed Armenians once took refuge. This scenario was played out in many regions of eastern Turkey: Zeytoun, Sirnak, Eruh, Lice, Dersim, and Bingöl.

But Cem, the young Armenian revolutionary from Dersim, self-proclaimed spiritual heir to the 1915 freedom fighters, has not joined the PKK. Kurdish rebels are not the only guerrillas active in Turkey today. These mountain summits, snow covered from November to May, and these Dersim villages, frozen under three to six metres at the height of winter, are TIKKO territory. A guerrilla organization as anachronistic as the PKK, TIKKO has an even longer history. In its heyday, it counted several dozen to a few hundred adherents armed with Kalashnikov rifles;

they would ambush Turkish troops in these mountains, clambering over them like goats. TIKKO is the armed wing of the TKP/ML (Türkiye Komünist Partisi/Marksist-Leninist) – the Communist Party of Turkey/Marxist-Leninist, itself a pro-Chinese offshoot of the Turkish Communist Party.

Founded in the early 1970s by Ibrahim Kaypakkaya, a charismatic young activist, the party is a blend of Maoism, Marxism-Leninism, and "anti-imperialism." Its armed struggle was inspired by the "People's War" strategy developed by Mao; it handles conspiracy theories as easily as it does explosives, and its ideology has been imprisoned in a glacier since the Cold War. Disciplined, hierarchical, and authoritarian, TIKKO requires its members to serve the revolutionary cause. Like the PKK, it has a political wing, a series of front groups that change names to sidestep prohibitions, and newspapers that serve to communicate its ideology and finance its operations. "To those interested in Turkey's far left and its many organizations, TIKKO is one of the most mysterious. Its origins and objectives are murky," says journalist Ahmet Şık, an expert in these matters. "Plunged in secrecy, TKP/ML-TIKKO has undergone splits, betrayals, and infiltration by the secret services. In 1994, the party split, giving rise to the TKP (ML), which later morphed into the Maoist Communist Party (MKP), requiring a constant settling of scores."

The next party to appear on the scene, in 2002, was the TKP-MLM (Türkiye Komünist Partisi/Marksist-Leninist Maoist), criticized for having turned its back on the legacy of Kaypakkaya. The People's Liberation Army of Turkey (Türkiye Halk Kurtuluş Ordusu, or THKO), embodying the pro-Cuban tendency of the revolutionary movement, has survived through the THKP-C, which became pro-Albanian. Alphabet soup, you might say, but let there be no mistake – these organizations are quite distinct from each other! On the ground floor of a building in downtown Tunceli is an office housing the Democratic People's Federation (DHF). Young activists sit in rows around a large table, but just one is authorized to speak. Signs, slogans, and pictures of Lenin, Mao, Stalin – and Ibrahim Kaypakkaya – are pinned to the walls. "We reject the opportunism of the TKP/ML," declares the spokesman, stiff as a poker. This organization is the political wing of the TKP-MLM and publishes a newsletter, *Özgür gelecek*

(Liberated future), not to be confused with *Partizan*, the newsletter of the TKP/ML.

Today, in the Dersim region, the least densely populated in Turkey, there is thus an unlikely assortment of dissenting and competing groups and guerrilla movements whose acronyms and symbols are painted on traffic signs lining the mountain roads. Most, if not all, claim to be descended from Ibrahim Kaypakkaya – "Ibo" – the local hero. His stencilled face, with its intense blue eyes, chiselled features, and cap, is plastered on walls and posters throughout the city of Tunceli. Kaypakkaya was born in 1949 to a farming family in Karakaya, near Çorum, north of Ankara. A brilliant student, he took classes in the physics department of Istanbul University's faculty of science and was active in various socialist organizations. During this period of intellectual and political unrest, his intelligence and charisma quickly set him apart from the crowd. After the widespread workers' strikes in June 1970, he joined TIIKP, the pro-Chinese Revolutionary Workers and Peasants Party of Turkey. Two years and a military coup d'état later, he led a rebellion against its leaders, who were accused of failing to act and complacency with the regime. Kaypakkaya fiercely denounced Kemalist Turkey as a "fascist regime" and advocated armed struggle. He founded TKP/ML and TİKKO, its armed wing.

The young revolutionary's fall was as meteoric as his rise. A few months after taking up arms, he was seriously wounded while leading guerrilla strikes in the Dersim region. On 24 January 1972, hunted by the military, he took refuge in a cave, where he hid out for five days in freezing temperatures. Eventually he was betrayed and captured, and some of his frostbitten toes were amputated. He was taken to Diyarbakır Prison, infamous for its brutal treatment of inmates and considered more a place of torture than of detention. In the 1970s and '80s, dozens of political prisoners died there. Kaypakkaya was tortured for three months but refused to speak. On 18 May 1973, at the age of twenty-four, he was shot and killed. Forty years later, "Ibo" is still a libertarian legend in Turkey, a martyr of the revolution.

What does all this have to do with the Armenian question and the memory of the genocide? One detail in this story caught our attention: Ibrahim Kaypakkaya founded TKP/ML and TİKKO on 24 April 1972, the anniversary of the Armenian genocide. In such underground political circles, everything is symbolic; the date could not have been an accident. Any doubts we may have had were laid to rest when some travel companions, former revolutionary strategists, told us that Kaypakkaya came from a family of converted Armenians. "Of course it was no coincidence," confirms Kemal, a Dersim ex-militant with an Armenian grandmother. He recites a list of former Armenian TIKKO members. That fact was carefully hidden since, at the time, Armenian origins had to be kept secret, even among left-wing circles. Any demands on behalf of Armenians were unthinkable. "There was always a consensus among left-wing movements against them," he says. "This country has never allowed Armenians to be Armenians," says Ayşe Günaysu, a former Trotskyist activist. "Whether in Trotskyist organizations or the Communist Party of Turkey (TKP), it was the same. At that time, if you were a socialist, you had to be an internationalist and forget about any ethnic or national identity. Being a leftist was incompatible with the affirmation of ethnicity." Salvation lay in revolution and only in revolution.

On the question of the Armenian genocide, Kaypakkaya's ideas differed from those of the other revolutionary far-left groups. Cafer, a former TIKKO leader who had moved to Europe as a political refugee and had agreed to speak to us in a café in Tunceli, explained: "Kaypakkaya's was the only organization to recognize the 1915 genocide and completely break with Kemalism, seen as a form of fascism. He was the first to ask the tough questions about Turkey." He continued: "When you are Armenian, when you belong to a nation that has suffered torture and massacres, and when you have grown up in the midst of a revolutionary struggle, you don't support people who are inspired by Kemalism. So the Armenians joined in great numbers because it was the organization that most distanced itself from Kemalist ideology."

Garbis Altinoğlu (Altinyan), for example, was one of the founders of TKP/ML before switching to the MKP, the Maoist Communist Party; he was imprisoned until 1991. Poet and painter Müzaffer Oruçoğlu, originally from Kars, fled Turkey after spending more than thirteen years in Turkish jails and "was very radical in his youth," according to Cafer. "There are not many left today, but at the time TIKKO was largely an Armenian movement."

To blend into the organization and hide their Armenian identity, many chose to Turkefy their names. Armenak Bakirciyan thus took the name Orhan Bakır. The son of a family from Sason, he grew up in an old basalt stone house in the *gavur mahallesi* district of Diyarbakir – the "infidels' quarter." His parents had named him after Armenak Ghazarian, better known as Hraïr Tjhokhk, an Armenian hero who died during the 1904 rebellion in the Sason region, a hotbed of revolutionary activity in the mountains south of Lake Van. Two generations later, following in the footsteps of this resistance hero, Bakirciyan became a leader of the TKP/ML. Every 24 April, on the anniversary of the genocide, a speech was traditionally made by the party. "He always refused to write it; he said he couldn't be objective," Cafer says with a smile. He continues: "Bakirciyan was a member of the central committee and leader of the armed wing – the commander of the guerrilla army. He was arrested and sentenced not only for being a communist but also for being Armenian. He was tried in Izmir and had to defend the fact that he was Armenian. In his defence, he said that he was honoured to be Armenian." Sentenced to death and thrown into prison, Bakirciyan somehow managed to escape. "The whole thing was orchestrated by the party," says Cafer. Limping and heavily bearded, Bakirciyan returned to fight with the guerrilla army in the Dersim region. A former political prisoner named Cemal tells us, "He was in love with my cousin, but at that time TİKKO members were not allowed to marry. Armenak was a likeable guy, really charismatic. In every café he visited, he made a positive impression. Many young men joined the movement because of him."

On 13 May 1980, Bakirciyan was in the town of Karakoçan in Elazığ Province. His mission that day was to assassinate the local police chief, a notorious torturer. Instead, it was Bakirciyan who was gunned down in the street. His body was secretly taken by security forces and dumped in a hole on the east bank of the Peri River. The Turkish army wanted to prevent his burial place from becoming a pilgrimage site, but that secrecy has led to the spread of many rumours. In the café of the neighbouring village, an elderly peasant nursing a beer claims that "the following year, his body was thrown in the water by soldiers. The officer said, 'He's an Armenian, a *gavur*, why would we give him a

gravestone?'" According to another version, "Orhan Bakir" had wanted
to be buried in the village of Faraş. His comrades in arms had stolen
his body and taken him there. The funeral had been conducted by an
imam close to TIKKO who said he was a converted Armenian. Cafer
smiles at the thought. "It's a beautiful story. It's true that he talked
about the village of Faraş, and there were two or three attempts to recover the body. But it's probably still there, somewhere along the river
bank."

A few months later, Bakirciyan's older sister, Suzi, who lives in Istanbul, confirmed that her brother had expressed a wish to be buried in
Faraş. "It's a village where he hid after his escape," she says, "a former
Armenian village where, during the 1915 genocide, the massacres were
particularly bloody." But, according to Suzi, many attempts to bury her
brother there have failed. "Right after his death, we planned a funeral
service. Our mother came especially from Sweden. We made a little
gravestone for Armenak, but the government destroyed it. And it probably destroyed his body too." She sighs. "There were three or four attempts to give him a gravestone. His family, his friends, his party,
everyone tried." On 13 May 2012, on the anniversary of his death, another memorial service was held secretly at night by a small group of
TIKKO militants. A simple marble rectangle with a plaque bearing his
name, "Armenak Bakirciyan – Orhan Bakır," was laid in the mountains.
The gravestone is symbolic only, since no body lies beneath it: more
than thirty years after his death, the remains of this TIKKO leader are
still a political hot potato, his true burial place unmarked. "They won't
let it happen," says Suzi.

But whether the government likes it or not, the place where the soldiers dumped Bakirciyan's body in 1980 has not been forgotten and,
in Dersim, he has become a legend. An hour's drive outside the city of
Tunceli, after climbing up into the mountains, then plunging down
into a valley, the traveller comes face to face with the Peri River, deaf-
ened by the roar of its rushing waters. A rickety bridge spans the river,
which marks the border between Tunceli province and Elazığ
Province to the east. On the metal guardrail, a slogan has been written
in blood-red letters: "TIKKO warriors are immortal."

In Istanbul, in the living room of her modest two-room apartment
at the foot of Kurtuluş Hill, a historically Christian neighbourhood,

Suzi has hung a framed black-and-white photograph of Armenak, literally "Little Armenian." The photo shows a young man with boyish good looks, his jet black hair cut in bangs. Since his disappearance, this is all she has left of him. When the photo was taken, her little brother was attending Sourp Khatch Tibrevank, the Armenian high school in Üsküdar, on the Asian shore of the Bosphorus. On the buffet, Suzi has a few photos of her brother surrounded by his school friends. "They often came to the house – they were all my little brothers," she recalls fondly. She points out Manuel Demir, Hayrabet Hançer, Noubar Yalim – and, in a larger photo, a fellow by the name of Hrant Dink. "Ah, Hrant," she sighs. "He was the smartest and sweetest of them all." They all attended the Tibrevank school in the 1970s, and like her brother, they all joined TIKKO. Later on, the Turkish government would make them pay heavily for this rebellion. Hayrabet Hançer, originally from the Armenian village of Gemarek, near Sivas, was killed in 1980 by far-right activists. Noubar Yalimian, known as "Recho," born in Mardin, was killed in 1982 in Amsterdam by a Turkish agent. Manuel Demir, born in the village of Bunyan, near Kayseri, was killed in 1988 at his home in Istanbul during a police operation. The small band of Tibrevank rebels has been annihilated.

The case of Hrant Dink was a little different. At school, he and Armenak were inseparable – best friends. Together with a third young rebel, Stepan, the comrades decided to legally change their names and join TIKKO. Armenak became Orhan; Stepan, Murat; and Hrant, Fırat. "Hrant was more of a sympathizer," says Yetvart Tomasyan, a colourful figure who heads the Aras Publishing House. "He was hot blooded back then, always ready for a fight. But he quickly distanced himself from the movement when he married Rakel. Together, we founded Aras. After that, Hrant became like a saint, so his militant past was forgotten." Cafer, the former TIKKO officer, agrees: "He didn't stay there long. He was just a sympathizer." But the Turkish government did not forget. Many believe that Hrant's youthful activism was one of the reasons he was murdered more than thirty years later. On 19 January 2007, he was shot three times in front of the office of his weekly newspaper, *Agas*, by Ogün Samast, a seventeen-year-old Turkish ultranationalist. It was a political assassination ordered from on high, according to Fethiye Çetin, the lawyer representing Hrant's family.

So, during the 1970s, between the 1971 and 1980 coups d'état, a period of political unrest and struggle between right- and left-wing political groups, was the Tibrevank school a hotbed of TIKKO activity?
"Undeniably," confirms a former boarder at the school, now living in
California. Suzi adds that at the time Tibrevank harboured a recruit-
ment cell for TIKKO's guerrilla army. Tomasyan, who also attended the
school, provides further details: "All of those young people were Armenians from Anatolia. From Sivas, Kayseri, Diyarbakir, and Malatya,
in the case of Hrant Dink … Young Armenians were sent to Tibrevank
from the interior of the country so they wouldn't lose their language.
But their culture was very different from that of Armenians in Istanbul. In the big city, they had more freedom, but they tended to keep to
themselves. They were all boarders. They never returned home on
weekends, and rarely during the holidays. They were poor, and they
never lost their country ways." To illustrate his point, he recalls an anec-
dote that makes him laugh out loud. "One day, Armenak brought me
a present. 'Here Tomo Abi [big brother Tomo], this is for you!' he said.
It was a rabbit. He had asked one of his friends to bring him a rabbit
from Diyarbakir. In those days, the bus trip took several days."

The 1980 coup d'état left the Armenian cell leaderless, and the former Tibrevank students – those who had not been killed – moved to
Europe or the United States. But TIKKO's guerrilla army, classified as a
terrorist organization by the European Union, and the implacable war
waged on it by the Turkish state, have survived the passing of the years,
the fall of the Berlin Wall, and the advent of globalization. In the villages of Dersim, confrontation is still a way of life.

In Alanyazı, in the hills of Mazgirt, the home of the Boztaş family is
riddled with bullet holes. The sound of the weapons still reverberates
in the elderly couple's ears. They had named their son Imam, thinking
that would offer him some protection, but on 8 March 2004, he was
shot down like a dog on their front doorstep. Two armed men in black
fatigues, scarves around their heads, had arrived at nightfall. "I was just
bringing in some wood to light the stove," says the old woman, her face
wrinkled by the sun. "They knocked at the door and wanted to take my
son. He resisted, saying he didn't know them. So they began to shoot.
They shot him six times." Other bullets tore through the home's tin
roof and pocked the stone wall of the house. The police confiscated

their son's cell phone. The authorities denied knowing anything about the execution, accusing the PKK, according to his mother. "On the day of the funeral," adds his elderly father, Hıdır, eyes red, "there were a lot of people. But also a lot of soldiers. The commander threatened us. He said, 'I gave you a chance, now get lost!'"

The family filed a complaint and has since been subjected to death threats and intimidation. At the cemetery on the edge of town, the headstone on which Imam's parents had engraved a poem by Nazim Hikmet and a tribute to their "martyred" son has been smashed to bits. Imam's widow fetches some papers from the kitchen to show us. "I filed a complaint with the European Court of Human Rights, and I'm waiting for justice to be done," she says. Imam Boztaş had been a TİKKO militant. In the 1980s, he served a long prison sentence in Malatya. At forty-nine, he had left behind the turmoil of the guerrilla war, but like almost everyone else in the village, the Boztaş are crypto-Armenians. In fact, just across from their home is a large empty field, perfectly flat, where nothing grows but grass. In one corner is a large basin, which might once have been a baptismal font. Until 1915, this was the site of a church. Based on the number of impeccably cut stones that have been taken from it to build homes, it must have been a large one.

TİKKO clearly has many roots, and it remains active in rural and mountainous regions such as Dersim. Like all underground revolutionary movements, it has gradually drifted toward sectarianism and violence, incorporating Mafia-like and criminal practices. But the legacy of Ibrahim Kaypakkaya is still that of an Anatolian workers and peasants' movement, profoundly anti-fascist and anti-Kemalist with, undeniably, a deep core of Armenianism. TİKKO continues to commemorate 24 April, and every year on 19 January, a group of partisans marches in the Istanbul parade to remember the murder of Hrant Dink. The spirit of Armenian resistance, that of the Sasun rebellion and Operation Nemesis, has survived, in part through the efforts of these guerrilla fighters. Former TİKKO members also participated in ASALA operations in Europe in the 1980s. In his rugged mountain home, young Cem, the "Armenian traitor," is the latest in this long line of rebels.

15

Hrant Dink:
The Armenian and His Turkish Heirs

"We killed a man whose ideas we could not accept." This statement by
Orhan Pamuk, recipient of the 2006 Nobel Prize in Literature, would
be a suitable epitaph for Turkish-Armenian journalist Hrant Dink.

Pamuk was not expressing posthumous regrets, which would be
pointless; he was simply describing a crime. The tens of thousands of
mourners who marched in Dink's funeral procession fully understood
the significance of his murder. On 23 January 2007, massive crowds assembled in front of the *Agos* newspaper offices and followed his hearse
through the city streets to the Balıklı Armenian-Gregorian cemetery,
not far from the Byzantine walls. This was the largest street protest ever
seen in Istanbul. Marchers brandished placards reading "We are all
Hrant Dink!" and "We are all Armenians!" In a country where being
called an Armenian is the worst possible insult, for Turks to make such
a declaration was unthinkable. Far more than a mere show of solidarity, they were saying that when you killed an Armenian, you were also
killing Turks. At least for this one day, Dink's ideas were uncontested,
and proponents of nationalist ideology did not dare show their faces.

At 3 pm on 19 January 2007, Hrant Dink fell to the ground in front
of the *Agos* building in the Osmanbey neighbourhood of Istanbul,
struck in the head by three bullets from the gun of an unknown as-
sailant. The news spread quickly. Incredulous but already in tears,
friends and strangers came running. On the sidewalk, under a white
sheet, just the soles of two black shoes visible, lay Turkey's Armenian
soul. In his last editorial, a bad omen on the morning of his death,

Dink had written that he had recently been inundated with threats. He had reported a troubling letter postmarked "Bursa" to the police, who had done nothing. And although the public prosecutor had appealed to have his conviction for "denigrating Turkishness" overturned by the Court of Cassation (Supreme Court of Appeals), the decision had been upheld.

Dink had shared his distress with his readers in his writings, because, as he said, his "only weapon [was] sincerity." "My torture begins, fuelled by worry and anxiety; on one side, vigilance, on the other, fear. I feel exactly like a dove: always looking to my left and my right, ahead and behind." Despite his fear, he declared, "It's not in my nature to abandon the flames of Hell to seek the pleasures of Heaven. I'm one of those men working to transform the Hell in which we are living into a Heaven." And, finally, this optimistic note: "The coming year [2007] will no doubt be even harder than the one just ended. The trials will continue and others will begin ... Who knows what injustices I will face? But there is just one truth that matters: although I live with the uncertainty of a dove, I know that the people of this country don't hurt the doves that live in cities in the midst of humans. They are fearful, yes, but free."[84]

We met Dink for the first time in October 2005 after he received a suspended six-month sentence under Article 301 of the Turkish Penal Code, which criminalizes the infamous "denigration of Turkishness." Taken completely out of context, one sentence in one of Dink's articles referring to "the poisoned blood associated with the Turk" was enough to justify throwing the book at him. Since the 2004 publication of a report titled "The Secret of Sabiha Hatun," in which Dink revealed that the adoptive daughter of Atatürk, Sabiha Gökçen, was an Armenian orphan, he had been in the cross-hairs of ultranationalist Turks. "My conviction was a warning: Be careful what you write," he told us. "Be careful what you do." He knew only too well that his six-month sentence represented much more than just a justice system fossilized in Kemalist ideology.

After his death, one of his friends told us that during Dink's trial at the Şişli courthouse in Istanbul, Veli Küçük, a retired general, had thrown a lighter at his feet: "It was a death sentence." Since then,

Küçük, the founder of Jitem, the special Turkish police unit involved in the "dirty war" against the Kurdish rebellion, has himself been thrown in prison, accused of being one of the leaders of the ultra-nationalist military organization dubbed "Ergenekon." Of course Dink never mentioned the frightening incident with the lighter to us. Eyes moist, he had simply said that he was "disturbed" by this "unjust" decision. "The battle between the democrats and the defenders of the status quo is intense these days. Opponents of democratic change speak up at every opportunity." As we spoke in his office, the telephone never stopped ringing, and *Agos* reporters kept popping in to ask his advice or get story approval.

Originally from Malatya, Dink was a charismatic, sensitive leader who inspired those around him to follow his lead in defending the rights of Turkish Armenians. In 1993, with Yetvart Tomasyan, he co-founded Aras, a publishing house specializing in Armenian history and literature. For twenty years, it has published works in Turkish on the Armenian genocide. (In November 2012, for example, *Armenians in the Ottoman Empire before 1915*, co-written by French-Armenian historians Raymond Kévorkian and Paul Paboudjian, appeared in Turkish twenty years after its publication in France.) Three years later, in 1996, Dink continued his efforts to dismantle anti-Armenian prejudices by founding *Agos* (The furrow), a small weekly newspaper that publishes in both Turkish and Armenian; the paper gives the Armenian community a voice and helps it to emerge from behind its barricade of fear.

Dink believed that only the democratization of the country, spurred on by calls for reform from the European Union, which Ankara is seeking to join, will enable Turkey to deal with its nationalist demons. He also thought the process should be carried out gradually. In 2006, after the French parliament voted on a bill penalizing the denial of the Armenian genocide, Dink declared that, if it were adopted, he would go to France himself to question the genocide, "all the while apologizing to [his] ancestors." Of course he knew all about the 1915 massacres, but he felt that Turkey was not yet ready to accept the truth. Sadly, this spirit of tolerance and understanding did not protect him.

Dink's assassination sent shock waves throughout Turkey, and a group of Turkish intellectuals picked up where he left off. Some were already among his circle of friends, while others had been following the Armenian question from a distance. But after his death, they honoured his courage and his memory by continuing the struggle, determined not to let his murderers win, not to surrender to nationalist hatred. In 2007, the political atmosphere was poisonous, with rumours of a violent attempt to overthrow the government disrupting the election campaign. The *Agos* staff was still in mourning, but their top priority was to keep the presses rolling. Etyen Mahçupyan, a tall, bearded, tired-looking fellow, took over management of the paper and courageously filled that position for three years. Born in Istanbul to a wealthy Armenian family, Etyen was a close friend of Dink. "We would call each other five or six times a day," he says. Every week, when they played the races together, the world might end, but they had thoughts only for the horses on which they had bet. It was a foregone conclusion that he would take Dink's place at the head of *Agos*, but it was not without risk. The conservative, Islamic-oriented newspaper *Zaman*, for which Etyen also writes columns, provides him with an armoured car and a bodyguard. At the entrance to his building in the trendy neighbourhood of Cihangir, a police officer is on duty twenty-four hours a day. In his white plastic sentry box, where he has hung a Turkish flag in plain sight, the officer spends his days reading the nationalist papers – the same ones that ran campaigns hostile to Dink.

The commitment of Turks to reveal the sufferings of Ottoman Armenians did not emerge full blown on 19 January 2007, of course. In 1995, Ayşe Nur Zarakolu, co-founder with her husband, Ragip, of the Turkish publishing house Belge, was sentenced to two and a half years in prison by Istanbul's State Security Court for publishing *The Armenian Taboo*, a translation of *Les Arméniens, histoire d'un génocide*, by French historian Yves Ternon. Mother Courage, as she was known by Armenians, stood on the front lines of every struggle on behalf of the Kurds and non-Muslim minorities and was imprisoned several times. In the last decade of the twentieth century, the articles written by academic Taner Akçam, author of *A Shameful Act: The Armenian Genocide and the Question of Turkish Responsibility* and a political refugee in Germany at that time, also began to raise the awareness of his Turkish colleagues.

In 2005, a committee of historians including Halil Berktay, Murat Belge, Selim Deringil, and Edhem Eldem defied the official Turkish version of history by organizing a conference innocently titled "Ottoman Armenians during the Decline of the Empire: Issues of Scientific Responsibility and Democracy." Initially scheduled for May, it was cancelled after justice minister and government spokesman Cemil Çiçek accused those associated with the event of "treason" and of "stabbing Turkey in the back" – threatening language that Armenians have heard since the early twentieth century. The meeting was rescheduled for September at Bogaziçi, a public university in Istanbul (known in English as Bosphorus University), but was once again cancelled at the last minute, this time because of a legal challenge. Organizers hastily shifted the conference to Bilgi University so that it could proceed. Then, on 24 September, a cordon of riot police faced hundreds of far-right and far-left ultranationalists shouting racist slogans and chanting "Turkey: Love it or leave it!" as they threw rotten eggs and tomatoes at arriving participants. In this tense political atmosphere, almost three hundred academics openly called into question the official Turkish version of events. The liberal *Radikal* newspaper wrote on its front page: "Even the word 'genocide' was uttered at the conference, but the world is still turning, and Turkey is still here." For Turkey, this was a major step: the genocide taboo had finally been lifted.

But the assassination of Hrant Dink pricked consciences. In the words of actor Halil Ergün, the Turks owe a debt of gratitude to their brother Dink, "the orphaned child of an orphaned people," killed for wanting to reconcile two enemies. The tens of thousands of individuals who marched in the funeral procession for this generous idealist showed that there was a thirst for truth, for democracy, among the people of Turkey. Hrant Dink was not the first intellectual to be assassinated in Turkey, but he was clearly one too many. The grieving crowds gave new impetus to his fight to unlock the secrets of the past. "Maybe we needed a martyr," suggested Robert Koptaş, then editor-in-chief of *Agos*, almost two years after Dink's death.

In late December 2008, four Turkish intellectuals, Cengiz Aktar, Ali Bayramoğlu, Ahmet Insel, and Baskin Oran, published a short online petition, "We Ask Forgiveness," written in the first person singular: "My conscience cannot accept that we remain indifferent to the Great Catastrophe that the Ottoman Armenians suffered in 1915, and that we deny it. I reject this injustice, I share the feelings and the pain of my Armenian brothers and sisters, and I ask their forgiveness." The site was immediately hacked, and the authors were inundated with hate mail and threats. Recep Tayyip Erdoğan, the prime minister, spoke out against the initiative: "I don't accept it. I don't support it. We have committed no crime, and we have nothing to apologize for."

But the apology was quickly signed by thirty thousand Turks. Its success proved that 1915 was no longer a subject of limited intellectual debate and had entered the public domain. The silence had been broken. "The important thing is that the Armenian question has become a subject of heated debate in Turkish politics," declared columnist Ali Bayramoğlu. "Now we know that something happened in 1915." As a known supporter of Dink, Bayramoğlu now has two bodyguards. Sketches of his apartment were found in the home of Ibrahim Sahin, the former head of the police special forces unit, who was arrested in connection with the investigation into Ergenekon. But Bayramoğlu says that his commitment to the cause is "for Hrant. I swore that I would do everything in my power." He believes that this new freedom to speak, made possible "thanks to *Agos* and the process of applying for membership in the European Union," is essential. "We must come face to face with our own history. Getting in touch with 1915 means getting in touch with the taboo of our Turkish identity. This is the only way democratization can proceed. On this subject, the important thing is not the position of the state but social legitimacy. For me, the most important thing is that society feel responsible for what happened."

The petition crossed borders and leapt oceans. Already, Dink's funeral had inspired members of the diaspora to travel to Turkey and set foot in the land of their ancestors for the first time, and they had been surprised to learn that Turks could be their allies. In January 2009, one month after the online apology appeared, some sixty representatives of Armenian communities in France and Canada published a text in the French daily newspaper *Libération* titled "Thank You, Turkish Citizens." After ignoring each other for almost a century, Turks and Armenians were starting to look past their deep-seated animosity and mistrust.

In the book *Dialogue sur le tabou arménien*,[85] journalist Ariane Bonzon brought together Ahmet Insel, one of the initiators of the

Turkish petition, and Michel Marian, a French philosopher and one of the members of the Armenian diaspora who have worked for rapprochement. On 14 October 2009, Marian attended the Turkey-Armenia football match in Bursa. Ankara and Yerevan had just signed a historic agreement in Zurich to normalize diplomatic relations, and the future looked bright. Insel, who heads the economics department at Galatasaray University in Istanbul, is a prominent member of Turkey's democratic left. In Bonzon's book, he courageously agreed to play the part of the bad guy, the Turk, discussing the progress he has made toward understanding the unacknowledged history of his country and the need to take ownership of it. Despite their disagreements, and each with his own viewpoint, the grandson of survivors from Erzurum and the great-grandson of a Muslim refugee from the Balkans were able to chart a path to reconciliation.

In a few years, the worst of the stench had begun to clear. In 2005, the celebrated Turkish novelist Orhan Pamuk had been tried in Şişli for a statement he made during an interview with the Swiss publication *Das Magazin*, a weekly supplement to a number of Swiss daily newspapers, including *Tages-Anzeiger*. In the interview, Pamuk stated, "Thirty thousand Kurds have been killed here, and a million Armenians." At the courthouse, the Nobel Prize-winning author was subjected to the jeers and insults of ultranationalist militants.

But progress is being made. Every 24 April, public commemorations are held in Istanbul to mark the start of the Armenian genocide. This tradition began on a Saturday in 2010, when hundreds of people gathered in Taksim Square around a large black banner on which the following words were written in Armenian, Turkish, and English: "We share this pain. We are all in mourning." Red carnations and candles created an atmosphere of solemnity. No government representatives attended the event, created by DurDe (Say Stop!), an organization founded in February 2007 to combat racism and nationalism in Turkey, but police officers were on hand to provide protection and keep dozens of hate-filled Grey Wolves at bay. "The genie is out of the bottle, and the time for action in Turkey has come," says Cengiz Aktar, one of the promoters of the gathering, which has become an annual event – with the agreement never to use the word "genocide."

"Of course it was genocide," he continues, "but that word will never be accepted. The only way to get around the denialism is to take action to develop a policy of memory, to educate the public." To demand that the genocide first be recognized would be unrealistic. That would put an end to all discussion. The group therefore replaces "genocide" with the much less inflammatory term "great catastrophe." This is also the expression used by US President Barack Obama in his annual 24 April address, to avoid diplomatic conflict with Ankara. The supporters of this approach explain that this is actually the translation of "Meds Yeghern," the term first used by the survivors to refer to the massacres. But "Meds Yeghern" can also be translated as "great crime."

The words "great catastrophe" eliminate all responsibility and criminal intent. It's no wonder the Turks aren't offended by their use, but they are criticized not only by Armenians but also by some Turkish intellectuals. On 24 April 2010, another commemoration was held at the Haydarpaşa Terminal, the starting point for trains headed to Asia. On the steps of the station, demonstrators held up signs bearing photographs of deported Armenians. It was from this station that convoys of some 250 Armenian leaders and intellectuals – deputies, doctors, lawyers, poets, and journalists – arrested during the night of 24–25 April 1915, were sent to two internment camps in Anatolia. This roundup of the Armenian elite symbolically marks the beginning of the genocide.

"We want to remember them, to explain to the Turks who they were," says Ayşe Günaysu, an activist with the Istanbul branch of the Turkish Human Rights Association (IHD), which organized this commemoration. For years, she has been fighting for various causes including the unconditional recognition of the genocide. "Recognition is a prerequisite, without which nothing else is possible," she says. "It's a moral and ethical position, and nothing must be expected in return. We must humbly make amends because it was our ancestors who carried out the genocide."

Vincent Duclert, a specialist in the Dreyfus affair and Turkish history at Paris's École des hautes études en sciences sociales, participated in the international workshop held at Istanbul's Sabancı University in 2009 to mark the centennial of the Adana massacres. The country, he observes, has two distinct groups of intellectuals, each emphasizing different approaches to dealing with Turkey's past: "The IHD, which has a tradition of fighting dictatorship, uses civic participation to address historic issues. It wants to put an end to the cautious approach that has prevented Turkey from progressing. On the other hand, with the request for forgiveness, we are dealing with republican intellectuals, some of whom have had trouble breaking with the history they have grown up with. They are looking for a compromise that doesn't humiliate the Turkish canon. But they are criticized for adopting a cause that is not too risky and that pleases Europeans."

Despite disagreements over strategy, the memory of the 1915 massacres has definitely entered the public domain. Hrant Dink dreamed of "replacing fear with desire," and that dream is now coming true. On 19 January 2007, the work of consciousness-raising began. Since then, there has been a surge in initiatives defying the official version of history, and bridges have begun to be built. The Armenia Turkey cinema platform, launched in 2008, supports co-productions between the two countries. Under the leadership of two professors, Leyla Neyzi and Hranush Kharatyan-Araqelyan, Turkish and Armenian students collected oral histories about 1915. This study of memory and its complexities led to the publication of a book, *Speaking to One Another*,[86] which, on page after page, reveals a Turkish society haunted by 1915. "In the private domain, first-hand witnesses may have disappeared, but what happened is an open secret," says Neyzi.

The younger generation of Turkish Armenians, self-confident and assertive, is continuing the work begun by *Agos*. Aris Nalcı, for example, who cut his teeth as a journalist alongside Hrant Dink, founded the *Van Times*, a monthly newspaper published in Kurdish, Turkish, Armenian, and English to give visibility to the multicultural life that once thrived in Van and the surrounding area. The work of French photographer Antoine Agoudjian, who has spent twenty years travelling in Anatolia and the Middle East documenting traces of the genocide, was exhibited in Istanbul in April 2011. The grandson of survivors, Agoudjian feels that showing his photos in Turkey is an important step. "Many people found the idea crazy, even rash. But I have come to understand that this story involves more than just

Armenians. It's something that concerns everyone interested in learning the truth." He adds that he hopes other members of the diaspora will contribute to the memory work begun by Turkish civil society.

What giant steps have been taken since the MerhaBarev project was launched in December 2006! MerhaBarev is a greeting in two languages: Turkish – *merhaba* – and Armenian – *barev*, both meaning "hello." The project was designed to create a photo-bridge between the two countries. Five Armenian photojournalists spent a week taking photos of Istanbul, while five Turkish photojournalists did the same in Yerevan. The results, exhibited in a gallery in Istanbul, extended a hand of friendship across the border, still closed, laying the groundwork for future meetings. The project seems innocuous today, but at the time it was revolutionary. And on opening day, as the gallery pulsed with the promise of a more peaceful future, Hrant Dink was there. It was just six weeks before 19 January 2007.

"Things are moving faster since the death of Hrant Dink," says Ahmet Insel. One man in particular has contributed more than any other to that acceleration: Osman Kavala. "For thirty years, he has played a silent but crucial role and has never abandoned his convictions," says Ayşe Günaysu. A promoter of intercultural dialogue, Kavala works quietly in the background to provide artists and intellectuals with the assistance they need. In person, he appears to be a shy man with impeccable manners, but he is absolutely determined. Born in Paris in 1957, he is one of the most powerful businessmen in the country and a board member of TÜSIAD, Turkey's largest business group. Kavala is known as the "red billionaire" – "billionaire" because, as a young man of twenty-five, he inherited the flourishing family business from his father, a ship owner; and "red" because, in thirty-five years, his often-radical politics have not changed one iota.

As a young student in Manchester, England, in the late 1970s, he formed friendships with members of the Irish Republican Army (IRA) and led student opposition to the policies of Prime Minister Margaret Thatcher. In Turkey, even before the 1980 military coup, he was one of the principal patrons of publications such as *Birikim*, the "socialist culture review" and the bible of left-wing intellectuals. Today, in his restaurant, Cezayir, located in a charming building in downtown

Istanbul, intellectual discussions and secret meetings on the most taboo subjects are held under his patronage. In addition, the "red billionaire" is often ahead of his time. Anadolu Kültür, a foundation he created in 1991, works through the medium of culture and the arts to help Turkey become a more democratic, pluralistic, and free country. Kavala had opened early cultural branches in Kars and Diyarbakir. Founded by Anadolu Kültür in 2009, DEPO, located in a former tobacco warehouse in Istanbul, is a cultural centre and platform for debate. In 2007, Kavala supported the election campaign of intellectual Baskin Oran. A member of TEMA (the Turkish Foundation for Combating Soil Erosion), the co-founder of the liberal think tank TESEV, and contributor to a research centre on the Kurdish question, Kavala has his finger in every pie. He rescues stray dogs, sponsors a festival devoted to Turkish-Greek rapprochement, and supports gay and lesbian associations.

Hasan Cemal, on the other hand, faced a double challenge: taking an unflinching look at the country's history while coming to terms with his own family background. In late 2012, he published *1915: The Armenian Genocide*, a shockingly straightforward account of this historic event. The book became a bestseller, piled high in bookstore windows and fuelling intellectual debate. At sixty-seven, Cemal is one of Turkey's leading journalists; his credibility is unquestioned. As he nears the end of a successful career, he is still an influential editorial writer for the *Milliyet* (The nation) newspaper,[87] with access to powerful government circles. His book is all the more remarkable in that he had everything to lose by venturing into the territory of the genocide. Comfortably ensconced in a luxurious mansion on the Asian side of Istanbul with a view of the Bosphorus and a live-in Filipino maid, he could have kept his distance from the story. But what makes Cemal's initiative so admirable is that, like it or not, he is part of that story. On the wall of the small second-floor room that serves as his office, Cemal has thumbtacked photos of his grandfather, an Ottoman dignitary born in 1872 on the island of Lesbos. This ancestor, whom he never met, is none other than Djemal Pasha, one of the Three Pashas, the military triumvirate that ruled the Ottoman Empire during World War I. As a top official of the Committee of Union and Progress, Djemal Pasha was seen as one of the perpetrators of the 1915 genocide. Convicted in 1919 and sentenced to death in absentia by the Constantinople courts martial, he fled to Germany and then Switzerland. In 1922, he was assassinated in Tbilisi, Soviet Georgia, by Armenian vigilantes.

For many years, Hasan Cemal knew nothing of all this. "As a child, I wasn't told much. I didn't know exactly why my grandfather had been assassinated," he said when we interviewed him in 2011. "At school, then at university, we learned only the official history: that Turkey had been at war, and the Armenians had collaborated with the enemy. So they were deported to Syria, and during the deportations terrible things had happened. That's all. Nothing about the fact that women and children were involved, or that Armenians from both western and eastern Anatolia had been deported. Nothing about the real reasons for this ethnic and cultural cleansing." Even at Ankara University's faculty of political science, Mülkiye, an anti-establishment hotbed, "there was no alternate history, not a word about the Kurds, the Alevis, the Armenians ... We spent a long time in the dark."

Cemal's first Armenian shock came in January 1973, when he was a young journalist. A university friend, Bahadır Demir, Turkey's deputy consul general in Los Angeles, was assassinated by a terrorist member of the Armenian Secret Army for the Liberation of Armenia (ASALA), the first in a long series of attacks on Turkish diplomats. "For the first time, the Turkish government was on the defensive. That was a clue. That's when I began to realize that something had happened," he said. Twenty years later came the collapse of the Soviet Union. "The left began to talk about identity, not just class struggle. We discovered that this country had erased identities, and the ice began to melt. It was in the early 1990s that the first articles by Taner Akçam began to appear. His courage marked a turning point. He unlocked my mind."

The other major shock for Cemal was the death of Hrant Dink in January 2007. "He's the one who awakened my conscience," said Cemal. "He helped me to understand the meaning of past suffering, that it's important to face it head on. He helped change attitudes on both sides – among both Turks and Armenians. And he paid with his life." Cemal and Dink had been among those who attended the first university conference on "the Armenian question" in Istanbul in 2005. Cemal wrote a critical article about government efforts to cancel the conference. Along with four other editorial writers, he was taken to court. Feeling threatened, he arrived at court with a bodyguard in a 4x4 armoured vehicle.

To ease his conscience, Cemal took advantage of the 2008 football game attended by Turkish president Abdullah Gül to visit Yerevan. At Tsitsernakaberd, the Armenian genocide memorial, he knelt and placed three white roses next to the eternal flame. A photo of this event, symbolizing the regret of a criminal's grandson, is on the cover of his latest book. In the museum's visitor's book, he wrote these words with a trembling hand: "To deny the genocide is to be an accomplice to that crime against humanity." Later, he wrote this: "I'll never forget that morning in Yerevan in September 2008. At the first light of day, Mount Ararat emerged and then melted into the mist. That morning I wrote that, for those who wish to see it, the hand of History will point the way."

While he was in Armenia, Cemal arranged another important encounter. One afternoon, he sat down for a cup of coffee with Armen Gevorkyan, the grandson of the man who had killed his grandfather. The meeting with Armen, a businessman of about fifty whose family was originally from Erzurum, was "strange." But it convinced him that such memory work must be done before any reconciliation is possible. His intellectual journey attracted the attention of the diaspora. Three years later, he was invited to attend a conference at the University of California, Los Angeles (UCLA), home of a large and highly activist Armenian community. Once again it was a meeting of grandchildren: the conference was organized by Pamela Steiner, a Harvard professor and the granddaughter of Henry Morgenthau, the American ambassador to the Ottoman Empire during the First World War, who had spoken out against the massacres. Cemal knew that expectations were high, and he felt somewhat nervous. The presence of armed guards posted in the lecture theatre was "both reassuring and disturbing," according to Harut Sassounian, publisher of the weekly *California Courier*. But, throughout the conference, Cemal used the word "genocide" without hesitation, putting everyone at ease by announcing that he had come to "open his heart."

This burgeoning of Turkish society could lead to renewal if it were supported by the government – and if the murder of Hrant Dink did not still go unpunished. The trial of his killer was a judicial farce, and the ramifications of the crime within the Turkish state were never explored. Ogün Samast, weaned on nationalism and just seventeen when he shot his victim at point blank range, was sentenced to twenty-three years in prison. Yasin Hayal, the man who provided him with the weapon and the money, was declared his only accomplice and sentenced to life in prison. According to the criminal justice system, these two men in Trabzon, at the far end of the country, planned the assassination of the editor-in-chief of *Agos* with no help whatsoever. On 17 January 2012, Istanbul's 14th Criminal Court cleared eighteen other suspects of being part of a criminal organization. The court also ruled that Erhan Tuncel, a police and gendarmerie informant believed to be a major player, had no involvement in the assassination. Throughout the five years of the trial, the court ignored the plaintiffs' demands to extend the investigation to military and police authorities. Neither the Trabzon police chief nor the Istanbul Intelligence Branch director was investigated. "We have everything we need," declared Fethiye Çetin, a Dink family lawyer, in 2011. "Evidence, documents, witnesses – everything but prosecutors with the political will to try the case."

Indeed, documents proving that intelligence services were aware of plans to assassinate Dink were ignored, and these were not the only clues left unexamined by investigators. Physical evidence, including videotapes from the surveillance camera of a bank near the crime scene, disappeared from the file. With these verdicts, Turkey has created yet another Armenian victim to whom it will one day have to render justice.

16

The Kurds: Pricking Turkey's Conscience

Yervant Bostancı, an Armenian in his fifties, bald as a billiard ball, leads us rapidly through the alleys of the old city of Diyarbakir, carefully avoiding children on bikes and delivery men with arms full of fresh-baked bread. He enters the *gavur mahallesi*, the "infidels' quarter," a neighbourhood he knows like the back of his hand. He spent his child-hood running along its narrow cobbled streets with their basalt stone houses, so characteristic of this great Kurdish city in southeast Turkey. Some of those houses have been destroyed. Yervant climbs to the top of a pile of rubble and garbage in an empty lot. "It was a beautiful, stur-dy old house. My aunt and uncle used to live here. They left around the same time we did, in 1976, first to Istanbul, then to Holland. My aunt died in Amsterdam. As you can see, there's nothing left." He sighs, hands on hips.

Yervant's family lived a little further down, on the corner of Black Sea Street. The two-storey house is gone now, a fig tree growing in its place. He walks around the lot, imagining the placement of the walls. "It began here, but the neighbours seem to have moved their property line a few metres. The door was there, and it opened directly onto the street. There were two floors. I put up a chinning bar to do gymnastics. I was very athletic," he says, miming pull-ups. "And there, right in front, was a pool. My father was a professional swimmer!" It's hard to im-agine a swimming pool at this abandoned intersection littered with garbage.

"Everything has changed. All of the dilapidated houses you see were owned by Armenians. My friend Sarkis lived there. And Garabet was over there." The neighbourhood he grew up in is now occupied by villagers who moved here from rural areas in the last three or four decades. On the opposite street corner, three generations of Kurdish women are chatting. Yervant, who speaks fluent Kurdish, calls to them, "Hello! How are you today?"

The eldest woman remembers him. "You're Hatun's son? Welcome back! You'll have to come back and build your house – the lot's waiting for you!" She gives him a toothless grin.

After a long exile, Yervant Bostancı, a world-renowned musician known in Turkey as Udi Yervant (Yervant the Oud Player), has come home. Twenty years ago, he moved to California, where he continued his career. His grandfather was a survivor of the 1915 genocide. "Kurdish leaders protected my grandfather. He came from the village to live in Diyarbakir, where the family lived for sixty years in a house that belonged to an Armenian group. So I grew up there, in the infidels' quarter, until 1976, when we moved to Istanbul." Yervant discovered music when he was five, played the darbouka at weddings, then took saz lessons from Turkish master Aşık Zülfi, perfecting his training as a Turkish classical musician on the banks of the Bosphorus.

In the 1980s, he could be seen strolling through the cosmopolitan streets of Istanbul, his smiling face sporting a thick paintbrush moustache. He accompanied the great names in Turkish music, including Zeki Müren, and performed in Greek and Armenian taverns. In the early 1990s he was appearing at the Mandra tavern, in the Armenian section of the Pangaltı district, not far from the big cemetery. "I was playing with a Greek soloist and a pianist, Ara Hamparian," he recalls. "We had lots of Armenian customers, so I would sing in Turkish and Armenian." One night in late 1991, he was leaving the tavern carrying his oud after an evening of revelry when someone came up and tapped him on the shoulder. "What language were you singing in?" he was asked.

"In Armenian," Yervant answered.

"Why were you singing in Armenian? Are you Armenian?"

"Yes …"

The man began to insult him: "I curse Armenia and the Armenians. I spit on you, your mother, and your children!" Yervant says, "I was getting ready to punch him in the face when the tavern owner came out and told me to calm down and keep my mouth shut. So then the other guy threatened me. 'I'm coming back tomorrow night, and if you sing again in Armenian, I'll kill you.'" That night, he says, he couldn't sleep a wink. "I was going crazy."

The next evening, he went back to play at the tavern, but he was frightened. "Instead of fifteen songs in Armenian, I played just four or five. After a while, the owner came up and asked me why I wasn't singing in Armenian. I reminded him that the night before that guy had insulted me in front of the tavern, and he had told me to keep my mouth shut. After that, I decided to stop. I felt that under those conditions I couldn't stay in Turkey any longer. On May 15th, 1992, I left for Los Angeles."

Twenty years later, even softened by a generous glass of raki, the memory of that incident still stings. The face of his aggressor is engraved on his memory. He shrugs. "He was a prominent figure, but I can't tell you his name."

Udi Yervant spent twenty years making a new life for himself in Los Angeles, home of a large Armenian community. He found there an audience for his songs, recording studios for his records – and a complete absence of death threats for being Armenian. "I have a life in the US, I'm known there, and I give concerts. But, of course, Diyarbakir has always been in my heart. Over there, I'm almost an ambassador for peace. Turks, Kurds, Armenians, and Assyrians living in Los Angeles all come and dance the halay together while I play." Then, in 2004, he was invited to return to his hometown to give a concert during the cultural festival. It was a troubling proposition. "I considered it from every angle. I hadn't set foot in Turkey for twelve years. I didn't want to go back. I decided I'd ask them to pay my travel and hotel expenses and a huge fee, so I wouldn't have to go. I sent them my answer, and they agreed to all my demands! So I went."

When Yervant's plane landed at the Diyarbakir military airbase, Şeyhmus Diken, a Kurdish writer and amateur historian, was waiting to welcome him. Diken has dreamed for years of returning (at least in his writing) to the days when the cosmopolitan city was a blend of all its ethnic and religious communities. It had been Diken's idea to bring Yervant back to Turkey, to give the festival an Armenian flavour. "We didn't know each other. At the terminal exit, he was waiting with a bouquet of flowers. And he shouted to me in Kurdish, 'Ula fille hoş geldin!' (Welcome, infidel!)" Yervant loved every minute of his visit: "The concert I gave was in the street where I was born! It was amazing!"

Adds Diken, "We grew up in the same neighbourhood, and we visited our childhood haunts together." Since then, Yervant has returned home every year to visit his Kurdish friend.

But it wasn't until 2012 that the two men discovered their secret bond. Diken tells the story: "When I was little, living in the 'infidels' quarter,' we had a close neighbour, a woman named Hatun. My mother, Ayten, had already lost five of her children. So when I was born, Hatun came to the house, prayed for me, and passed me under her clothing three times – an Armenian custom. She said to my mother, 'May God protect him, your son, who is now my son.'" He stops, letting the suspense build, then continues. "Our family was poor. The men in Hatun's family worked in the rice fields and brought us rice. We never had to pay." It was only recently that Diken and Yervant made the connection. When Yervant asked his mother if she'd ever heard of a woman named Ayten who had lost five children, she told him the whole story. "In fact, Hatun was Yervant's mother," says Diken, "and Yervant was the little boy who came to bring us rice! We are brothers. That's when I fully understood just how closely Kurds and Armenians are tied, even though history has separated us."

Following this joyful reunion, Diken decided to write a book, accompanied by a CD of Yervant's music. *Infidel! Welcome* was published in October 2012. Since then, Yervant has visited Diyarbakir more and more often. "I am first a resident of Diyarbakır, then an Armenian and a Christian," he says. "I may be crazy, but I want to move back here."[88]

Yervant's return to his lost homeland may signal a wave of such returns. In any case, that's the hope of Osman Baydemir, the charismatic mayor of Diyarbakır Metropolitan Municipality, a lawyer and member of the Peace and Democracy Party (BDP), a party close to the

Kurdish nationalist movement. On 25 September 2012, on the sidelines of a conference of Turkish and Armenian journalists, he expressed his dream: "An Armenian, an Assyrian, and a Chaldean, whose grandfathers or great-grandfathers were born in Diyarbakır, have the same right to live in Diyarbakır as I have. I would like to invite all the ethnic groups whose ancestors lived in Diyarbakır to come back to live here again. Come back to your city! Kurds, Armenians, Chaldeans, Yazidis and all the ethnic groups that once lived in Diyarbakır helped build Diyarbakır's city walls. So all of these people have a right to this city."

Baydemir's invitation is extended to the tens of thousands of exiles who have fled the threats and massacres since 1915. Talaat Pasha's notebooks, published by historian Murat Bardakçı, indicate that there were 56,166 Armenians living in Diyarbakır before the events of 1915. According to the Patriarchate of Constantinople, 106,867 Armenians lived in 250 villages throughout the province. In the bazaars surrounding Diyarbakır's old Ulu Cami mosque, they ran jewellers' shops, copper workshops, and forges. They tended vineyards. Yet the evidence of their existence has all but vanished. The old silkworm market, a magnificent building with a carved façade, now houses the Turkish post and telephone office (PTT). Silk farming, once a specialty of the municipality, has not survived. During the 1895 massacre, the entire marketplace, now known as the "burned bazaar," was torched to drive out the Christians. At the time of the genocide, almost half of the walled city belonged to Armenian families and foundations, but over the past century Diyarbakir lost much of its life's blood; many activities have been abandoned for lack of the necessary skills.

Many genocide survivors who sought refuge in Syria, Armenia, France, and the United States were originally from Diyarbakir, but few have dared to return. In the minds of Armenians, it is still the city where, in 1915, people played street soccer with the head of an Armenian priest and the bell tower of the Sourp Giragos church was destroyed by cannon fire because it was taller than the minarets. The city's governor at the time was Dr Mehmed Reshid, known as the "butcher of Diyarbakır"; he embodied the most extreme wing of the Young Turk movement. In June 1915, writes Raymond Kévorkian, "Armenian men were systematically rounded up and taken daily in groups of between 100 and 150 to the Marden Gate or the road to Gözle (today's Gözalan), where their throats were slit."[89] The members of the leading Armenian families, the Kazazians, the Terpandjians, the Yegenians, and the Handanians, were taken to a place south of the city, where their throats were cut. "Five hundred and ten women and children were killed and thrown into the underground cisterns at Dara, vestiges of the Byzantine period." Children under three were thrown off the old bridge spanning the Tigris. A few craftsmen were able to save themselves by paying substantial sums to the *mufti* Ibrahim for attestations of their conversion to Islam. The largely Kurdish Muslim population participated willingly in the massacres, destruction, and pillaging that devastated Diyarbakir. The few survivors who remained in the 1960s and '70s ended up moving to Istanbul or fleeing the country, leaving a city that had been bled dry.

Since the "departure" of the Armenians,[90] Diyarbakir has grown to more than a million inhabitants. Considered the "political capital" of Turkey's Kurds, it is a militant stronghold where the PKK's campaign is looked upon with a benevolent eye. Political unrest has been a constant here since the creation of the republic, doing nothing to ease the minds of its former inhabitants. The Kurds have been in perpetual rebellion against the state, especially since Cheikh Saïd, the leader of a local insurrection, was hanged at the foot of the city wall in 1925. Following Arab conquests in the seventh century, the region was occupied by the Bakir tribe and became known as Diyar Bakr – "landholdings of the Bakr tribe" in Persian. When it was visited by Atatürk in 1937, he deemed it not sufficiently Turkish and renamed it Diyarbakir – land of copper. The Kurds call it Amed. And, under the Ottoman Empire, the Armenians called it Tigranakert. Today, the city is seriously thinking of adopting yet another name, a combination of its Armenian and Kurdish names: Tigranamed.

Renaming the city to reclaim part of its stolen identity is the latest scheme of Abdullah Demirbaş, the mayor of Sur, which includes the historic centre of Diyarbakir inside the city walls. Since his election in 2004, Demirbaş, a Kurdish Armenophile and relentless activist for cultural rights, has been working to reintroduce Armenian symbols into the local landscape. When we visited him in his large town hall office in October 2012, he had just returned from Yerevan, the capital of Armenia, with which he wishes to form partnerships and develop cultural projects. A few months earlier, he had signed a twinning agreement with Gumri, Armenia's second-largest city. On open shelves occupying a full wall of his office is an Armenian alphabet presented to him by Yerevan municipality.

"I know what it's like not to be able to speak your own language," Demirbaş says. "When I was seven, I couldn't speak Turkish, and my teacher would hit me. I have always fought to preserve linguistic identities." As a young philosophy teacher, he was fully aware of the tragedy that struck his city in 1915, and of the silent suffering endured by the Armenians in his neighbourhood. He also grew up in the "infidels' quarter." "I remember that, when I was little, there was an Armenian lady who gave us painted Easter eggs. But since we were poor, we ate them," he says with a smile. "My father, who was very religious, always said that God would take his revenge for what was done to the Armenians."

One day in 2004, soon after Demirbaş was elected, an Assyrian man went to see him at city hall. "He made a real impression on me. He came and he asked me, 'Are you going to continue the same system of oppressing minorities?' I knew I had to do something." He began to reintroduce the use of multiple languages in municipal affairs and had brochures and postcards printed in seven languages, including Kurdish, Assyrian, and Armenian. He launched a project called "A Story for Each Night and Every Home a School," aiming to publish 365 stories for children in Kurdish and other minority languages. Armenian became an official working language at city council, but nobody spoke it. So the mayor introduced Armenian lessons at city hall, attended by growing numbers each year. With each new initiative, court cases were brought against him in an attempt to stop him – more than twenty-five in all.

In 2007, he was removed from office, together with the entire city council, for using the Kurdish language in official business. Having printed children's books and tourist brochures in Kurdish, he was accused of misusing municipal resources. In 2009, he was re-elected with an even stronger majority than in 2004, but a month later he was again tried for "spreading terrorist propaganda." He had appeared on Roj TV, a satellite television station linked to the PKK. The judicial harassment continued in 2009. On Christmas Eve, he was arrested, handcuffed, and imprisoned along with dozens of other Kurdish mayors in the region, all accused of belonging to the PKK's shadow administration. His fragile health made headlines, however, and international pressure resulted in his being freed, whereupon he immediately took up the struggle again.

"I want the Armenians to return, but not as tourists. This is their home," he says. The Diyarbakir municipality wants to reverse the genocidal policy of the Turkish state, which has systematically erased all evidence of minorities. Another of Demirbaş's projects was the "Streets of Culture." His goal was to renovate a mosque, a synagogue, an Armenian church, and a Chaldean church; he also renamed a lane in the old city after Mıgırdiç Margosyan, a local Armenian writer. It was largely under his leadership that the sixteenth-century Armenian Sourp Giragos (St Giragos) Church, said to be the largest Armenian church in the Middle East, was restored. During the First World War, the German army had headquartered there. In 1915, while Christians throughout the district were being massacred, artillery cannon from across the city took aim at the hated bell tower and shot it to pieces. Later the building was used as a textile warehouse for a government-owned corporation. Since the genocide, no religious service had been held there. In the early 1990s, after heavy snowstorms, sections of the neglected roof collapsed.

Finally, on 23 October 2011, Sourp Giragos, the property of an Istanbul-based Armenian foundation, was returned to the Armenian Apostolic Church and its community. On the day of the grand reopening, dozens of Armenians from Istanbul and the diaspora sat together on heavy wooden benches, intoxicated by clouds of incense and religious fervour. Osman Baydemir, mayor of Diyarbakir, and Abdullah Demirbaş, mayor of its old city, were there to welcome visitors. "Welcome to your home," read a banner in four languages. About one-third of the cost of the restoration had been covered by the city council.

More discreetly, dozens of Diyarbakir Muslims also attended this first service. Among them were many converts for whom the time had come to reveal their hidden identity: at least a dozen were baptized that day. Since then, the renovations have continued, and, despite still-strong opposition from neighbours, the bell tower is being rebuilt. Religious services are now being held, and, on 4 November 2012, a bronze bell weighing 150 kilograms, custom made in Moscow, was installed, with deputy patriarch Aram Ateşyan, originally from Diyarbakir, in attendance. Bells had not been heard in the church for almost a century.

The restoration of Sourp Giragos was spectacular, but it contrasted sharply with the neglected state of the six or seven other Armenian churches in the old city of Diyarbakir. Some have been commandeered by the state, for which promoting multiculturalism is not a priority. The Sourp Sarkis Catholic Church, for example, is used as a copper workshop by students at a training centre, a project initiated by the subprefecture in 2012. The Protestant church across the street from it now serves as a textile factory, with veiled teenagers working at looms set up on the ground floor and in the balconies. The building is in the process of assimilation: the walls have been plastered, and the stained glass has been replaced with PVC. Mustafa Toprak, the nationalist governor of Diyarbakir, and Ertuğral Günay, the minister of culture, both came to give their blessing to this transformation. In contrast, they have never set foot in Sourp Giragos.

The policy of denial is still at work, as demonstrated by the refusal of the Ministry of the Interior to grant the request of Aram Tigran's family in 2009. A celebrated Armenian musician, Tigran had wanted to be buried in Diyarbakir, the homeland of his ancestors. Born in Syria after his parents had been deported there in 1915, he later moved to Armenia, where he worked at Radio Yerevan for eighteen years; then, in the 1990s, he settled in Athens. In the summer of 2009, age seventy-five, he died there. Near the end of his life, Tigran briefly visited his ancestral homeland. During a historic visit, he said, "It was the dream of a lifetime to return to Diyarbakir. I was always praying, 'God! Before I die, will I ever see the home of my ancestors?'"

A visit to his parents' village reduced Tigran to tears: "When I see these mountains, these trees, these rivers, and these houses, my soul aches, and I feel a searing pain. I remember my father and my mother, what they endured. I am saddened by the fact that they could not live in their homeland." And he was denied the right to go to his final rest there. Ankara refused to allow Tigran's funeral to be held in Diyarbakir, and he was finally buried in the Armenian cemetery in Brussels. Mayor Baydemir was infuriated by this refusal. "They would not allow him to return to his homeland. But on behalf of the people of Diyarbakir, we will take a handful of earth from this cemetery, where he wanted to be buried, and, even though it's only symbolic, we will sprinkle it on his grave. That way, we will be at peace, knowing we have done our best to honour his wishes."

This episode pricked the conscience of the Kurdish authorities, who organized a symbolic ceremony at the Armenian cemetery near the Urfa Gate. "If Tigran had been buried here today, this ground would have been the richer for it," declared Fırat Anlı, provincial head of the pro-Kurdish Democratic Society Party (DTP). "Because we uprooted and rejected them ... Perhaps this would have been a kind of apology to the Armenians and Assyrians and all the Mesopotamian peoples whose value was not appreciated and whose lives were extinguished ... With Aram Tigran, we could have seized the opportunity to face the past and build a future."

It is to ensure that the suffering of the past is finally recognized that Abdullah Demirbaş wishes to erect a monument in the old city[91] – "A monument dedicated to the victims, to face the past and encourage the state to assume its responsibility," he says. Could the Kurds take the first step toward collective repentance? It seems that won't happen any time soon. Like many of his constituents, Demirbaş believes the central government is solely responsible for the "calamity" that occurred in their region. Many want to believe that the Kurds were simply used, encouraged to take up arms against their Armenian "brothers." By depicting themselves as the people who just "did the dirty work," the Kurds hope to limit their responsibility. Yet religious intolerance, tribal mechanisms, and greed pushed many of them to participate in the genocide.

Mayor Baydemir has nevertheless laid the groundwork for some serious introspection. "We refuse the legacy of the grandparents who participated in this massacre; we refuse to be a part of that history; and we honour those of our grandparents who opposed the massacre and the cruelty," he declared in September 2012. "To deny the crimes committed by some of our grandparents would be to perpetuate them in some way. We must first acknowledge the suffering of the people so we can start to heal the wounds." A few months earlier, he had given a moving speech on the subject to a group of historians and activists working for the Armenian cause during a conference organized in his city by the Hrant Dink Foundation. Baydemir, a former lawyer who was one of the first defenders of Abdullah Öcalan,[92] did not hesitate that day to denounce the actions of his ancestors. "We must begin by confronting the past. The time for reparation has come; the time to heal wounds. Each one of us must investigate their own family history ... For myself, I denounce the actions of my grandparents, of my ancestors who served in the Hamidye regiments." Baydemir was referring to the light cavalry regiments established by and named after Sultan Abdul Hamid II in 1891, which were guilty of massacres in the late nineteenth century.

These signs of Kurdish repentance are of course not without ulterior political motives. "Obviously, it's also a strategy on the part of the Kurdish nationalist movement," says Kurdish activist Yildiz Önen, the granddaughter of an Armenian and originally from Derik. The PKK and its legal front have a clear interest in goading the Turkish state about its past. The 1915 genocide was a founding action that, once laid bare, could remind people of more recent atrocities and further shake the country's foundations. With this in mind, Abdullah Öcalan has long pushed for the establishment of a Truth and Reconciliation commission that would deliver justice to the victims of both the Armenian genocide and the "dirty war" against the Kurds.

This desire to explore the past is echoed in high circles. As part of the effort to rewrite the Turkish constitution, the pro-Kurdish Peace and Democracy Party (BDP) proposed that the new text include the following paragraph about the "right to learn the truth": "Everyone has the right to learn the truth, to access substantive information about the country's history, and to request that documents and information about this history be made public, including government archives. There is no statute of limitations on genocide or crimes against humanity." The entire administration of the pro-Kurdish party is thus on board, and its political strategy includes the recognition of 1915.

"Within this strategy, the role of Abdullah Demirbaş, for example, is to spread a positive message about multiculturalism," says a resident of Diyarbakir who has recently "come out" as an Armenian.

Of course there is also some opportunism among Kurds who, by identifying with the genocide victims, hope to draw attention to their own plight. But it would be unfair to think they are not sincere. "The war the Kurds are fighting gives them real empathy for the Armenians," says Gülisor Akkum, a Kurdish sociologist and the Diyarbakir correspondent for the *Armenian Weekly*, a publication of the American diaspora. "This war has had at least one positive impact: the Kurdish nationalist movement is prepared to shoulder its share of the responsibility." The outspoken, chain-smoking Akkum tells us how she followed the trail of the Armenian deportees in an attempt to understand what happened. "I went to Der-Zor, but also to Anjar, Lebanon," she says. "It's impossible to remain insensitive to that pain."

For both the Kurds and the Turks, assuming responsibility would mean paying reparation and compensation. "I'd say that about 80 per cent of Diyarbakir once belonged to Armenians," says Akkum. "The Kurds took all their property. In his memoirs, Kurdish writer Musa Anter talks about the pillaging. Now it's those wealthy families who hold all the power." Şeyhmus Diken agrees with this estimate. Almost a century later, the clans who, in 1915, collaborated with the forces of the governor, Dr Mehmed Reshid, to strip the Armenians of their wealth are still viewed by authorities with a benevolent eye. "They must be held accountable."

This is precisely what the Diyarbakir Armenian Foundation has set out to do. "The state is now telling us that we can reclaim properties that were confiscated after 1936," says Abdulgaffur Türkay, the foundation's secretary. "We have filed claims for 168 buildings. Some are owned by the state, others belong to the municipality, and still others are privately owned ... Some of the properties are being used for schools, a water treatment facility ... And those are just the church properties for which we've been able to find documents, deeds, land registry certificates ... In all, we found the names of 190 properties in a dusty register that was discovered by accident in the Sourp Giragos church during renovations. The Armenian cemetery near the Urfa

Gate used to measure 20,000 square metres – now it measures just 1,000 square metres ... The rest has been covered over by streets and houses."

Adds Vartkes Ergün Ayık, the foundation's president: "When we began our investigation, we were constantly searching the archives of the land registry office. Every time we went in, the official in charge of the registers was amazed. One day, he told us, 'There was a time when half of Diyarbakir belonged to you.'"

17

Death of a Sub-Prefect

"We must take decisive action, eliminate all non-Turkish elements from the population," declares one of the characters, an Ottoman pasha. "Later, we'll say that nothing happened. If anyone argues, we'll shut them up." The audience at Diyarbakir's municipal theatre roars with laughter at this caricature of the bloodthirsty Turk in *The Armenian Concert, or the Turkish Proverb*. Written by Gérard Torikian, a French director and grandson of an Armenian survivor, the play is groundbreaking: this is the first time the genocide has been depicted on a Turkish stage.

At the stage door, a bewildered-looking man stands motionless in the middle of the empty corridor. Eyes shining, he tells us that his name is Abdurrahim Zorarslan, and he is an Islamized Armenian. He came to see the play without telling his wife, a Muslim who wears the chador and is exasperated by her husband's identity crisis. Happy to escape his loneliness and find a sympathetic ear, he is our first contact with Lice, his birthplace and home to one of the genocide's best-kept secrets.

Ninety kilometres of fertile countryside separate Lice from Diyarbakir. The area is rife with memories of historic events that Turkey would rather forget; of course, they are not mentioned in any guidebook. With its cinderblock hovels and satellite-covered rooftops, the village of Fis looks like any other Kurdish village in the region. It was in a small cafe here that Abdullah Öcalan met with his comrades and founded the Kurdistan Workers' Party (PKK), the armed movement that is still at war with Ankara. In the 1990s, along with more than 3,000 other villages,[93] it was forcibly evacuated by the Turkish army and occupied by "village guards," militiamen armed by the government – retribution for the hamlet's friendliness with the "terrorists." Only recently have a few families been allowed to return.

Sixty kilometres from Diyarbakir, on the road to Lice, we arrive in Karaz. At first glance, it is as unremarkable as Fis, although we observe that the small mosque advertises its support for the governing party, something not often seen in regions sympathetic to the Kurdish cause. Suphi, a solidly built farmer bronzed by the Mesopotamian sun, leads us off the main road down a lane rutted by tractor tires. He yells into his cell phone as he stops next to an ancient tree near a pile of hay covered with a tarp and a few old tires. In the village, this spot is known as the "Sub-Prefect's Spring." Wearing a hooded jacket against the biting wind that sweeps through the valley, he gestures. "That's where Hüseyin Nesimi was killed. People come here often to visit him." In the Islamic and Kurdish tradition, quiet contemplation near a grave is a sign of respect for the deceased. Nesimi's memory has thus not been completely erased; it still flows like an underground stream, in silence. Just a few initiates know where to find him.

In 1915, Hüseyin Nesimi was the *kaïmakam*, or sub-prefect, of the Lice district. When he learned of the decision to deport the Armenians, he asked the governor for an official letter. Then he made the rounds of all the Armenian homes and ordered the Muslims and police under his authority not to harm Christians. "Furious, the governor, summoned him to Diyarbakir," says author Şeyhmus Diken. "Nesimi set off on his horse with an escort. No doubt he feared being attacked. In those days, it took two days to travel the ninety kilometres between Lice and Diyarbakir. The governor arranged for him to be ambushed in Karaz. These facts are a matter of record, but they were hidden." Nesimi was shot to death on 23 June. Telegrams in the Ottoman archives confirm the official version, that he was killed by Armenian bandits. "We must right this wrong by revealing what really happened and the compassion of this Ottoman official," says Diken. "A woman in his employ reported that she had seen him crying about his inability to save the Armenians." The records show that the governor in question, Dr Mehmed Reshid, one of the founders of the Committee of Union and Progress, was known for his extreme cruelty, a matter of complete indifference to the central government. Obsessed with the quest for racial purity, Reshid had also ordered a squadron of Circassians to execute another sub-prefect, Raşid Bey, posted in Derik, who had requested confirmation of the deportation orders from Istanbul. Ali Sabit Es-Süveydi, the deputy *kaïmakam* of Beşiri, was killed for the same reason.

The region's turbulent history has conspired to erase the memory of the courageous sub-prefect from Lice. In 1975, an earthquake devastated the town, levelling eight thousand homes. Waves of emigration took with them the few remaining Armenians. More departures occurred in the 1990s, during the darkest hours of the civil war between the PKK and the state. The departing inhabitants, replaced by villagers from the surrounding area, took with them the memory of Hüseyin Nesimi. Even Fikriye Aytın, Lice's mayor, a member of the pro-Kurdish Peace and Democracy Party (BDP), had never heard of him. She was touched to learn of Nesimi's act of resistance and suggested that the town could pay posthumous tribute to his courage, perhaps by naming a street after him.

In the midst of the market stalls on Lice's main street, a glimmer of light emerges from a forge. It once belonged to an Armenian who left the area after the earthquake in search of a less hostile environment. Today, a Kurdish blacksmith tends the fire with an enormous, ancient bellows. As a teen, the blacksmith had apprenticed with the original owner, and he can still summon snatches of Armenian from the depths of his memory. *Tchour per*: "Bring water." *Egour kezi mi pan esem*: "Come here; I want to tell you something." A small group of onlookers spills out onto the street. "His grandmother was Armenian," someone says. "Of course, there are other families like his." It takes a lot to stop such tongues from wagging. A Turkish tank rolling slowly along the potholed street is a call to order, urging loiterers to move along.

Abdurrahim's family lives outside Lice's centre. In the small garden, under metal sheets forming an arbour, a mosaic of religion and identity produced by a century of turmoil can be seen. Two veiled little girls, a neighbour's children, enter the kitchen: it's time for their Quran lesson from Abdurrahim's sister-in-law. "My wife observes Ramadan for all of us," laughs Talhat, one of Abdurrahim's brothers,

who visits the mosque only on Fridays, "to put in an appearance." A
Bible in Turkish and Arabic, given to them by a missionary, is brought
out to show the visitors and passed from hand to hand. The Bible is
never opened, but it's not thrown away, either. "I'm first a Kurd, then
an Armenian, but I never go to church," says young Zozan. Her cousin,
Abdullah, chimes in: "I'm 100 per cent Armenian," he says. Among the
Zorarslan family, identity is not a matter of religion – except for Hasan,
Abdurrahim's son. "Thank God, I'm Muslim," he declares as his father
tries to hide his pain.

The blue-eyed young man, an English student at a university in
western Turkey, was educated at a Gülen school – part of a movement
based on the teachings of Fethullah Gülen, a powerful Turkish Islamic
preacher. "I can't be Armenian, because that would mean being Christian," he explains. "That's impossible, because I'm Muslim, like my
mother. But that didn't save me from being called a 'filthy infidel'
when I was little." His distress is palpable. For Hasan, living in this
conservative region, being the son of one of Lice's last remaining
Armenian families is a curse. He would give just about anything to
forget about the Christian roots of his father's family.

Akif, Abdurrahim's other brother, borrows the city hall's pickup
truck to show us the old Armenian houses. At dusk, we head up into
the mountains above Lice. The Turkish army's combat helicopters are
just returning from operations, flying low over the rocky peaks. The
PKK guerrillas are not far away. At the end of a deeply rutted road, we
can make out in the half light some ruins, stark remnants of a
neighbourhood levelled by the 1975 earthquake. Nothing has been
touched since then – everything was simply abandoned. An odd-
looking two-storey building, partly flattened, is the remains of a
sixteenth-century watermill-mosque, built over a river whose waters
thunder down the mountainside. A little higher up, there was a
church, but it is out of bounds now, behind military lines. Across from
it, facing the valley, is a marble pool and a few stones among the
brambles, the remains of the sub-prefect's house. There was a time
when the official's rented Ottoman home was impressive. It possessed
a *salemlik*, the part of a Muslim household reserved for the master of
the house, open to male servants and visitors, and a *haremlik*, the part
reserved for women. Its white stones, skilfully carved by Assyrians and

brought here from the city of Mardin near present-day Syria, were the most beautiful in the region. After the earthquake, the army confiscated them to build the barracks that circle the city. One of these barracks can be seen in the restricted military area that extends past the road along the steep rock face. This is all that remains of Lice's courageous sub-prefect.

We return to Diyarbakir and its one million inhabitants. The exodus triggered by the civil war has transformed the city, which has spilled over the five kilometres of black lava stone walls surrounding the old city, cramming its refugees into soulless warehouses. Their numbers include many from Lice. In the concrete jungle, memory fragments of Nesimi's story teeter on the edge of oblivion. Time is the unfailing accomplice of the Turkish authorities and their denial of history.

Each day, elderly men from Lice gather at the Özay teahouse, a tiny room with yellowed walls, the old black-and-white television in the corner tuned to the races. The Turkish law forbidding smoking in public places is disregarded here. Playing cards and dominoes are slapped down on rickety tables amidst thick clouds of smoke. Nihat Işik, elegantly attired in a three-piece suit dating from the 1980s, comes here every day to drink tea with his cronies. Selim, his father's nephew, an eminent Kurd, owned the house that was rented by the sub-prefect. The two men respected each other.

"One day in the 1950s, a man named Süleyman came to see me," says Işik. "I was working at the civil status office of the Lice sub-prefecture. He wanted to talk to me because he had something weighing on his conscience. He told me that he was one of the men who had shot the *kaïmakam* – and that the leader of the *çete* [gang] had written a report saying that Armenian bandits had killed him but that the order had actually come from the governor." Nihat is relieved to be able to tell this story, which he has guarded like a precious secret for more than half a century because he obviously couldn't "talk openly" about it to just anyone. "His body stayed there all night," he adds. "Selim Bey called some villagers to look after the body, and they buried it there." He had heard this story from the sub-prefect's mother. He also remembers a few other details: Nesimi, a Turk originally from the island of Crete, at that time an Ottoman possession, had enjoyed drinking wine in his garden and used to dine with Armenians.

Author Şeyhmus Diken came across Işik while researching the story of the sub-prefect. Diken, fifty-eight, is acutely sensitive to the historic presence of Armenians in this region, which is now mostly Kurdish. "The two communities shared these lands for centuries," he says. "Perhaps the Armenians are no longer physically here, but their homes and churches remain. For me, their soul is still present, in these streets." Diken is nostalgic for the cultural mosaic that Diyarbakir used to be. His hometown was once peopled by Kurds, Syrians, Jews, and Armenians; a few still remained in the 1960s. He recalls a childhood incident that may have planted the seed for this nostalgia. One afternoon as he was leaving school, a gang of kids began to beat up his friend, Artin. When he tried to defend his pal, the other boys scornfully accused him of siding with a *gavur*. His grandmother consoled the two boys with thick slices of bread smeared with tomato paste. One day, Artin and his family left Diyarbakir, hoping, like other Armenians, to make a new life for themselves in a more welcoming environment. Over time, Diken's memories of his friend faded, but a few years ago he met Aram Ateşyan, the deputy patriarch of the Armenian Patriarchate in Istanbul, who was visiting Diyarbakir. Ateş-yan was his childhood friend, Artin.

Diken says he's "on the side of the oppressed." He believes it is vital to rehabilitate the memory of the sub-prefect. "There's no point saying that a million and a half Armenians were killed but that has nothing to do with us because the Turkish Republic did not exist at the time." Sincere repentance is in the details. Moreover, "if the state were smart, it could use its archives to show that not all governors carried out the orders; there were exceptions." But is it possible for a state to be smart? Diken, who graduated with a degree in political science from Ankara University, has experienced the answer first-hand. After graduation, he also became a sub-prefect, but he lost his position after the coup d'état on 12 September 1980 when his Kurdish origins caught up with him. "It's true," he says; "I too was a *kaïmakam*, and I too was sacked. Nesimi was looking after Armenians. For me, it was Kurds. The Turkish and Ottoman states have the same mentality."

Beylikdüzü is a newly developed area on the European side of Istanbul stretching as far as the eye can see. From the centre of town, it takes us a good hour to drive there. The asphalt on roads leading to factories and high-rises has barely cooled, and bulldozers are busily digging up the earth. The Turkish contractors are in a hurry: the area's rapid growth spells profits for them. A white Porsche Cayenne is parked in front of a building; we enter and wind our way past hot-tub models to the CEO's office. This is the empire of the sub-prefect's descendants, who have made their fortune in bathroom fixtures, exporting them around the world.

Nesimi's two grandsons greet us under the watchful eye of a huge portrait of Mustafa Kemal. The latest issue of *Forbes* magazine is displayed on a coffee table. Sporting a gold watch and a head of white hair, the elder son is the proud guardian of his namesake's legacy. He tells us his grandfather grew up in a respected family, with a great-uncle who was a Sufi shaikh, in Crete. At that time, the Ottoman Empire prohibited Turks from leaving the island, then rocked by pro-independence rebellions. There was one exception, however: every year, the two top high-school students were authorized to pursue their studies in Istanbul – the first at military college and the second at the Mekteb-i Mülkiye, or School of Civil Administration. Hüseyin Nesimi, in whom a rebellious spirit was already deeply rooted, had studied to become an administrator. One Friday, he stood at the front of a crowd lining the street where the imperial procession was about to pass. When Sultan Abdülhamid II drew up in front of him, he threw into the carriage a letter containing a list of proposed reforms for the empire. "That's why he was sent to eastern Turkey, as a punishment," explains Hüseyin Nesimi Jr. "Those Kurdish lands, rebellious to the central authority, were already seen as thankless postings."

"My nanny witnessed it all," he says. "In Lice, she was the one who raised my father, Abidin. She told me that the Armenians were so desperate to save themselves that they offered their gold to my grandfather. Of course, he refused to take it. She also told us that he ordered his soldiers to protect the Armenians. To those who wanted to kill them, he said, 'Take their property, but don't kill them.'" After the sub-prefect was killed, Fatma, his widow, and Abidin, his son, were also threatened by bandits. "They were hidden by the owner of the house where they lived."

Orphaned at four, Abidin was clearly his father's son. As an active militant for the Communist Party, he was imprisoned several times –

the last for writing an essay on land reform and the need to redistribute the lands confiscated by the biggest landowners. "When my father was not in prison, the house overflowed with visitors," his son recalls. "He had lots of Armenian friends. We always knew what had happened to our grandfather, but we didn't talk about it much outside the family." But today Hüseyin is clearly proud and happy to recall his memory. "My grandfather is a hero to me. He sacrificed himself to save others." He chooses his words carefully, avoiding all mention of the state's responsibility for what happened. Business is business, after all. But times are changing. Hüseyin has never gone in search of the past and knows the region only through one of his sales outlets in Diyarbakir. Now, however, he plans to erect a mausoleum near the old tree where his grandfather was murdered.

18

The Righteous Turks

Guests hand their Louis Vuitton bags to obsequious bellhops before entering the revolving doors. With its stunning views of the Bosphorus – especially at sunset, the water tinged with pink – Istanbul's luxurious Swissotel is a favourite of rich tourists from the Arabian Peninsula, government ministers and diplomats, and businesspeople from around the world. On their way to the hotel, taxis drive past the stadium of the Beşiktaş football club, then along a winding avenue. It is here, just a few dozen metres from the hotel entrance, that Kemal Ceyhan believes his grandfather, Mehmet Celal Bey, is buried – under the asphalt. Before building the road, the authorities did not bother to move the grave, enclosing it in a concrete tomb.

A park with a small private cemetery once occupied the land where the Swissotel stands today. The Celal family, a branch of the Ottoman dynasty, were the owners of this green space, which they donated to the Istanbul municipality in the 1920s. "There were two conditions for the gift: a mosque was to be built, and the cemetery was to remain untouched," says Ceyhan. But in their haste to realize the profits inherent in this prime location, developers ignored those conditions, he says, and "lawsuits launched to recover the property have all been lost." Who remembers that today?

Celal (Djelal) Bey was a senior official in the Ottoman Empire. His name should be well known to all Turkish students, yet it is not found in any textbook. Both his body and his memory have been carefully buried. Like all children of his generation, Fikret Ali Ceyhan knew nothing about his illustrious ancestor. He was twelve when he first heard the name. While helping his parents sort through the belongings of a great-uncle, an eccentric bachelor who had just died, Fikret discovered some yellowed documents inside a wood box inlaid with mother of pearl. The man pictured on the ID card wore a tie and a fez, the traditional headgear under the Ottoman Empire. Narrow glasses balanced on his nose framed a tired brow and an austere expression. His profession was given as "Former Governor General of Conieh."[94] Puzzled, Fikret asked his father, Kemal Ceyhan, about this man he had never heard of. "Your great-great-grandfather was a respected official, the governor of several provinces," was the reply. Ceyhan, an engineer with a Daliesque moustache, was "a little uncomfortable; it was a touchy subject." Pressed for answers by his son, he finally broke his silence.

It was 1915. The deportations had begun and were unstoppable. The Young Turks had sent telegrams and emissaries to every province. At that time, Mehmet Celal Bey was governor of Aleppo, the natural meeting-place of all roads in Asiatic Turkey and thus the convergence point of the convoys. Skeletal survivors dressed in rags and infested with vermin were marched into the city. Conscience-stricken and opposed to the deportations, Celal Bey did his best to slow down the convoys. On 18 June he was removed from his post as governor of Aleppo and transferred to Konya, a city in the central Anatolian region of Turkey. There, he continued to disobey orders.

As far as he could, this Turkish bureaucrat protected the Armenians, prohibited the looting of their property, and tried to reduce the suffering of the tens of thousands who passed through the railroad station on their way to the Syrian Desert. In his memoirs, he wrote this about the experience: "In Konya, I was like a person sitting by the side of a river, with absolutely no way to save anyone. Blood was flowing in the river and thousands of innocent children, blameless old people, helpless women, and strong young men were carried down this river toward oblivion. Anyone I could save with my bare hands, I saved; the others, I suppose, were carried down the river, never to return."

The Ceyhans tell us that, when he died in 1926, tens of thousands of Armenians attended the funeral of the Muslim Turk who had risked his life for them. Yet his great-great-grandson knew nothing about it until he opened the mother-of-pearl-inlaid box.

"At home, we don't talk much about politics," he says. "I had heard a little about the Armenians, but not much." His father knew that, in a country hostile to Armenians, the memory of this ancestor would be a heavy burden that could hurt Fikret's prospects. Then, in 2005, a conference innocently titled "Ottoman Armenians during the Decline of the Empire" was held at Bilgi University in Istanbul, and the taboo was finally broken: the word "genocide" was spoken in public. Still, the atmosphere was tense, and the participants required police protection. In a nationalist backlash, the writer Orhan Pamuk was dragged into court.

Now nineteen, Fikret is pursuing his studies at Princeton University in the United States, and he has begun to write a book about his ancestor. "I want to understand how my origins intersected with history and to let people know that there were brave men who defied orders," he says. His father is a bit apprehensive about the project, but he is proud of his son.[95]

Like Celal Bey, other Ottoman bureaucrats throughout the empire disobeyed orders and refused to participate in the extermination of a people. Many government officials, such as the *vali* (governors) of Kastamonu and Ankara, were dismissed for not carrying out the deportation orders. Like the sub-prefects of Lice and of Bafra in the Black Sea region, others paid with their lives. Mustafa agha Azizoğlu, the mayor of Malatya, was murdered by his own son, an ultra-conservative infuriated by his father's efforts to save Armenians. Many more lives were saved by brave men and women who hid their neighbours or helped them to escape.

We are not referring here to men who stole children for their own purposes or forced beautiful young girls to marry them. Neither are we talking about those who, motivated by greed, offered their "protection" – a service that often dried up when the money did. We're talking about those selfless individuals who, inspired by faith or humanity, chose a more dangerous route. These "righteous Turks" are the genocide's forgotten heroes. Their invisibility is understandable, for their very existence is evidence of the crime that, almost a century later, Ankara still tries to deny.

In Turkey, the subject is just starting to be explored. The Hrant Dink Foundation awards scholarships to researchers investigating such acts of conscience. "The righteous Turks are still a taboo subject," says Betül Tanbay, a professor of mathematics at the prestigious Bosphorus University and project head at the foundation. "In Turkey, a period of denial followed that of silence. Knowing about the righteous Turks would allow people to open a forbidden door and catch glimpses of what really happened. The goal is not to prove the innocence of all their ancestors, but it's the same mechanism as for the French: it's easier to acknowledge Nazi collaboration if you believe your grandfather was a resistance fighter." The existence of the righteous Turks is an effective rebuttal to the oft-repeated argument that "our ancestors couldn't possibly have committed such atrocities."

But how many people were saved? What happened at the individual level in Turkey? "We really don't know, because there are no local histories," says historian Taner Akçam, who dedicated his book *A Shameful Act* "to the memory of Haji Halil, a devout Muslim Turk, who risked his life to save the members of an Armenian family from deportation and death by keeping them safely hidden for over half a year. This courageous act continues to show us the path to creating a different relationship between Turks and Armenians."

That such acts were not isolated cases is suggested by a telegram sent by the commander of the Third Army to the governors of several provinces: "We have learned that, in certain villages, the population of which has been sent to the interior, certain [elements] of the Muslim population have given Armenians shelter in their homes. Since this is a violation of government orders, heads of households who shelter or protect Armenians are to be executed in front of their homes, and it is imperative that their houses be burned down. This order shall be transmitted in appropriate fashion and communicated to whom it may concern. See to it that no as yet undeported Armenian remains behind and inform us of the action you have taken. Converted Armenians must also be sent away. If those who attempt to protect Armenians or maintain friendly relations with them are members of the military, their ties with the army must be immediately severed, after their superiors have been duly informed, and they must be prosecuted. If they are civilians, they must be dismissed from their posts and tried before a court-martial."[96]

Among the diaspora, there is talk of cattle cars loaded with Armenians that were uncoupled from deportation trains. During a casual conversation, we learned of a local dignitary, Wahabi Effendi,[97] who hid all the children he could find in tree trunks. In the Kurdish southeast, villagers told historian David Gaunt that the night before a planned massacre of neighbouring Armenians, the women stuffed the barrels of their husbands' guns with bread crumbs.

While travelling through Dersim's "rebel land," we made the acquaintance of Cafer Tayhani, an Armenian beekeeper who makes ends meet behind the grill of a greasy spoon. During the summer, he devotes his time to his beehives, placed on land owned by the descendants of Temur Agha, a tribal chieftain buried in a small cemetery in the middle of the fields. Cafer's family was among those whose lives were saved by the chieftain. "He saved two hundred Armenians. They say that the general in charge of military operations in Dersim tried several times to have him killed because he refused to hand over the Armenians who had hidden on his land."

Of Temur Agha's extensive property, only a few small plots remain; the rest was divided up following disputes among his heirs. His beautiful stone house is still standing, however, and is now inhabited by Haskar Cağli, an elderly woman who strives to keep her ancestor's memory alive. "Emissaries were sent, offering to make him governor if he would stop protecting the Armenians," she says. "But he refused." She takes a few steps toward the barn, stops, and hits the ground with her cane. "The hiding place was down there, underground. They had everything they needed down there – beds, blankets, food. When it became too dangerous, they began to evacuate the Armenians to the Russian front, near Erzincan. They were led north in small groups of ten." The authorities were furious, and the army burned Temur's crops. "Temur's face was plastered on posters all over the region – he was wanted for collaborating with the Armenians." In the end, he was killed. "Temur was a good and pious man," says Haskar. "Unfortunately, the truth is that many of us were very bad to the Armenians."

The Armenian diaspora is another valuable source of information. Véronique Agoudjian's paternal grandmother, Varvar, was eighteen in 1915. The daughter of a boilermaker named Kouyoumdjian, Varvar lived in Kütahya, a small western town famous for its pottery. Perhaps one day it will be known for the courage of its governor. Supported by two prominent families, Faïk Ali Bey refused to deport the five thousand Armenians living in his district and ordered his Turkish citizens to protect them. They were all spared. Thousands of deportees also found refuge in the province. "My grandmother told me that, one morning, some Turks knocked at their door, saying, 'Leave quickly, get out of the country, your lives are in danger.' It was probably the neighbours," says Véronique, now a pharmacist in Paris.

The Kouyoumdjians left their home at dawn, headed west, then further west, knowing they would never return. The women had sewn gold coins into the hems of their skirts. The family's first stop was in Salonica, Greece, and, in 1923, they set sail for the New World. A large community of refugees from Kütahya had settled in Buenos Aires – it still meets once a month to remember its shared history. Varvar disembarked with her husband in Marseille, but her parents, along with her two brothers and her sister, continued on their way. Varvar died in 1986, age ninety-three, without ever seeing her family again. All her life, she kept a chipped pottery ashtray from Kütahya, decorated with black, yellow, and blue stripes, in a place of honour on her table – a fellow exile.

Like all the survivors, Varvar tried to bury the past under a cloak of silence. When she was pressed to speak, tears would often flow before words. She would talk about women who made their daughters look ugly to protect them from kidnappers, but she also acknowledged that her family's relations with their Turkish neighbours were good. They would drink tea in each other's homes. "She often said that her life was saved by Turks," recalls Véronique. "She was very grateful. She knew that a political decision had conditioned some Turks to do the worst but that others were able to think for themselves and didn't want to kill their neighbours."

The details of these heroic acts were often lost from one generation to the next. Michel Marian, a philosophy professor at Sciences Po in Paris,[98] had always heard that his grandparents, originally from Bayazid, in the far east of the Ottoman Empire, had reached the Caucasus after crossing the Russian front. In doing so, they escaped the terrible fate of many of their fellow Armenians, thrown from cliffs into the Euphrates or gutted with the bayonettes of *çete*, gangs of bandits and thieves in the government's pay. Michel's entire family survived, except for one uncle serving in the Ottoman army, who disappeared during the Great War. Doubtless he suffered the same fate as most Armenian conscripts: disarmed and then murdered.

The story passed down in the Marian family was accurate but incomplete. Michel's grandfather, Agop, an ironmonger, had indeed sought refuge in what would become Soviet Armenia with his young wife, Luçik, and the rest of his family, but what happened in the fateful hours before they fled the country was forgotten. That morning, emissaries from the Young Turk government had arrived in Bayazid with deportation orders, which they immediately delivered to the governor. As soon as they left, "the governor went to see the leading Armenians and told them to leave town that very night," says Michel. "I didn't know about the role played by that man. My grandfather never mentioned him. I only learned about his existence recently from a distant cousin, a historian. I was astonished!" In the 1970s, when Michel decided to find out what really happened in 1915, he learned about the atrocities suffered on his mother's side of the family, originally from Erzurum, in eastern Anatolia; of children who died from typhus during the deportation or were kidnapped by Turks; of a great-grandmother whose husband and two of her children were murdered before her eyes. In this province, where fighting between Turks and the Russians was fierce, the extermination was particularly thorough.

Taner Akçam understands about these forgotten details, these missing pages of history. "How did Turks save the lives of Armenians?" he asks. Learning that he is both a Turk and on their side, the descendants of survivors have often shared their stories with him. He finally concluded that this is "an open secret. They just aren't ready to share it yet." The survivors are put off by Turkey's denial of the genocide, fearing the state could use the stories to its advantage. Telling those stories "could be helpful, because it could offset the overall negative image," agrees Michel. "But as long as Turkey takes no official step, Armenians fear the stories of those brave Turks would simply offer a diversion. That the actions of those courageous few would eclipse stories of the massacre itself and overshadow the survivors' number one priority: Turkish recognition of the genocide."

Beyond the reluctance to share them, the stories also raise more philosophical questions: "Who were the righteous Turks?" "What inspired them to do what they did?" To these questions, historian Raymond Kévorkian replies that "such behaviour was often motivated by very simple factors – such as friendship or professional ties. In Adana, for example, freemasons protected their Armenian brothers, but that didn't stop them from participating in the overall liquidation. In Erzurum, Turkish merchants whose Armenian partners had been deported sometimes took in their children. The human factor was key."

Take the extraordinary story, preserved at the Zoryan Institute,[99] of Mehmet Effendi, known as the Turkish Schindler. In 1915, Mehmet, an industrialist in Malatya, saved most of the extended Piloyan family by hiding them in his own home and secretly employing the men in his factory, which produced tents and blankets for the Ottoman army. He was also able to have one of the younger boys released from prison, saving him from certain death. Finally, in 1923, Mehmet provided armed guards to escort the family to Syria. In 1925, they emigrated to Mexico.

The background to this story was a monetary loan that was converted by this kind man into a moral debt. In 1897, when Mehmet Effendi was twenty, he had asked Sarkis Piloyan, then the owner of a leather tanning business, for a loan of 20 gold lira to pay his *bedel* (waiver fee) to keep him out of the Ottoman army. Mehmet wanted to avoid doing his military service because he needed to protect his business interests at home. At the time, this tidy sum could buy a small house in Malatya. The Piloyans were not the only ones who benefited from the help of this influential entrepreneur; however, he also employed other Armenians in his factory, leading us to believe that his actions were disinterested.

The same can be said of Hasan Mazhar Bey, the governor of Ankara who was relieved of his duties when he refused to obey the deportation orders. After the war, he headed the administrative committee charged with investigating officials who were guilty of crimes against Armenians and preparing the trial records for their court martial. In his statement to the court explaining what had happened in the province of Ankara in 1915, he declared, "When I received orders from the Ministry of the Interior concerning the deportation of Armenians, I pretended not to understand. As you know, other provinces had finished the deportations before I had even begun. Then, one day, Atif Bey[100] came to see me and orally delivered the orders from the Ministry of the Interior requiring that Armenians be murdered during the deportation. 'No, Atif Bey,' I said, 'I'm a governor, not a bandit; I can't do that. I would rather leave my post, and you can come and do it yourself.'[101]

Armen Marsoobian, a philosophy professor at Southern Connecticut State University, told us the story of his grandfather, Tsolag Dildilian, the only professional photographer in the Black Sea region. As was sometimes the case with tradespeople such as bakers and blacksmiths, Tsolag's profession may have saved his life and those of his family, for his skills were needed by the Turkish army. How did it happen? "It was likely a combination of factors," says Armen. "But one man in particular stands out."

According to the family history, pieced together largely through the meticulous research of Armen's Parisian cousin, the Dildilians, who lived in the town of Merzifon, benefited greatly from the daring of Mahir Bey, the chief of police,[102] who had the words "Stays here" written on the doors of many Armenian homes. Perhaps he was paid to do so, but the fact remains that Mahir eventually lost his position, which went to his zealous assistant. On 6 August 1915, when the sign on the door was no longer enough to protect the inhabitants, Mahir paid Tsolag Dildilian a secret visit. Maritsa, the cousin of Armen's mother, then in her teens, wrote down what happened: "At 5 p.m. on that Friday afternoon, the doorbell rang, and I went to answer it. A high-ranking official was standing there. While he was walking the twenty or thirty metres from the gate to the front door, we had had time to warn my uncle and, since it was forbidden for girls to be seen by Turks, I then made myself scarce." Mahir's message was simple: "First thing tomorrow, apply to convert to Islam; that's the only way out." Dildilian followed his protector's advice.

On 10 August 1915, there was a full moon. At 5:30 am, Maritsa was woken "by the creaking of ox carts in the street." The last convoys of Armenian deportees were leaving Merzifon. By late August, the deportations were finished. Before the war, the city was home to 10,381

Armenians. Only 307 remain today, all Islamized. Armen found the names of eight of his family members on a document listing the converts. A man with the first names "Ahmed Nuri," a photographer by trade, was no doubt his grandfather. A daughter named Hatice Leman was Armen's mother, Alice.

Armen wonders about the actions of Mahir Bey. "Does a righteous act make the person who does it a righteous person? Were his actions inspired by pragmatism or morality? What else did he do to save Armenians? What more could he have done?" These are all relevant questions. Raymond Kévorkian's research has revealed a less admirable side to the man. The reports of William Peter, the US consul in Samsun, show that the police chief took advantage of the Armenians' despair to extort money from them in exchange for promises – promises that he did not keep – not to deport them. Was he a man without scruples – or a man who endangered his career to ease his conscience? Only Allah can say.

Despite the uncertainty surrounding the motives of his family's benefactor, Armen believes it is "important for modern Turkish society to hear" these rescue stories. They provide "evidence of the genocide, since these people knew that a crime against humanity was being committed, that a people was being exterminated, and that it was not simply a matter of relocating them in the interests of national security." Finally, while "too many Turks still identify with the perpetrators of the crime," who have been absolved by the official ideology, the righteous Turks offer people a new possibility, that of taking a position on past events for which they do not assume responsibility and of asking themselves, "Who do I identify with? If I had been in their shoes, what would I have done?"

The children of 1915 might find some comfort in these stories, but for the most part they are still in too much pain to hear them. Turkey has denied them their status of victim, so they are left to deal with their suffering on their own. That, at least, cannot be taken from them, and they do not want to hear stories of "righteous Turks." "If we mention them, we're treated like gullible fools," says Véronique Agoudjian, whose grandmother was saved in Kütahya. The rejection of such accounts "is symptomatic of the pathology of a people whose suffering has been denied," Véronique says. "The descendants are tormented souls. Some are completely unable to listen to these stories – yet they can be healing, not just for the Turks but for us as well."

The image of the righteous Turk could show us another side of that mythological figure – the bloodthirsty and barbaric Turk – and perhaps appease the ghosts who, for the past century, have haunted the consciousness of their descendants, crying out for justice.

Conclusion

In November 2008, we were standing on the hill of Tsitsernakaberd in Yerevan, Armenia's capital city. The winter sky was pierced by the granite spire of the memorial to the 1915 genocide. University students from Istanbul, a few journalists, some Turks, a German, and a Frenchman strolled solemnly along the avenue lined with pine trees planted by visiting dignitaries, through the rooms of the genocide museum, and around the forty-four-metre high grey stele. The small group were guests of the Turkish Economic and Social Studies Foundation (TESEV), a liberal think tank promoting the democratization of Turkey, which was holding a series of meetings with its Armenian counterpart, the Caucasus Institute.

This was the first time that most of these visitors, genocide experts, had set foot in Armenia. The visit to the memorial complex with Turkish citizens was a symbolic event that we did not want to miss. We were surprised to see that, during a long pause in front of the eternal flame, some of the Turkish visitors pulled out digital cameras and began snapping photos, as tourists might do in front of the Eiffel Tower or the Trevi Fountain. The Frenchman was uncomfortable and his German colleague outraged. Clearly unaware of the inappropriateness of their behaviour, the visitors taking souvenir photos were reminded that this was not the place for it, and the conversation quickly turned to the question of collective responsibility.

"What should we feel responsible for?" asked the Turks in surprise. The journalist from Germany explained that, in his country, every high school student visits the Nazi concentration camps at least three times. He himself has led tours of Auschwitz. To him, the visitors' casual attitude toward this memorial to the 1.5 million victims of the Armenian genocide was intolerable.

The photo-taking incident at Tsitsernakaberd highlights the special sensitivity of both the Germans and the French to the recognition of the Armenian genocide as a result of their own collective history. In those countries, three generations have been raised to feel the weight of history since the Second World War. That work has yet to begin in Turkey, where the people have a long road to travel to assimilate their historic responsibility and collectively carry out their duty to remember.

In 2015, the hundredth anniversary of the Armenian genocide could mark a turning point, a key step along the path to awareness and recognition of the crime. The dialogue begun a few years ago between civil societies, both Turkish and Armenian – in Armenia and also among the diaspora – has created unprecedented openings. The year will be marked by numerous demonstrations and commemorations – in Armenia, of course, where a "central committee" has been formed to coordinate events, but also in Europe and the United States, and even in Turkey.[103]

A Hollywood film on the genocide is in the works. A memorial museum may be opened in Sèvres, no doubt rekindling tensions between Paris and Ankara. In turn, the Turkish state is preparing its rebuttal and promises to flood the market with revisionist books, pamphlets, and movies. But this defensive approach is in itself an admission of guilt, and Turkish leaders know that. In July 2012, on the flight back from Paris after the first official visit following the France-Turkey diplomatic crisis, Turkey's foreign affairs minister Ahmet Davu-toğlu spoke more openly to the journalists who had accompanied him: "We must sit down together and talk. Our goal is to break the ice. Now there will be someone who will sit across from the Armenians and listen to them. I'm not the type of foreign affairs minister to say, 'No, nothing happened in 1915' ... We are preparing new messages for 2015. We're looking for new ways to talk about 'truthful memory.' I am also working on a book on the history of the Ottoman Empire. I don't call it a 'genocide,' but when someone says there was one, I don't deny it."

Recognition of the genocide is not on the agenda for 2015; Turkey will not likely do an about-face regarding 1915 in honour of the centennial. But perhaps a different reading of history will become possible.

Notes

TN *indicates a translator's note.*

1 Jürgen Habermas, "Die Utopie des guten Herrschers," in *Kultur und Kritik* (Frankfurt: Verstreute Aufsätze, 1973), 386–7.

2 Elias Siberski, *Untergrund und Offene Geselschaft, Zur Fragen der strukturellen Deutung des sozialen Phaenomens* (Stuttgart: F. Enke, 1967), 51.

3 "Forums avec Pierre Vidal-Naquet," *Le Nouvel Observateur*, 24 January 2005.

4 TN: The 100th anniversary of Bastille Day in France.

5 "Révolution française et Jeunes-Turcs," *Revue du monde musulman et de la Méditerranée* 52–3 (1989): 160–72.

6 Vidal-Naquet, *Assassins of Memory: Essays on the Denial of the Holocaust*, translated and with a foreword by Jeffrey Mehlman (New York: Columbia University Press, 1992).

7 Albert Londres, *Marseille, porte du Sud* (Paris: Editions de France, 1927).

8 TN: The Colbert decree (1669) in France set up formal training for French-born students as interpreters for Turkish, Arabic, and Persian, leading to the founding of the Constantinople school of translators.

9 TN: Today, the word "Bey" is still used informally as a social title for men (somewhat like the English "Mr"). Unlike "Mr," however, it is generally used with first names and not with last names. As with most Turkish titles, it follows the name rather than precedes it, e.g., "Ahmet Bey" for "Mr Ahmet."

10 The predominantly (76 per cent) Armenian-populated province of Nagorno (Upper) Karabakh was attached to Azerbaijan during the Soviet era, but was claimed by Armenia after the collapse of the Soviet Union. The armed

conflict, frozen since 1994, claimed almost twenty thousand lives and created a million refugees.

11 TN: Pied-Noir, literally meaning "Black-foot," a person of European origin who lived in Algeria during French rule, especially one who returned to Europe after Algeria was granted independence.

12 Former name of the city of Antep.

13 A *vilayet* is an Ottoman administrative division corresponding to a province.

14 Raymond Kévorkian, *The Armenian Genocide: A Complete History* (London: I.B. Tauris, 2011), 533.

15 Authors' interview with Köker.

16 Named after a Turkish tribe that ruled Asia Minor from the eleventh to the twelfth centuries.

17 Alevism, a heterodox branch of Islam that incorporates elements of Shamanism and Christianity, is followed by 15 to 20 per cent of the Turkish population. This minority, persecuted under the Ottoman Empire, is still greatly discriminated against.

18 Kévorkian, *Armenian Genocide*, 543.

19 Interview.

20 The names of the grandmother and her grandson have been changed.

21 Çetin, *My Grandmother: A Memoir* (New York: Verso, 2008). First published in 2007.

22 Ibid.

23 Ibid.

24 Çetin and Ayşe Gül Altınay, *The Grandchildren* (New Brunswick, NJ: Transaction Publishers, 2014).

25 An ethnic group living primarily in eastern Turkey and speaking the Zazaki language.

26 An armed group that carried out attacks in the 1970s and '80s.

27 The Shafi'i school of thought is one of the four schools of law of Sunni Islam. Most Kurds in Turkey belong to the stricter and more conservative Shafi'i school of Sunni Islam, whereas most Turks belong to the Hanafi school.

28 In this chapter, all first names have been changed, except those followed by a family name.

29 The PKK, or Kurdistan Workers' Party, is a Marxist-Leninist movement founded in 1978 by Abdullah Öcalan. It fought an armed struggle against Turkey from 1984 to 2013.

30 TN: The atrocities of the 1890s are often called the Hamidian massacres, to distinguish them from the greater atrocities associated with the 1915 Armenian genocide.

31 Kévorkian, *Armenian Genocide*, 515.

32 Leslie A. Davis, *The Slaughterhouse Province: An American Diplomat's Report on the Armenian Genocide, 1915–1917*, edited by Susan K. Blair (New Rochelle, NY: Aristide D. Caratzas, 1989).

33 Kévorkian, *Armenian Genocide*, 514.

34 "Genocide of the Kurds," in *The Widening Circle of Genocide*, vol. 3 of *Genocide: a Critical Bibliographic Review*, edited by I.W. Charny (London: Transaction, 1994), 165–91.

35 The Grey Wolves, the ultranationalist militants of the MHP's youth organization, the Idealist Youth, are known for their racist ideology and violent methods.

36 "Turkey Renames 'Divisive' Animals," BBC *News*, 8 March 2005.

37 Sinan (1489–1588) was the chief architect of the Ottoman Empire. His masterpiece was the Süleymaniye mosque in Istanbul, although his most famous work was the Selimiye mosque in Edirne. A converted Christian, he is believed by some to have had Armenian origins.

38 TN: Co-authored with his wife, Müjde Nişanyan.

39 TN: Küçük was released from jail on 12 March 2014 under a newly passed law abolishing specially authorized courts (ÖYM) and reducing to five years the maximum period of detention before a final verdict on an appeal.

40 Nişanyan, *Yanlış Cumhuriyet* (Istanbul: Everest, 2012).

41 TN: In January 2014, Nişanyan began serving a jail sentence of one year and forty-five days for "openly denigrating the religious values held by a certain portion of the population."

42 Twice a year, this committee brings together members appointed by the European and Turkish parliaments to consider issues related to Turkey's accession to the European Parliament.

43 See chapter 9.

44 Franz Werfel, *The Forty Days of Musa Dagh*, translated by Geoffrey Dunlop and James Reidel, with a preface by Vartan Gregorian (Boston: David R. Godine, 2012). Original title: *Die Vierzig Tage des Musa Dagh*.

45 Kévorkian, *Armenian Genocide*, 757–8.

46 See Bardig Kouyoumdjian and Christine Siméone, *Deir-Zor: On the Trail of the Armenian Genocide of 1915*, translated by Michele McKay Aynesworth

with a preface by Yves Ternon. (Published with support from the association Le renouveau Tebrotzassère, 2010.)

47 TN: *demirci* = blacksmith.

48 TN: Turkmens are members of a group of Turkic peoples inhabiting the region east of the Caspian Sea and south of the Aral Sea, now comprising Turkmenistan and parts of Iran and Afghanistan.

49 Mayor elected by the villagers, with the status of civil servant.

50 TN: Israel's official memorial to the Jewish victims of the Holocaust, established in 1953.

51 TN: A popular belief that outside forces, particularly the West, are conspiring to weaken and carve up Turkey.

52 TN: Peace treaty between the Ottoman Empire and the Allies at the end of World War I; it was annulled during the Turkish War of Independence and replaced by the Treaty of Lausanne.

53 TN: On 24 May 2011, Baku lost this record by just three metres to Dushanbe, the capital of Tajikistan.

54 TN: The threat was made in response to non-binding US and Swedish votes branding World War I–era killings of Armenians by Ottoman Turks as genocide.

55 TN: *Pasha* or *pascha* was a high rank in the Ottoman Empire political and military system, typically granted to governors, generals, and dignitaries. Within the Ottoman Empire, the Ottoman sultan had the right to bestow the title of *pasha*.

56 TN: *Tanzimat* means "reforms," "rearrangement," and "reorganization," and in Ottoman history, the Tanzimat period refers to a time of westernizing reforms from 1839 until 1876.

57 Between 1920 and 1922, a covert operation by the Armenian Revolutionary Federation (Dashnaktsutyun), Operation Nemesis, named after the Greek goddess of vengeance, carried out the assassination of eight top-level officials of the Committee of Union and Progress and "Armenian traitors" who had fled the country and were convicted in absentia by the Constantinople courts-martial in 1919. The sentences handed down by the court, which had tried some of the crimes committed in 1915, were carried out by these self-appointed dispensers of justice.

58 TN: Together with other prisoners, Doğu Perinçek was released from prison in March 2014.

59 TN: Robert Faurisson is a French academic and Holocaust denier.

60 Vidal-Naquet, *Assassins of Memory*, 161.

61 *Le Nouvel Observateur*, 24 January 2005.

62 *Le Monde*, 7 January 2012.

63 Taner Akçam, *A Shameful Act: The Armenian Genocide and the Question of Turkish Responsibility* (New York: Metropolitan Books, 2006).

64 *Le Monde*, 7 January 2012.

65 TN: The stated intention of ASALA was "to compel the Turkish Government to acknowledge publicly its responsibility for the Armenian Genocide in 1915, pay reparations, and cede territory for an Armenian homeland" (US Department of State, "Appendix B," *Patterns of Global Terrorism Report –1996*).

66 In *Talaat Pasha's Report on the Armenian Genocide*, 1917, edited and introduced by Ara Sarafian (Gomidas Institute, 2012), historian Ara Sarafian arrives at very different conclusions.

67 TN: Following the Hamidian massacres, Aivazovsky threw the medals given to him by the Ottoman Sultan into the sea and told the Turkish consul in Feodosia, "Tell your bloodthirsty master that I've thrown away all the medals given to me, here are their ribbons, send them to him and if he wants, he can throw them into the seas painted by me."

68 TN: Gül's mandate as president of Turkey ended on 28 August 2014, when he handed over the post of head of state to Prime Minister Recep Tayyip Erdoğan.

69 TN: A Muslim legal expert who is empowered to give rulings on religious matters.

70 Kévorkian, *Armenian Genocide*, 621.

71 TN: Some five to seven million Muslim migrants from hostile regions arrived in Ottoman Anatolia from 1783 to 1914; the influx of migration during the early twentieth century was due to the loss of almost all Ottoman territory during the Balkan War of 1912–13 and World War I. These *muhacirs* (refugees) saw the Ottoman Empire, and subsequently the Republic of Turkey, as a protective "motherland."

72 Uğur Ümit Üngör and Mehmet Polatel, *Confiscation and Destruction: The Young Turk Seizure of Armenian Property* (London/New York: Continuum, 2011), 125.

73 Ibid., 128

74 Buğra, *State and Business in Modern Turkey: A Comparative Study* (Albany: SUNY Press, 1994), 82.

75 Ibid.

76 TN: Quoted in Üngör and Polatel, *Confiscation and Destruction*, 79.

77 TN: Ibid.

78 TN: Ibid., 167–8.

79 Ibid.

80 TN: On 14 March 2012, the Armenian Patriarchate filed a landmark suit in Ankara for the return of the Sanasarian School.

81 Asquith and Baldwin, memorandum to Prime Minister Ramsay MacDonald, 26 September 1924, cited in André Mandelstam, *La Société des Nations et les Puissances devant le problème arménien* (Beirut: Association Libanaise des Universitaires Arméniens, 1970), 489–93.

82 TN: On 13 June 2012, the Turkish Supreme Court of Appeals upheld this decision. But on 30 September 2013, Prime Minister Erdoğan announced that the land would be returned to the Syriac community in Turkey.

83 TN: Yaşar Kemal, *Salman the Solitary* (London: Harvill Press, 1997), translated by Thilda Kemal.

84 In *Chroniques d'un journaliste assassiné* (Paris: Galaade, 2010), the writings of Hrant Dink are collected by Günter Seufert and translated into French by Bernard Banoun, Haldun Bayrı, and Marie-Michèle Martinet.

85 Ahmet Insel and Michel Marian, *Dialogue sur le tabou arménien*, coordinated by Ariane Bonzon (Paris: Liana Levi, 2009).

86 Leyla Neyzi and Hranush Kharatyan-Araqelyan, *Speaking to One Another* (Bonn: Institut für internationale Zusammenarbeit des deutschen Volkshochschul-Verbandes, 2010).

87 TN: Cemal resigned from the newspaper *Milliyet* in 2013 when his work was censored.

88 TN: He did so in June 2013. See http://www.armenianweekly.com/2013/06/25/armenian-musician-udi-yervant-returns-to-diyarbakir/.

89 Kévorkian, *Armenian Genocide*, 363–4.

90 Şeymus Diken's book *Gittiler Iste* (Here they are gone) is a collection of essays in Turkish (Istanbul: Aras Publishing, 2011) telling the story of Diyarbakir in the time of peaceful coexistence between Armenians, Kurds, Assyrians, Chaldeans, Kurdish Yezidis, Greeks, Jews, and other ethnic and religious groups more than a century ago.

91 TN: The Sur Municipality of Diyarbakir inaugurated the Monument of Common Conscience on 12 September 2013, with Mayor Abdullah Demirbaş

apologizing in the name of Kurds for the Armenian and Assyrian genocides. The inscription reads, in six languages including Armenian, "We share the pain so that it is not repeated."

92 TN: One of the founding members and jailed leader of the Kurdistan Workers' Party (PKK), listed as a terrorist organization internationally by some states and organizations. On 21 March 2013, Öcalan declared a ceasefire between the PKK and the Turkish state.

93 Human Rights Watch, http://www.hrw.org/reports/2002/turkey/Turkey 1002.htm.

94 *Konya* in modern Turkish.

95 TN: Fikret's book is titled *Mehmet Celal Bey: One Era, One Man (1863–1926)*. See www.mehmetcelalbey.com/en.

96 Quoted in Raymond Kévorkian, *Armenian Genocide*, 314.

97 TN: Efendi (or Effendi) is a title of respect or courtesy that was used in the Ottoman Empire. It follows the personal name and was generally given to members of the learned professions and high-ranking government officials. In the Ottoman era, it was the most common title affixed to a personal name after that of Agha.

98 TN: A university with a strong international dimension.

99 TN: The Zoryan Institute for Contemporary Research and Documentation was established in Cambridge, Mass., in 1982, followed by the Zoryan Institute of Canada, Inc., incorporated in Toronto in 1984 as a non-profit research institute.

100 Member of the Committee of Union and Progress who replaced Vali Mazhar and implemented the program to exterminate the Armenians.

101 Archives of the Armenian Patriarchate of Jerusalem, box 21, file M, no. 492. Quoted in Akçam, *A Shameful Act*, 164.

102 In fact, Mahir Bey was the commander of the gendarmerie.

103 TN: The Armenian Genocide Centennial Committee of Canada is headquartered in Montreal.

Index

Acknowledgments

This publication was made possible by grants from the publications program of the Dolores Zohrab Liebmann Fund, the AGBU Lawrence Terzian Fund and the Armenian Genocide Centennial Committee of Canada (thanks in particular to Mheir Karakachian).

Laure Marchand and Guillaume Perrier express their gratitude to His Eminence Nareg Alemezian, the Archbishop of the Armenian Apostolic Church in Cyprus, for facilitating the sponsorship of the book's translation into English through the generous donations of the following individuals in memory of the victims of the Armenian genocide: Father Jirayr Tashjian (France), Mr and Mrs Garo Aghazarian (Lebanon), Mr and Mrs Khatchig Aprahamian (Lebanon), Mr and Mrs Alex Demirdjian (Lebanon), Mr and Mrs Ardziv Der Khatchadourian (Lebanon), Mrs Véronique Garévorian (France), Mr and Mrs Movses Hergelian (Lebanon), Mr and Mrs Hagop Kassardjian (Lebanon), Mr and Mrs Arthur Nazarian (Lebanon), Mr and Mrs Sam Rakoubian (Lebanon), Mr and Mrs Hrant Sahakian (Russia), the Salkhanian brothers (Lebanon), and an anonymous donor (Switzerland).